CASEBOOK SERIES

D1099968

JANE AUSTEN: *Emma* (Revised) David Lodge
JANE AUSTEN: *'Northanger Abbey'* & *'Persuasion'*
JANE AUSTEN: *'Sense and Sensibility'*, *'Pride and Prejudice'* & *'Mansfield Park'*
  B. C. Southam
BECKETT: *Waiting for Godot* Ruby Cohn
WILLIAM BLAKE: *Songs of Innocence and Experience* Margaret Bottrall
CHARLOTTE BRONTE: *'Jane Eyre'* & *'Villette'* Miriam Allott
EMILY BRONTE: *Wuthering Heights* (Revised) Miriam Allott
BROWNING: *'Men and Women'* & *Other Poems* J. R. Watson
CHAUCER: *The Canterbury Tales* J. J. Anderson
COLERIDGE: *'The Ancient Mariner'* & *Other Poems* Alun R. Jones & W. Tydeman
CONRAD: *'Heart of Darkness'*, *'Nostromo'* & *'Under Western Eyes'* C. B. Cox
CONRAD: *The Secret Agent* Ian Watt
DICKENS: *Bleak House* A. E. Dyson
DICKENS: *'Hard Times'*, *'Great Expectations'* & *'Our Mutual Friend'* Norman Page
DICKENS: *'Dombey and Son'* & *'Little Dorrit'* Alan Shelston
DONNE: *Songs and Sonets* Julian Lovelock
GEORGE ELIOT: *Middlemarch* Patrick Swinden
GEORGE ELIOT: *'The Mill on the Floss'* & *'Silas Marner'* R. P. Draper
T. S. ELIOT: *Four Quartets* Bernard Bergonzi
T. S. ELIOT: *'Prufrock'*, *'Gerontion'* & *'Ash Wednesday'* B. C. Southam
T. S. ELIOT: *The Waste Land* C. B. Cox & Arnold P. Hinchliffe
T. S. ELIOT: *Plays* Arnold P. Hinchliffe
HENRY FIELDING: *Tom Jones* Neil Compton
E.M. FORSTER: *A Passage to India* Malcolm Bradbury
WILLIAM GOLDING: *Novels 1954-64* Norman Page
HARDY: *The Tragic Novels* (Revised) R. P. Draper
HARDY: *Poems* James Gibson & Trevor Johnson
HARDY: *Three Pastoral Novels* R. P. Draper
GERARD MANLEY HOPKINS: *Poems* Margaret Bottrall
HENRY JAMES: *'Washington Square'* & *'The Portrait of a Lady'* Alan Shelton
JONSON: *Volpone* Jonas A. Barish
JONSON: *'Every Man in his Humour'* & *'The Alchemist'* R. V. Holdsworth
JAMES JOYCE: *'Dubliners'* & *'A Portrait of the Artist as a Young Man'* Morris Beja
KEATS: *Odes* G.S. Fraser
KEATS: *Narrative Poems* John Spencer Hill
D.H. LAWRENCE: *Sons and Lovers* Gamini Salgado
D.H. LAWRENCE: *'The Rainbow'* & *'Women in Love'* Colin Clarke
LOWRY: *Under the Volcano* Gordon Bowker
MARLOWE: *Doctor Faustus* John Jump
MARLOWE: *'Tamburlaine the Great'*, *'Edward II'* & *'The Jew of Malta'* J. R. Brown
MARLOWE: *Poems* Arthur Pollard
MAUPASSANT: *In the Hall of Mirrors* T. Harris
MILTON: *Paradise Lost* A. E. Dyson & Julian Lovelock
O'CASEY: *'Juno and the Paycock'*, *'The Plough and the Stars'* & *'The Shadow of a
  Gunman'* Ronald Ayling
EUGENE O'NEILL: *Three Plays* Normand Berlin
JOHN OSBORNE: *Look Back in Anger* John Russell Taylor
PINTER: *'The Birthday Party'* & *Other Plays* Michael Scott
POPE: *The Rape of the Lock* John Dixon Hunt
SHAKESPEARE: *A Midsummer Night's Dream* Antony Price
SHAKESPEARE: *Antony and Cleopatra* (Revised) John Russell Brown
SHAKESPEARE: *Coriolanus* B. A. Brockman

Shakespeare

The Sonnets

A CASEBOOK

EDITED BY

PETER JONES

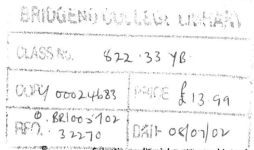

Published by
PALGRAVE
Houndmills, Basingstoke, Hampshire RG21 6XS and
175 Fifth Avenue, New York, N. Y. 10010
Companies and representatives throughout the world

PALGRAVE is the new global academic imprint of
St. Martin's Press LLC Scholarly and Reference Division and
Palgrave Publishers Ltd (formerly Macmillan Press Ltd).

ISBN 0–333–21237–1

This book is printed on paper suitable for recycling and
made from fully managed and sustained forest sources.

A catalogue record for this book is available
from the British Library.

Transferred to digital print 2002

Printed and bound in Great Britain by
Antony Rowe Ltd, Chippenham and Eastbourne

CONTENTS

2. Critical Studies

Part Four: *Recent Studies, 1952–76*

ACKNOWLEDGEMENTS

The editor and publishers wish to thank the following who have kindly given permission for the use of copyright material: William Empson, extract from *Seven Types of Ambiguity* (1930; 3rd ed., revised 1935, repr. 1953 by Chatto & Windus), reprinted by permission of the author and Chatto & Windus Ltd. Inga-Stina Ewbank, extracts from 'Shakespeare's Poetry', from *A New Companion to Shakespeare Studies*, ed. Muir and Schoenbaum (1971), reprinted by permission of the author and Cambridge University Press. Stefan George, extract from 'Shakespeare Sonnette', from *A New Variorum Edition of Shakespeare: The Sonnets*, ed. Hyder Edward Rollins, © 1944 by the Modern Language Association of America, reprinted by permission of the publisher, J. B. Lippincott & Co. Robert Graves and Laura Riding, extract from 'A Study in Original Punctuation and Spelling' (1926), reproduced in Robert Graves, *The Common Asphodel*, reprinted by permission of the authors and A. P. Watt & Son. Joan Grundy, 'Shakespeare's Sonnets and the Elizabethan Sonneteers', from *Shakespeare Survey*, No. 15, ed. Allardyce Nicoll (1962), reprinted by permission of the author and Cambridge University Press. G. K. Hunter, 'The Dramatic Technique of Shakespeare's Sonnets', from *Essays in Criticism*, III (April 1953), reprinted by permission of the author and *Essays in Criticism*. W. G. Ingram and Theodore Redpath, extract from *Shakespeare's Sonnets* (1964), reprinted by permission of the publisher, Hodder and Stoughton Educational Ltd. G. Wilson Knight, 'Symbolism', from *The Mutual Flame*, published 1955 by Methuen & Co., reprinted by permission of the author and Curtis Brown Ltd. L. C. Knights, 'Shakespeare's Sonnets', from *Explorations* (1946), originally published in *Scrutiny* (1934) by Cambridge University Press, reprinted by permission of the author and Chatto & Windus Ltd. Jan Kott, extracts from 'Shakespeare's Bitter Arcadia', from *Shakespeare our Contemporary* (1964) translated by Boleslaw Taborski, reprinted by permission of the publisher, Methuen & Co. Molly M. Mahood, 'Love's

Confined Doom', from *Shakespeare Survey*, No. 15, ed. Allardyce Nicoll (1962), reprinted by permission of the author and Cambridge University Press; and extract from 'The Sonnets', from *Shakespeare's Wordplay* (1957), reprinted by permission of the publisher, Methuen & Co. Winifred M. T. Nowottny, 'Formal Elements in Shakespeare's Sonnets', from *Essays In Criticism*, II (January 1952), reprinted by permission of the author and *Essays in Criticism*. F. T. Prince, 'The Sonnet from Wyatt to Shakespeare', from *Stratford-upon-Avon Studies*, II (1960), reprinted by permission of Edward Arnold (Publishers) Ltd. John Crowe Ransom, extracts from 'Shakespeare at Sonnets', from *The World's Body*, © 1938 by Charles Scribner's Sons, reprinted by permission. A. L. Rowse, extract from *Shakespeare's Sonnets: The Problems Solved*, 2nd ed. (1973), by permission of the author. Lytton Strachey, extracts from 'Shakespeare's Sonnets', from *Spectator* (1905), reprinted in *Spectatorial Essays by Lytton Strachey* (1964), reprinted by permission of the author's literary estate and Chatto & Windus Ltd. C. F. Williamson, 'Themes and Patterns in Shakespeare's Sonnets', from *Essays in Criticism*, XXVI (July 1976), reprinted by permission of the author and *Essays in Criticism*. Yvor Winters, extract from 'Poetic Styles, Old and New', from *Forms of Discovery* (1967), © Yvor Winters, reprinted by permission of The Swallow Press.

GENERAL EDITOR'S PREFACE

The Casebook series, launched in 1968, has become a well-regarded library of critical studies. The central concern of the series remains the 'single-author' volume, but suggestions from the academic community have led to an extension of the original plan, to include occasional volumes on such general themes as literary 'schools' and genres.

Each volume in the central category deals either with one well-known and influential work by an individual author, or with closely related works by one writer. The main section consists of critical readings, mostly modern, collected from books and journals. A selection of reviews and comments by the author's contemporaries is also included, and sometimes comment from the author himself. The Editor's introduction charts the reputation of the work or works from the first appearance to the present time.

Volumes in the 'general themes' category are variable in structure but follow the basic purpose of the series in presenting an integrated selection of readings, with an Introduction which explores the theme and discusses the literary and critical issues involved.

A single volume can represent no more than a small selection of critical opinions. Some critics are excluded for reasons of space, and it is hoped that readers will pursue the suggestions for further reading in the Select Bibliography. Other contributions are severed from their original context, to which some readers may wish to turn. Indeed, if they take a hint from the critics represented here, they certainly will.

A. E. DYSON

INTRODUCTION

In a sonnet on the sonnet form, Wordsworth exclaimed:

> . . . with this key
> Shakespeare unlocked his heart . . .

Robert Browning was moved to retort, in his poem 'House':

> Hoity-toity! A street to explore,
>   Your house the exception! '*With this same key*
> *Shakespeare unlocked his heart,* once more!'
>   Did Shakespeare? If so, the less Shakespeare he!

The impulse to reply is healthy. But we learn that the volume of critical writing on Shakespeare's *Sonnets* is surpassed only by that on *Hamlet*: not a reassuring fact. Criticism and investigation of *Hamlet* have helped elucidate an inexhaustibly rich text; research on the *Sonnets* has often lapsed into a quest for some missing link – usually conceived as a biographical secret – which, if found, would solve all the problems the poems raise, a key to all the 'hidden meanings'. This sort of research has entertained many fanciful sleuths without bringing them any nearer the poems. The essays collected in this book attempt in various ways to clear a route through the undergrowth of speculation towards an understanding of the poems and towards an appreciation of the workings of Shakespeare's creative mind.

With Thomas Thorpe, the first publisher of the *Sonnets* (1609), serious critical problems begin. After the title-page of his edition he added the notorious dedication (reproduced in Part One below): a mere thirty words which gave birth to controversial speculative tomes, essays, and acrimony: who was W.H.? Was he the youth addressed in the *Sonnets*? Once the game had begun, the players tried to identify the other 'personalities' addressed and

evoked, the Dark Lady and the Rival Poet. In spite of what L. C.
Knights calls the 'superior attractiveness of gossip', it is salutary
to find that most modern critics ignore this aspect of the
work.

Even had the dedication been omitted, more important
problems would have remained. Is there a pattern in the ordering
of the poems? Did Shakespeare write all of them? When did he
write them? Were they merely a literary exercise or passionate
statements compelled by actual experience? 'They are hot and
pothery', Walter Savage Landor wrote. So – we are tempted to
add – are some of the critics who have come at them from
various directions. The most helpful critics are those who keep
two objectives foremost in mind: to read the poems *as poetry*; and
to see what light they cast on the problems of creative work
within conventional form, and on Shakespeare's creative approach in particular.

There are few facts, and speculation is a continual temptation.
The first mention of the *Sonnets* occurs in *Palladis Tamia: Witt's
Treasury* (1598), a book compiled by Francis Meres, a Cambridge
schoolmaster and cleric, cataloguing the English writers of the
day and their Latin and Greek parallels. It lists Shakespeare's
plays written at the time and speaks of his 'sugred sonnets among
his private friends'. Later it refers to Shakespeare, among other
sonneteers, as one 'most passionate among us to bewaile and
bemoane the perplexities of Love'. The sonnets referred to need
not be those we have and accept as Shakespeare's; but in the
following year (1599) versions of sonnets CXXXVIII ('When my
love sweares that she is made of truth') and CXLIV ('Two loves I
have of comfort and dispaire') appeared in a miscellany of
poems, *The Passionate Pilgrim*. The title-page erroneously ascribes
contents to Shakespeare. Of the twenty lyrics included, fifteen are
by other poets and three are extracts from Act IV of *Love's Labour's
Lost* (without indication of source). The book seems to have been
popular and ran to three editions, the third (1612) including
work by Thomas Heywood (extracts from his *Troia Britannica*)
still under the supposed authorship of Shakespeare. Heywood
protested in his *Apology for Actors*, adding that Shakespeare was
also 'much offended'. William Jaggard, the publisher, sub-

sequently printed a cancel title-page, removing Shakespeare's name.

The only authoritative text of the *Sonnets* (hereinafter referred to as Q) was published in 1609. '20 Maij Thomas Thorpe Entred for his copie vnder thandes of master Wilson and master Lownes Warden A Booke called Shakespeares sonnettes.' Thus the entry in the Stationers' Register. The printer was George Eld. The edition appears to have been divided between two booksellers: the imprint on seven of the surviving thirteen copies is that of John Wright, on four that of William Aspley. The other two lack title-pages. The British Museum copy's title-page reads: 'SHAKE-SPEARES / SONNETS. / Never before Imprinted. / AT LONDON / By *G. Eld* for *T. T.* and are / to be solde by *William Aspley* / 1609.' The dedication follows (p. 27), and then a hundred-and-fifty-four numbered sonnets and a forty-seven stanza poem entitled 'A Lovers Complaint. / BY / WILLIAM SHAKESPEARE.'

The fact that only thirteen copies of Q survive is significant. It is rare for a seventeenth-century book. This has given rise to speculation that it may have been withdrawn. The text as such is good – as reliable at least as a good Quarto of the plays. Whether it is based on Shakespeare's manuscript or not is a further problem on which critics are divided. The unevenness – poetically – of the sonnets has led to uncertainty over Q: some critics prefer to regard the weaker pieces as not Shakespeare's at all. A few critics go so far as to suggest that the sequence is altogether the work of other hands – Sidney, Barnabe Barnes, William Warner, Donne and others have all been suggested. The basic authority of the 1609 text was most interestingly questioned by L. C. Knights in his essay reprinted in this volume (Part Three).

Acceptance or otherwise of the authority of the Q text is not merely a matter of scholarly interest. It throws into relief the problem of the sequential order of the *Sonnets*, and hence of the over-all 'organisation' of the sequence, the inter-relations of imagery, the possibility of a latent plot, and so on. The nature of the problem is highlighted by the next extant edition, that of 1640, which appeared after Shakespeare's death. Under the title

'POEMS: / WRITTEN BY / WIL. SHAKE-SPEARE. / Gent. / Printed at London by Tho. Cotes, and are to be sold / by Iohn Benson, dwelling in St Dunstans / Church-yard. 1640' appeared a miscellaneous collection including all but eight of the sonnets from Q, a couple of songs from Shakespeare's plays, the whole of 'The Passionate Pilgrim' in its 1612 version, a reprinting of 'The Phoenix and the Turtle', and poems by Milton, Ben Jonson and Herrick, among others. The venture is clearly a piracy. The publisher jumbled the Q order, grouping two or three sonnets together under titles such as 'Injurious Time' or 'A Bashfull Lover', as if they were separate poems. He changed some of the pronouns: the young man becomes a young woman. But, according to J. Dover Wilson in the introduction to his 1966 edition of the Sonnets, J. B. Leishman checked the text and found, beyond one or two pronoun changes, possibly misprints, 'no evidence of deliberate falsification of this sort'.

More significant is that John Benson appears to have been able to deceive his contemporaries over the existence of Q. The paucity of copies of Q indicates that the poems were not widely known and that Shakespeare most probably had no hand in the original publication. This in turn casts doubt on the authority of the ordering of the sonnets in Q. There is also, as Martin Seymour-Smith has pointed out in the admirable introduction to his 1963 edition, the possibility that publication of love poems addressed by a man to a man might have placed the poet in jeopardy. Seymour-Smith writes,

The fact that Shakespeare may have felt apprehension about the publication of the Sonnets does not in itself imply that there had actually been an 'illegal' association between himself and his friend. It does, however, very strongly suggest that the Sonnets were essentially personal and private compositions: there is nothing else in Elizabethan literature in which a man so openly avows love for another man.

Benson was so successful in his enterprise that even as recently as 1924 T. G. Tucker in his edition suggested that Benson might have had access to unknown manuscripts.

The first edition of the Sonnets not based on Benson was issued by Bernard Lintott (1711), edited by an unknown hand. Undoubtedly the outstanding scholarly edition in the eighteenth century was Edmond Malone's (1780), firmly establishing the authority of the Q text and adding a commentary superior to many more recent ones. The faults with his edition are in his emendations, largely in the area of punctuation. His emendations have been followed by many modern editions. This is no mere pedantic complaint: as Robert Graves and Laura Riding illustrate in their essay (Part Three), slight variations in punctuation lead to changes of emphasis and meaning.

Most rewarding of twentieth-century editions are H. C. Beeching's (1904), Sidney Lee's (1905), R. M. Alden's variorum (1916), T. G. Tucker's (1924 – especially for introductory matter), H. E. Rollin's *New Variorum* in two volumes (1944) and J. Dover Wilson's (1966). Martin Seymour-Smith's edition (1963) is recommended not only for its introduction but for the text, which retains the old spellings.

When were the *Sonnets* written? Most attempts to date them are guesswork, yet what little evidence there is proves important if we wish to relate them to Shakespeare's world and to his plays. Theories abound, often grounded on the doubtful hints of historical allusion thrown out by an image or a single line, and then generalised to apply to the whole sequence. The facts are few: all the sonnets were written by 1609; two of them had been written by 1599.

Theories about the dating of the *Sonnets* fall into two categories: whether the detective believes the sonnets to be autobiographical; or whether he takes them to be merely literary exercises. If the former, then the investigator will tend to date by contemporary 'references', by possible Friends and Dark Ladies; if the latter (see Sidney Lee's *Life of William Shakespeare*, enlarged edition, 1915) he dates by style and the main vogue for sonnet sequences.

A large tribe of Friends has been suggested by different critics. The salient candidates are listed by Ingram and Redpath. Those whom patient historians have exhumed through research are usually young Elizabethans for whom parents or protectors are trying to arrange marriages. Such candidates are less glamorous (though perhaps more credible) than the inspired guesses of Oscar Wilde, say, or John Masefield. Wilde excitedly points to one of the boy actors in Shakespeare's company (see *A Portrait of Mr W. H.*, 1889), William Hews. Masefield, in his Romanes Lecture on 'Shakespeare and Spiritual Life' (1924) took a similar view. The 'lovely boy' of sonnet CXXVI was an actor who remained small enough to play the diminutive parts of Moth and Ariel.

Dark Ladies are even more hypothetical: Queen Elizabeth is the most preposterous suggestion, a negro prostitute the most unlikely. The most plausible suggestion is Mary Fitton, the Maid of Honour who was Pembroke's mistress. But this supposes Pembroke to have been the Friend. A. L. Rowse has found yet another Dark Lady, Emilia Lanier (*Shakespeare's Sonnets: The Problems Solved*, 1964).

In the preface to his play *The Dark Lady of the Sonnets*, George Bernard Shaw comments that Shakespeare 'rubbed in the lady's complexion in his sonnets mercilessly; for in his day black hair was as unpopular as red hair was in the early days of Queen Victoria. Any tinge lighter than raven black must be held fatal to the strongest claim to be the Dark Lady. . . .'

Rival Poets are generally taken from among Marlowe, Chapman and Greene, though again here there is a library of speculation.

A preconceived biographical interpretation can force the *Sonnets* into a dating, but cannot solve many of the poetic problems of the poems. The *Sonnets* may confess passion; they do not confess fact. Even the 'name' they set out to immortalise is never spoken. A biographical situation has been translated into a human situation, with a poetic veracity and depth of authority. That is the unarguable fact, and more important than any putative *dramatis personae*.

We may wish to date the *Sonnets* by relating them to the plays. *Love's Labour's Lost* contains seven sonnets (1588–94), some of them woven into the dialogue of the play, others as independent lyrics. There are also parallels in *Midsummer Night's Dream* and *Romeo and Juliet*. Sidney Lee found further parallels in the narrative poems and other early plays. Some critics have confused the issue, finding connections with the later plays (Beeching, for example, in 1904). C. S. Lewis in *English Literature in the Seventeenth Century* (1954) writes of this problem:

I can hardly conceive a poet moving from the style of the best sonnets . . . to that of *Venus and Adonis*, but can easily conceive one who had achieved Shakespeare's mature dramatic technique still writing some of the sonnets we have . . . If Shakespeare had taken an hour off from the composition of *Lear* to write a sonnet, the sonnet might not have been in the style of *Lear*.

Dating by contemporary allusion is certainly entertaining but can be misleading. The most notorious 'contemporary allusion' is in sonnet CVII, 'The mortall moone hath her eclipse indur'de'. The variety of interpretations invalidates the approach. 'Moon' has been taken variously to refer to the crescent formation of the advancing Armada (1588–9), to the Queen's recovery from serious illness (1596), to danger threatening the Queen (1601) and to her death (1603).

Samuel Butler in his edition (1899) and Leslie Hotson in 'Shakespeare's Sonnets Dated' (1949) plump for 1585–8; but this verdict fails to take into account the actual mature authority of the poetry, superior in many ways to the verse in *Venus and Adonis* and *The Rape of Lucrece* (1593–4). The more widely accepted dating, between 1594 and 1599, fits better with the poetic evidence, the relation with the early plays, and the main vogue for sonnet sequence writing, which extended from Sir Philip Sidney's *Astrophel and Stella* (written about 1580, first and unauthorised edition 1591) through Samuel Daniel's *Delia* (1592), Henry Constable's *Diana* (1592), and others until, shortly before the turn of the century, fashions changed.

Shakespeare's choice of the sonnet form for his love poems has been criticised by some, most notably John Crowe Ransom (Part Three). He stresses the inherent inflexibility of the form, its tendency to impose a specific organisation on the experience that seeks expression through it. But as other critics have replied,

Shakespeare's control of the form is not merely technical. He adapts the rigid structure to his own needs. M. M. Mahood (Part Four) points out that we should first look in a sonnet 'not for the kind of logic which could be reduced to a prose syllogism, but for a satisfying organisation of sound and sense that conveys the ordered movement of thought into which the emotion has been shaped'. And Winifred Nowottny (Part Four) sensitively identifies 'form' as 'that in virtue of which the parts are related one to another' or 'that which manifests itself in the relationship of the parts'. In this sense, 'the *Sonnets* reveal Shakespeare's strong sense of form'. Yvor Winters suggests that Shakespeare seldom took the traditional sonnet form 'with any real seriousness' – his sonnets 'never achieve the closely organized treatment of the subject which we find in the best of Jonson and Donne'. This is a much more serious consideration than the identity of Mr W. H.

The first seventeen sonnets seem to indicate that Shakespeare intended to write a sequence true to the conventions of the day, probably following the model of Daniel's *Delia*, and then took command of the convention and transcended it as his experience became more complex. There are obvious stresses in his attempt to reconcile the acutely real emotions to the traditional, basically logical, sonnet form. Service and bondage are terms often employed by the critics: 'imagery is subordinated to the creation of the form of the whole' writes Nowottny; 'the thinking is put at the service of the symbol' writes Wilson Knight; and Ewbank says, 'Explicitly, then, in the sonnets, Shakespeare is striving for the subordination of the style to the subject matter.' Content – the poet's experience – is in conflict with the conventions of the sonnet. This is what distinguishes the sequence from the work of Shakespeare's contemporaries. G. K. Hunter rightly remarks (Part Four) that it is 'the approach to the *Sonnets* as lyric, narrative, or metaphysical exercises that is misdirected'. The tensions of Shakespeare's complex experience drive the 'drama' of the sonnets not necessarily forward in a linear narrative progression but inward, into a paradoxically expanding awareness of the nature of love, beset by the different mutabilities of time, fickleness and rivalry.

Ransom stresses that the 'metrical pattern of any sonnet is

directive', and that if 'the English sonnet exhibits the rhyme-scheme ABAB CDCD EFEF GG, it imposes upon the poet the following requirement: that he write three co-ordinate quatrains and then a couplet which will relate to the series collectively'. True, schematically. But if the content is intractable, the form must become a little malleable, as it does in Shakespeare's usage. Patrick Cruttwell in *The Shakespearian Moment* (1960) has highlighted this point. He says that we misread not only the sonnets but the literature of the age itself if we ask for a narrative, 'an objective sequence with a fictional story'. To see the Elizabethan age 'as a solid, unchanging unity is utterly misleading. Within it there were two generations and (roughly corresponding to those generations) two mentalities. In the 1590s the one "handed over" to the other . . . there *was* an old, and there *was* a new, and the task of criticism is to analyse and distinguish.' The *Sonnets* belong to the transition and are a key to our understanding of it. The sonnet sequence form is old, the use Shakespeare puts it to is new.

The first sonnet sequence of real note was by Francesco Petrarca (1304–74) – *Canzoniere*, which included longer poems as well, but is predominantly sonnets. That sequence established many of the conventions, formal and thematic. Petrarch followed Dante, who had employed the form in *La Vita Nuova*, preferring the rhyme scheme ABBA ABBA CDECDE (or, in the sestet, CDCD CD), all the lines decasyllabic. A final couplet was avoided. Sir Thomas Wyatt, after visiting Italy in 1527, developed an English form close to Petrarch's but often introduced a final couplet. The Earl of Surrey began using the form we now call Shakespearean or English: i.e., fourteen decasyllabic lines divided into three quatrains and a concluding couplet, rhymed ABAB CDCD EFEF GG or ABBA CDDC EFFE GG. Spenser in the *Amoretti* had used the final epigrammatic couplet, but his sonnets often did not break between octave and sestet (and are sometimes called the 'link' sonnet). Shakespeare commonly places a strong pause at the end of each quatrain, with a double pause at the end of the second.

From Petrarch (but also from Horace and Ovid) Shakespeare

borrowed the 'eternising' theme, to protect the beloved against
the ravages of time. He spares us many of the conventional
excesses of Petrarch and other sonneteers, the woes of the rejected
suitor, the tenuous and then dashed instants of hope. The
substance is more authentic, it seems: the best sonnets reanimate
convention altogether. He goes so far in sonnet CXXX as to reverse
the convention of comparing the beloved favourably with objects
of natural beauty: 'My Mistres eyes are nothing like the Sunne'.

There *were* conventions to be accepted or rejected, of course;
but it is misleading to suggest as M. J. Wolff does (*Englische
Studien*, XLIX, 1916) that the *Sonnets* are entirely conventional,
tracing each theme back to Italian predecessors. Sidney Lee
(Part Three) explored this field in a masterly way in his *Life*,
particularly Shakespeare's debt to Golding's translation of
Ovid's *Metamorphoses*. Lee overstates his case, but it was a
salutary excess, for it marked the turning-point in the critical
history of the *Sonnets*. It was an attempt to read them as poetry, to
get beyond the fruitless debates about the 'characters'. Benedetto
Croce perhaps best summarises the nature of Shakespeare's use of
convention in his *Ariosto, Shakespeare and Corneille* (1920) where he
says that, despite his models,

Shakespeare does not cease to be a poet, because he is never altogether
able to separate himself from himself, everywhere he infuses his own
thought and modes of feeling, those harmonies peculiar to himself, those
movements of the soul, so delicate and profound. This has endowed the
Sonnets with the aspect of biographical mystery, of a poem containing
some hidden moral and philosophical sense.

The 'biographical mystery' is bound to be in our minds when we
consider the actual sequential arrangement of the *Sonnets*. The
order of Q is now generally accepted for convenience, but there
are objections. It is strange, for example, for the sequence to build
up to, and conclude with, two of the weakest sonnets (CLIII and
CLIV); there is no logical plot; there is no consecutive 'emotional'
or 'internal' drama; and there is a great unevenness of quality in
the writing. But attempts at regrouping the poems have failed to

produce anything better: they are necessarily subjective. T. W. Baldwin in *The Literary Genetics of Shakespeare's Poems and Sonnets* (1950) suggests that, thematically, every sonnet in Q grows out of the one before it. This is a profitable study, but more profitable is J. B. Leishman's approach in *Themes and Variations in Shakespeare's Sonnets* (1961). He does not argue for the correctness of the Q ordering, but for the inter-connectedness of the entire *oeuvre*. Failing an authoritative alternative, Q must be accepted. Jan Kott (Part Four) finds himself, perhaps a little fancifully, able to look at the full sequence broadly as a 'drama'.

It is possible to divide the sonnets, as presented in the Q text, into two separate groups: I– CXXVI and CXXVII–CLIV, the former addressed to one (or more?) young man, the latter to the Dark Lady. In the first seventeen, as they stand, the poet urges the young man to marry and propagate; but the relationship changes in tone and manner, the speaker becomes 'involved', suffers the trials of rivalry when another poet solicits his friend, and when the friend falls in with the poet's mistress and the two men share her favours unbeknown to each other. The truth emerges, the poet forgives his friend, breaks with the lady. Perhaps that is as far as we dare to go. L. C. Knights cautions us (Part Three): 'we tend to assume that the collection is more homogeneous than in fact it is, and we tend, therefore, to make rather sweeping generalizations about "The Sonnets" as a whole'. In a footnote, he adds:

The tendency is encouraged by the fact that the Sonnets are printed in a numbered sequence, without titles. And remembering the part played by verbal habit in directing thought, we may consider the effect of the mere repetition of the phrase, 'The Sonnets'.

We may be able to appreciate the *Sonnets* more readily than nineteenth-century readers. They were concerned for Shakespeare's moral reputation. 'O my son!' cries Coleridge, 'I pray fervently that thou may'st know inwardly how impossible it was for Shakespeare not to have been in his heart's heart chaste.' Even Samuel Butler, conceding that Shakespeare's affection may have amounted to more than a 'typical Renaissance friendship', protects the poet by the idea that 'Mr W. H. must have lured him on.' Coleridge blames the 'very inferior women of that age'. The approach was biographical first. Lee helped to change that, and the moral climate has changed sufficiently for prescriptive censure to cease to mar our reading of the poems. Apart from A. L. Rowse's recent efforts, there is less serious attention paid to the unverifiable biographical source of the work, more to the human and poetic source and nature of the sequence. In the middle of the twentieth century, critics – notably Wilson Knight in *The Mutual Flame* (1955) (Part Four) – began to examine the symbolic elements, and to re-examine the perennial thematic elements.

This book, in its last section, reveals that a continual dialogue and debate is taking place among the critics, and with each encounter we are made aware of further poetic qualities in the *Sonnets*. The value of the criticism they have received this century is often great. It is no longer impressionistic criticism nor moral apologetics but close attention to text and to the poetic milieu from which that text emerged; an attention, too, to the human aspects of the poetry, a belief that, though the *Sonnets* are not a key to Shakespeare's biography, they take us closer than any other work of his to the creative intelligence that brought about the verse of the plays.

PART ONE

Relationships

1. Two uses of sonnet form in an early play, *Romeo and Juliet*

I

CHORUS Two households, both alike in dignity,
In fair Verona, where we lay our scene,
From ancient grudge break to new mutiny,
Where civil blood makes civil hands unclean.
From forth the fatal loins of these two foes
A pair of star-cross'd lovers take their life;
Whose misadventur'd piteous overthrows
Do with their death bury their parents' strife.
The fearful passage of their death-mark'd love,
And the continuance of their parents' rage,
Which, but their children's end, nought could remove,
Is now the two hours' traffick of our stage;
The which if you with patient ears attend,
Where here shall miss, our toil shall strive to mend.

Prologue

II

ROMEO If I profane with my unworthiest hand
This holy shrine, the gentle sin is this;
My lips, two blushing pilgrims, ready stand
To smooth that rough touch with a tender kiss.
JULIET Good pilgrim, you do wrong your hand too much
Which mannerly devotion shows in this;
For saints have hands that pilgrims' hands do touch,
And palm to palm is holy palmer's kiss.
ROMEO Have not saints lips, and holy palmers too?
JULIET Ay, pilgrim, lips that they must use in prayer.
ROMEO O! then, dear saint, let lips do what hands do;
Then pray, grant thou, lest faith turn to despair.
JULIET Saints do not move, though grant for prayer's sake.
ROMEO Then move not, while my prayers' effect I take.

I v 96ff.

2. Two references to sonnets from early plays

I

BEROWNE   O! but for my love, day would turn to night.
Of all complexions the cull'd sovereignty
Do meet, as at a fair, in her fair cheek;
Where several worthies make one dignity,
Where nothing wants that want itself doth seek.
Lend me the flourish of all gentle tongues, —
Fie, painted rhetoric! O! she needs it not:
To things of sale a seller's praise belongs;
She passes praise; then praise too short doth blot.
A wither'd hermit, five-score winters worn,
Might shake off fifty, looking in her eye:
Beauty doth varnish age, as if new-born,
And gives the crutch the cradle's infancy.
O! 'tis the sun that maketh all things shine.
KING   By heaven, thy love is black as ebony.
BEROWNE   Is ebony like her? O wood divine!
A wife of such wood were felicity.
O! who can give an oath? where is a book?
That I may swear beauty doth beauty lack,
If that she learn not of her eye to look:
No face is fair that is not full so black.
                          Love's Labour's Lost, IV iii 230ff.

II

PROTEUS   As much as I can do I will effect.
But you Sir Thurio, are not sharp enough;
You must lay lime to tangle her desires
By wailful sonnets, whose composed rimes
Should be full-fraught with serviceable vows.
DUKE   Ay,
Much is the force of heaven-bred poesy.
PROTEUS   Say that upon the altar of her beauty

You sacrifice your tears, your sighs, your heart.
Write till your ink be dry, and with your tears
Moist it again, and frame some feeling line
That may discover such integrity:
For Orpheus' lute was strung with poets' sinews,
Whose golden touch could soften steel and stone,
Make tigers tame and huge leviathans
Forsake unsounded deeps to dance on sands.

Two Gentlemen of Verona, III ii 66ff.

The 1609 Dedication by Thomas Thorpe

TO. THE ONLIE. BEGETTER. OF.

THESE. INSVING. SONNETS.

Mr. W. H. ALL. HAPPINESSE.

AND. THAT. ETERNITIE.

PROMISED.

BY.

OVR. EVER-LIVING. POET.

WISHETH.

THE. WELL-WISHING.

ADVENTVRER. IN.

SETTING.

FORTH.

T. T.

W. G. INGRAM AND THEODORE REDPATH

A Note on the Dedication

This apparently straightforward dedication of a volume of
poems, signed with the initials of the publisher (Thomas
Thorpe), and seemingly addressed to somebody only indicated
by initials, has raised a welter of ingenious speculations and
conflicting interpretations. There is no evidence that the Dedication stimulated attention until very late in the eighteenth
century, but since then it has been the playground of theorists
who have allowed it to distract their interest from the poems as

poems. As the late Professor Rollins wrote in 1944: 'No doubt the sonnets would be more often read for their poetry today if Thorpe had discarded his own thirty words!'

The chief enigmas embodied in the wording are as follows:

    (1) What is a 'begetter'?
    (2) What does 'onlie' mean?
    (3) Who was Mr. W. H.?
    (4) Who was the Well-wishing Adventurer?
    (5) What is the meaning of 'setting forth'?
    (6) What does 'promised' mean, and to whom was the 'eternitie' 'promised'?
    (7) Who was T. T.?
    (8) What is the syntax of the Dedication?

1 *Begetter*] The chief answers have been: (*a*) 'inspirer'; (*b*) 'procurer' (i.e. of the manuscript for the publisher).

Linguistic usage favours 'inspirer'. Although the *verb* 'beget' had earlier borne the sense 'to get, to acquire', no example is cited in *OED* after 1393, other than a sentence from Hamlet's advice to the players: 'You must acquire and beget a temperance that may give it smoothness', where the word does not mean *procuring* something external but *engendering* a quality in oneself. A further point is that the examples cited by *OED* always connote acquiring some thing or goods *for oneself*. This would argue against 'begetter' meaning 'procurer *for another person*', though it would still leave *possible* the sense 'procurer for himself'.

The passage from Dekker's *Satiromastix* often cited in support of the sense (of the *verb* 'beget') 'procure for another' is, in fact, as Samuel Butler pointed out, spoken by a Welshman, Sir Rhys Ap Vaughan, who is held up to ridicule throughout the play by his travesties of English speech. The passage reads as follows: 'If I fall sansomely upon the Widdow, I have some cossens German at Court, shall beget you the reversion of the Master of the Kings Revels.' Other words in this very passage make it hardly respectable evidence of correct English usage.

Moreover, the *noun* 'begetter' is only cited by *OED* as having two senses: (1) 'a procreator'; (2) 'the agent that originates, produces or occasions'. This passage is cited under (2), where in all the other examples the word bears a figurative, theological sense, e.g. in Golding, *De Mornay's Work concerning the Trueness of the Christian Religion*, iii, 28: 'The onely one God . . . the Begetter of the Soules of the other Gods'. In no case cited there or elsewhere could the word mean 'procurer'.

Thus, whatever the dedicator may have intended the word to mean, it would not to the contemporary reader have conveyed the meaning 'procurer'. If the dedicator intended such a meaning he would, therefore, have been writing in a cryptic and private language. In any case, however, since he was himself of that time, the probability against his having even *intended* such a meaning is tremendous.

Against the meaning 'inspirer' it has been urged that the *Sonnets* are not all addressed to the same person. In answer, however, it has been pointed out that the first 126 sonnets (or, at all events, almost all of them) seem to be addressed to the same person, and that those addressed to a woman are printed at the end of the book; so that the allusion in the Dedication would be substantially accurate if 'begetter' meant 'inspirer'.

2 *Onlie*] This is taken by almost all commentators to mean 'sole', whether they think the reference is to the 'inspirer' or to the 'procurer'. There is, however, an alternative sense, namely, 'incomparable', 'peerless' (cf. *OED*, sense 5), and, as William Sharp, who has anticipated us in suggesting this meaning, points out (*Songs, Poems and Sonnets of Shakespeare*, Newcastle, 1885; Introduction, p. 23), the word is used in this sense in Sonnet 1, line 10. This meaning would possibly sort somewhat better with 'inspirer' than with 'procurer'.

3 *Mr. W. H.*] What Rollins called the 'guessing contest' about Mr. W. H. was started by Tyrwhitt and Farmer in the late eighteenth century. The chief candidates nominated by commentators for the honour of the designation have been: (*a*) William Herbert, Third Earl of Pembroke (1580–1630); (*b*) Henry Wriothesley, Third Earl of Southampton (1573–1624), whose initials would then be reversed; (*c*) William Hall, a piratical printer; (*d*) William Hervey, stepfather of the Earl of Southampton; (*e*) William Hathaway, Shakespeare's

brother-in-law; (*f*) William Hughes (Hewes), who has been variously identified; (*g*) William Himself. As stated in our Preface, we have no intention of adjudicating between their rival claims.

4 *The Well-wishing Adventurer*] There seems to be pretty general agreement that this was Thomas Thorpe, who, as the publisher of the *Sonnets,* was 'venturing' some capital.

5 *Setting forth*] The high-flown language of the Dedication is characteristic not only of the time but also, in particular, of Thorpe himself. Just as 'adventurer' would have suggested the enterprises of merchant venturers, so 'setting forth' would have suggested the sailing of one of their ships, though it would also have suggested the process of printing and publishing a book.

6 (*a*) *The meaning of 'promised'*] Two meanings are possible: (i) 'promised in the specific words of the poems' (e.g. in Sonnets 18 and 19); (ii) 'augured by the quality of the poet's work'.

(*b*) *To whom was the 'eternitie' 'promised'?*] (i) If Mr. W. H. was the *inspirer* it was 'promised' to him in whichever sense is the right one; (ii) if he was not the *inspirer* but only the *procurer,* it was 'promised' to him in sense (*a*) (ii), not in sense (*a*) (i), in which, indeed, it was 'promised' only to the *inspirer.*

7 *T. T.*] Undoubtedly Thomas Thorpe, the publisher of the *Sonnets.*

8 *The syntax of the Dedication*] The printing of the Dedication is lapidary, i.e. closely similar to that of many inscriptions in stone. It has a full stop after every word. The pointing, therefore, does not help in determining the syntax. Some scholars have seen 'wisheth' as concluding a sentence, and having 'Mr. W. H.' as its subject. The French scholar Chasles based this view on the leading between the central five lines, but, as Massey has pointed out, this no more divides them from what follows than from what precedes. It seems, indeed, pretty evident that the subject of 'wisheth' is 'T. T.'.

SOURCE: extract from the Ingram and Redpath edition of *Shakespeare's Sonnets* (1964) pp. 3—5.

A. L. ROWSE

The Publisher's Mr W. H.

The first thing to realise is that the Sonnets were not published until many years after the experiences they relate were over. That is very understandable when we come to consider the nature of the experiences, whom they affected and how near the bone they were. They were not published until 1609, only seven years before Shakespeare's death; the experiences they describe go back to the years 1592 to 1594–5, a decade or more before.

We need not go into details about publication, printing, typography: we need only to say that the people involved – publisher, printer, booksellers – were all reputable people. The publisher, Thomas Thorpe, was rather remarkable among publishers. He was himself literary-minded, he had a notably distinguished list, published a number of famous plays, particularly Ben Jonson's and Chapman's, as well as Marlowe's translation of Lucan; and Thorpe was a friend of Edward Blount, Marlowe's friend.

Shakespeare cannot have had anything to do with the publication. Thorpe had got the manuscripts from 'Mr. W. H.' – this was regular enough in Elizabethan publishing – and it was Thorpe who wrote the somewhat flowery dedication to 'Mr. W. H.', full of gratitude for having got the manuscript of the Sonnets for him, as well he might be. A study of Thorpe shows that eloquent dedications were characteristic of him. But the essential point to remember is that 'Mr. W. H.' – we shall come to him later – was not Shakespeare's man at all, but Thorpe's, the publisher's.

Scores, if not hundreds, of books and articles have been written under the misapprehension that 'Mr. W. H.' was the young lord to whom Shakespeare wrote the Sonnets. All these books are beside the mark. We need not consider any of them, merely point out that such eminent Shakespeare scholars as Sir Edmund Chambers and Professor Dover Wilson, let alone others, incomprehensibly overlooked this elementary fact and ruined their work in this regard by trying to find a 'Mr. W. H.' who fitted the character of Shakespeare's young 'Lord of my love'.

Let us repeat: 'Mr. W. H.' was simply Thorpe's dedicatee. We shall note later who he was – a matter of secondary importance – in its proper place at the end of the story. But the realisation of this obvious fact is the indispensable condition to getting the Sonnets right: it opens the way to common sense about them and their correct interpretation.

SOURCE: *Shakespeare's Sonnets: The Problems Solved*, 2nd ed. (1973) pp. xiii–xiv.

NOTE

[The first sentence of the third paragraph has been revised by Dr Rowse for this Casebook – Ed.]

PART TWO

Early Comment
1598—1799

FRANCIS MERES (1598)

As the soul of Euphorbus was thought to live in Pythagoras: so the sweete wittie soule of *Ovid* lives in the mellifluous & hony-tongued *Shakespeare*, witness his *Venus and Adonis*, his *Lucrece*, his sugred Sonnets among his private friends, &c.

SOURCE: *Palladis Tamia* (1598).

JOHN BENSON (1640)

To the Reader,
I here presume (under favour) to present to your view, some excellent and sweetely composed Poems, of Master *William Shakespeare*, Which in themselves appeare of the same purity, the Authour himselfe then living avouched; they had not the fortune by reason of their Infancie in his death, to have the due accommodation of proportionable glory, with the rest of his everliving Workes, yet the lines of themselves will afford you a more authentick approbation than my assurance any way can, to invite your allowance, in your perusall you shall finde them *Seren*, cleere and eligantly plaine, such gentle straines as shall recreate and not perplexe your braine, no intricacie or cloudy stuffe to puzzell intellect, but perfect eloquence; such as will raise your admiration to his praise: this assurance I know will not differ from your acknowledgement. And certaine I am, my opinion will be seconded by the sufficiency of these ensuing Lines; I have beene somewhat solicitus to bring this forth to the perfect view of all men; and in so doing, glad to be serviceable for the continuance of glory to the deserved Author in these his Poems.

SOURCE: 'Epistle to the Reader', POEMS: / WRITTEN / BY / WIL. SHAKE-SPEARE. / Gent. (1640).

NOTE

[Benson here is deliberately misleading his readers, pretending to present to them hitherto unprinted poems. The sonnets are in a shuffled

order, and his urging of their authenticity by comparison with the
openly acknowledged *Venus and Adonis* and *Lucrece* merely adds to his
attempts to cover his tracks of piracy. Benson also altered pronouns
making the young man appear a woman; but see Intro., p. 13 – Ed.]

ANONYMOUS (1683)

An Allusion to Sonnet LV

. . . and wherever they shall for the future happen to come, I
doubt not but they will make good that of the incomparable
Shakespear:

> Not Marble, nor the gilded Monument
> Of Princes shall out-live this powerful Line;
> But you shall shine more bright in this Content,
> Than dusty Trophies soil'd with sluttish time,
> 'Gainst Death and all oblivious Enmity,
> Still shall you live, Your Praise shall still find room
> Ev'n in the Eyes of all Posterity;
> Were this frail World sunk to its final Doom.
> So till in Judgement you again shall rise,
> You live in this, and dwell in Lovers Eyes.

SOURCE: from the Dedication of *Eronema: Or, The Noble
Stranger. A Novel* (London, 1683).

ANONYMOUS (1774)

If Shakespeare's merit as a poet, a philosopher, or a man was to
be estimated from his Poems, though they possess many instances
of powerful genius, he would, in every point of view, sink beneath
himself in these characters. Many of his subjects are trifling, his
versification mostly laboured and quibbling, with too great a
degree of licentiousness.

SOURCE: from *Preface to the Poems*: supplementary volume to
The Plays in 8 Volumes, ed. J. Bell and C. Etherington (1774).

NOTE

[This edition contains John Benson's corrupt and muddled grouping again – Ed.]

EDMOND MALONE (1780)

Many of the thoughts that occur in his dramatic productions are found here likewise; as may appear from the numerous parallels that have been cited from his dramas, chiefly for the purpose of authenticating these poems. Had they therefore no other merit, they are entitled to our attention, as often illustrating obscure passages in his plays.

I do not perceive that the versification of these pieces is less smooth and harmonious than that of Shakespeare's other compositions.

SOURCE: from *The Poems*; supplementary volume (1780) to Johnson's and Steevens's 1778 edition of *The Plays of William Shakespeare*.

NOTE

[This edition shows the first attempt at textual emendation and intelligent critical notes – Ed.]

GEORGE STEEVENS (1793)

We have not reprinted the Sonnets, &c. of Shakespeare, because the strongest act of Parliament that could be framed, would fail to compel readers into their service; notwithstanding these miscellaneous Poems have derived every possible advantage from the literature and judgement of their only intelligent editor, Mr Malone, whose implements of criticism, like the ivory rake and golden spade in Prudentius, are on this occasion disgraced by the objects of their culture. – Had Shakespeare produced no other works than these, his name would have reached us with as little celebrity as time has conferred on that of Thomas Watson, an older and much more elegant sonnetteer.

SOURCE: from *Advertisement to The Plays of William Shakespeare* (1793).

GEORGE CHALMERS (1799)

Of those Amatory Verses [the sonnets], it may be truly said, that as a whole poem, which is often tied together by a very slight ligature, they have two of the worst faults, that can degrade any writing; they are obscure; and they are tedious. Spenser, who furnished the model of them, has his obscurities, and tediousness; but he has withal, more distinctness, in his topicks, and more facility, in his style: Shakspeare plainly endeavoured to go beyond the mark of his rivalry; but, in affecting the sublime, he sunk, by a natural cadence, into the unintelligible. Spenser having no rival, and only a single object, caught at such topicks of praise, as he thought would please the most, and adopted such a style, as he could most easily manage. Of such a poet, as Shakspeare, it may easily be conceived, that he has many happy phrases, and elegant lines, though they are generally darkened by conceit, and marred by affectation; with as many happy phrases, and elegant lines, Spenser has fewer conceits and less affectation; having from inheritance, as fruitful a garden of images, which he watered from a deeper fountain of learning. Shakspeare 'fancy's sweetest child', shows sometimes a manifest superiority in *imagination* over Spenser, when this wonderful poet is forming the same images. By an effort of his creative powers, Shakspeare appears to have carried away the palm, in this great quality of a true poet, from his illustrious rival, even when Spenser put forth his whole strength, in cultivating the same field.

SOURCE: from *A Supplemental Apology for the Believers, in the Shakspeare-papers* (1799).

PART THREE

Comment and Criticism
c. 1803–1938

1. CRITICAL COMMENT

[Wordsworth]

These sonnets beginning at CXXVII to his mistress, are worse than a puzzle-peg. They are abominably harsh, obscure, and worthless. The others are for the most part much better, have many fine lines[,] very fine lines and passages. They are also in many places warm with passion. Their chief faults – and heavy ones they are – are sameness, tediousness, quaintness, and elaborate obscurity.

[Coleridge]

I can by no means subscribe to the above pencil mark of W. Wordsworth; which, however, it is my wish should never be erased. It is *his*: and grievously am I mistaken, and deplorably will Englishmen have degenerated if the being *his* will not in times to come give it a value, as of a little reverential relic – the rude mark of his hand left by the sweat of haste in a St Veronica handkerchief! . . . My sweet Hartley! if thou livest, thou wilt not part with this book without sad necessity and a pang at heart. Oh, be never weary of reperusing the first four volumes of this collection, my eldest born! . . . These sonnets thou, I trust, if God preserve thy life, Hartley! thou wilt read with a deep interest, having learnt to love the plays of Shakespeare, co-ordinate with Milton, and subordinate only to thy Bible. To thee, I trust, they will help to explain the mind of Shakespeare, and if thou wouldst understand these sonnets, thou must read the chapter in Potter's *Antiquities* on the Greek lovers – of whom were that Theban band of brothers over whom Philip, their victor, stood weeping; and surveying their dead bodies, each with his shield over the body of his friend, all dead in the place where they fought, solemnly cursed those whose base, fleshly, and most calumnious fancies had suspected their love of desires against nature. This pure love Shakespeare appears to have felt – to have been in no way ashamed of – or even to have suspected that others could have suspected it. Yet at the same time he knew that so strong a love would have been made more completely a thing of permanence and reality, and have been blessed more by nature and taken under her more especial protection, if this object of his love had been at the same time a possible object of desire – for nature is not soul only. In this feeling he must have written the twentieth sonnet; but its possibility seems never to have entered even his imagination. It is noticeable that not even an allusion to that very worst of all possible vices (for it is wise to think of the disposition, as a *vice*, not of the absurd and despicable act, as a *crime*) not even any allusion to it [occurs] in all his numerous plays – whereas Jonson, Beaumont and Fletcher, and Massinger are full of them. O my son! I pray fervently that thou may'st know inwardly how impossible it was for a Shakespeare not to have been in his heart's heart chaste. I see no elaborate obscurity and very little quaintness – nor do I know any sonnets that will bear such frequent reperusal: so rich in metre, so full of thought and *exquisitest* diction. S. T. Coleridge, Greta Hall, Keswick, Wed. morning, half past three, Nov. 2, 1803.

> SOURCE: from Marginalia in the set of Robert Anderson's *Poets of Great Britain* (13 vols, 1793–1807) in the Folger Shakespeare Library, Washington D.C.

NOTE

[Wordsworth's marginal comment is undated. Coleridge wrote his on the day of Hartley Coleridge's christening, the boy being then 'more than seven years of age' – Ed.]

WILLIAM WORDSWORTH (1815)

. . . There is extant a small Volume of miscellaneous poems, in which Shakespeare expresses his own feelings in his own person.

It is not difficult to conclude that the Editor, George Steevens, should have been insensible to the beauties of one portion of that Volume, the Sonnets; though in no part of the writings of this Poet is found, in an equal compass, a greater number of exquisite feelings felicitously expressed.

Source: from *Essay, Supplementary to the Preface to 'Lyrical Ballads'* (1815).

s. t. coleridge (1817)

I

. . . Shakespeare's evenness and sweetness of temper were almost proverbial in his own age. That this did not arise from ignorance of his own comparative greatness we have abundant proof in his Sonnets, which could scarcely have been known to Mr Pope when he asserted that our great bard 'grew immortal in his own despite'. Speaking of one whom he had celebrated, and contrasting the duration of his works with that of his personal existence, Shakespeare adds:

> Your name from hence immortal life shall have,
> Though I, once gone, to all the world must die;

[S.T.C. quotes rest of Sonnet lxxxi – Ed.]
    I have taken the first that occurred; but Shakespeare's readiness to praise his rivals, *ore pleno*, and the confidence of his own equality with those whom he deemed most worthy of his praise   are   alike   manifested   in   the   eighty-sixth Sonnet . . . [quoted by S.T.C. – Ed.].

II

. . . It has been before observed that images, however beautiful, though faithfully copied from nature, and as accurately represented in words, do not of themselves characterize the poet. They become proofs of original genius only as far as they are modified

by a predominant passion; or by associated thoughts or images
awakened by that passion; or when they have the effect of
reducing multitude to unity, or succession to an instant; or lastly,
when a human and intellectual life is transferred to them from the
poet's own spirit,

> Which shoots its being through earth and air.

In the two following lines, for instance, there is nothing
objectionable, nothing which would preclude them from forming, in their proper place, part of a descriptive poem:

> Behold yon row of pines, that shorn and bow'd
> Bend from the sea-blast, seen at twilight eve.

But with the small alteration of rhythm, the same words would be
equally in their place in a book of topography, or in a descriptive
tour. The same image will rise into a semblance of poetry if thus
conveyed:

> Yon row of bleak and visionary pines,
> By twilight-glimpse discerned, mark! how they flee
> From the fierce sea-blast, all their tresses wild
> Streaming before them.

I have given this as an illustration, by no means as an instance, of
that particular excellence which I had in view and in which
Shakespeare, even in his earliest as in his latest works, surpasses
all other poets. It is by this that he still gives a dignity and a
passion to the objects which he presents. Unaided by any
previous excitement, they burst upon us at once in life and in
power. [S. T. C. quotes from Sonnets xxxiii and cvii -- Ed.]

As of higher worth, so doubtless still more characteristic of
poetic genius does the imagery become when it moulds and colors
itself to the circumstances, passion or character present and
foremost in the mind. For unrivalled instances of this excellence
the reader's memory will refer him to the *Lear*, *Othello*, in short to
which not of the 'great, ever living dead' man's dramatic works?
Inopem me copia fecit. How true it is to nature, he himself finely
expressed in the instance of love in Sonnet xcviii . . . [quoted by
S.T.C. – Ed.].

SOURCE: extracts from *Biographia Literaria* (1817): extract I
from ch. 2; extract II from ch. 15.

s. t. COLERIDGE (1833)

. . . I believe it possible that a man may, under certain states of
the moral feeling, entertain something deserving the name of love
towards a male object – an affection beyond friendship, and
wholly aloof from appetite. In Elizabeth's and James's time it
seems to have been almost fashionable to cherish such a feeling;
and perhaps we may account in some measure for it by
considering how very inferior women of that age, taken generally, were in education and accomplishment of mind to the
men. . . . I mention this with reference to Shakespeare's sonnets,
which have been supposed, by some, to be addressed to William
Herbert, Earl of Pembroke, whom Clarendon calls the most
beloved man of his age, though his licentiousness was equal to his
virtues. I doubt this. I do not think that Shakespeare, merely
because he was an actor, would have thought it necessary to veil
his emotions towards Pembroke under a disguise, though he
might probably have done so, if the real object had perchance
been a Laura or Leonora. It seems to me that the sonnets could
only have come from a man deeply in love, and in love with a
woman; and there is one sonnet which, from its incongruity, I
take to be a purposed blind. These extraordinary sonnets form, in
fact, a poem of so many stanzas of fourteen lines each; and, like
the passion which inspired them, the sonnets are always the same,
with a variety of expression, – continuous, if you regard the
lover's soul – distinct, if you listen to him, as he heaves them sigh
after sigh.

These sonnets, like the Venus and Adonis, and the Rape of
Lucrece, are characterised by boundless fertility and laboured
condensation of thought, with perfection of sweetness in rhythm
and metre. These are the essentials in the budding of a great poet.
Afterwards habit and consciousness of power teach more
ease – *praecipitandum liberum spiritum.* . . .

SOURCE: extract from *Table Talk* (14 May 1833).

JOHN KEATS (1817)

. . . One of the three Books I have with me is Shakspear's Poems:
I ne'er found so many beauties in the Sonnets – they seem to be
full of fine things said unintentionally – in the intensity of
working out conceits. Is this to be borne? Hark ye!

> When lofty trees I see barren of leaves
>   Which erst from heat did canopy the herd,
> And Summer's green all girded up in sheaves,
>   Borne on the bier with white and bristly beard.

He has left nothing to say about nothing or anything: . . . He
overwhelms a genuine Love of Poesy with all manner of abuse,
talking about –

> a poet's rage
> and stretched metre of an antique song.

Which by the by will be a capital Motto for my Poem, won't it?
He speaks too of 'Time's antique pen' – and 'april's first born
flowers' – and 'death's eternal cold'. . . .

> SOURCE: from letter to John Hamilton Reynolds (22
> November 1817) in *Letters*, ed. M. B. Forman (1931) pp.
> 69–70.

PERCY BYSSHE SHELLEY (undated)

That famous passage in that pathetic sonnet in which, addressing
a dear friend, he complains of his own situation as an actor, and
says that his nature is (I quote from memory)

> Subdued
> To what it works in, like the dyer's hand.

Observe these images, how simple they are, and yet animated
with what intense poetry and passion.

SOURCE: 'Note on the Hundred and Eleventh Sonnet of Shakespeare', in *The Works of Percy Bysshe Shelley*, newly edited by Roger Ingpen and Walter E. Peck (1965) vol. VII, p. 152.

WILLIAM HAZLITT (1815)

. . . M. Sismondi professes to have a prejudice against Petrarch. In this he is not, as he supposes, singular; but we suspect that he is wrong. He seems to have reasoned on a very common, but very false hypothesis, that because there is a great deal of false wit and affectation in Petrarch's style, he is therefore without sentiment. . . . It is not improbable, that if Shakespear had written nothing but his sonnets and smaller poems, he would, for the same reason, have been assigned to the class of cold, artificial writers, who had no genuine sense of nature or passion. Yet, taking his plays for a guide to our decision, it requires no very great sagacity or boldness to discover that his other poems contain a rich vein of thought and sentiment. We apprehend it is the same with Petrarch. . . .

SOURCE: extract from review of Sismondi's *Literature of the South, Edinburgh Review*, XXV (June 1815).

WILLIAM HAZLITT (1817)

. . . Of the Sonnets we do not well know what to say. The subject of them seems to be somewhat equivocal; but many of them are highly beautiful in themselves, and interesting as they relate to the state of the personal feelings of the author. . . .

[Hazlitt quotes as among 'the most striking', and under theme-labels, sonnets XXV ('Constancy'), XXIX ('Love's Consolation'), CII ('Novelty') and LXXIII ('Life's Decay') – Ed.]

In all these, as well as in many others, there is a mild tone of

sentiment, deep, mellow, and sustained, very different from the
crudeness of his earlier poems.

SOURCE: extract from *Characters of Shakespear's Plays* (1817)

WILLIAM HAZLITT (1821)

... Shakespear's [Sonnets], which some persons better-informed
in such matters than I can pretend to be, profess to cry up as 'the
divine, the matchless, what you will', – to say nothing of the
want of point or a leading, prominent idea in most of them, are I
think overcharged and monotonous, and as to their ultimate
drift, as for myself, I can make neither head nor tail of it. Yet
some of them, I own, are sweet even to a sense of faintness,
luscious as the woodbine, and graceful and luxuriant like it. Here
is one:
From you have I been absent in the spring
[H. goes on to quote the whole of Sonnet xcviii – Ed.]

SOURCE: extract from Essay xvii: 'On Milton's Sonnets', in
Table Talk (1821).

WILLIAM HAZLITT (1826)

... we find Milton quoted among those authors, who have left
proofs of their entertaining a high opinion of themselves, and of
cherishing a strong aspiration after fame. Some of Shakespear's
Sonnets have also been cited to the same purpose; but they seem
rather to convey wayward and dissatisfied complaints of his
untoward fortune than anything like a triumphant and confident
reliance on his further renown. He appears to have stood more
alone and to have thought less about himself than any living
being. . . .

SOURCE: extract from Essay xii: 'Whether Genius is
Conscious of its Powers?', in *The Plain Speaker* (1826).

WALTER SAVAGE LANDOR (1828)

I

Porson: . . . In the poems of Shakespeare, which are printed as sonnets, there sometime is a singular strength and intensity of thought, with little of that imagination which was afterward to raise him highest in the universe of poetry. Even the interest we take in the private life of this miraculous man cannot keep the volume in our hands long together. We acknowledge great power, but we experience great weariness. . . .

II

Landor: . . . A few of Milton's *Sonnets* are extremely bad: the rest are excellent. Among all Shakespeare's not a single one is very admirable, and a few sink very low. They are hot and pothery: there is much condensation, little delicacy; like raspberry jam without cream, without crust, without bread, to break its viscidity. But I would rather sit down to one of them again, than to a string of such musty sausages as are exposed in our streets at the present dull season. . . .

SOURCE: extracts from *Imaginary Conversations*, Third Series (1828): extract I from 'Southey and Porson'; extract II from 'Southey and Landor'.

EDWARD DOWDEN (1875)

. . . The Shakspere whom we discern in the Sonnets had certainly not attained the broad mastery of life which the Stratford bust asserts to have been Shakspere's in his closing years. Life had been found good by him who owned those lips, and whose spirit declares itself in the massive animation of the total outlook of that face. When the greater number of these Sonnets were written Shakspere could have understood Romeo; he could have understood Hamlet; he could not have conceived

Duke Prospero. Under the joyous exterior of those days lay a craving, sensitive, unsatisfied heart, which had not entire possession of itself, which could misplace its affections, and resort to all those pathetic frauds, by which misplaced affections strive to conceal an error from themselves. . . .

SOURCE: extract from *Shakspere: A Critical Study of His Mind and Art* (1875).

J. A. NOBLE (1880)

. . . Shakspeare has this and that quality which belonged to his predecessors – the insight of one, the imagination of another, the expressional felicity of a third; but he writes them all in a new synthesis, and for the product of this synthesis we are bound to make a new definition. Until Shakspeare has a compeer he is a class by himself, and as the world seems to have decided that the compeer has not yet arrived, he remains above all else Shakspearian. And in his poems, notably in these so-called sonnets, which are the richest and completest of them, this unique personal note is as clearly discernible as in the noblest of the plays, and much more discernible than in some of those earlier dramatic efforts which mark the tentative stage of his development. If we could imagine the existence of a person of cultivated taste who was still ignorant of the recognised place of Shakspeare in literature, he could not pass from the sonnet work of Shakspeare's contemporaries to that of the master himself without an instant sense of an enlarged outlook, of a freer, clearer air, of a more impressive spiritual presence. There is the recognition of an unmistakable amplitude of treatment, a large utterance, and ensuing upon this a feeling of fellowship with a soul wealthy enough to disdain the smaller economies of the intellect. In these sonnets there is no sense of strain; we do not feel, as in reading Drummond, that the poet has touched his possibilities, but that even in his farthest reaches they are still long ahead of him. Even when the intellectual level attained by an author is not absolutely high, as it is here, there is always a felt charm in his work if it leave such an impression as this; a charm like that which belongs to the feats of some trained athlete who performs what seem muscular miracles with the graceful ease of effortless strength.

Coleridge has spoken of the 'condensation of thought' in these sonnets, Dyce of their 'profound thought', Archbishop Trench of their being 'double-shotted with thought'; but, if we mistake not, the thing which gives to them their specific gravity is not what is usually understood by thought, but what may rather be described as intellectualized emotion – that is, the incarnation of pure emotion, which is itself too rare and attenuated an essence to be adequately and at the same time sustainedly expressed, in a body of symbol or situation which is supplied by the intellect. The simple pouring out of passion is apt to become tiresome to all save the lover and the beloved; but in reading Shakspeare's sonnets we are sensible of no such loss of gusto; the last is as piquant as the first; and this because the mere passion, which is in itself an ordinary thing – though the passion of a Titan must needs be Titanesque – is supplemented by the tremendous intellectual force which lies behind and beneath it, and bears it up as the foam-bell is borne on the bosom of the great sea. . . .

SOURCE: extract from 'The Sonnet in England', *Contemporary Review*, XXXVIII (1880).

DANTE GABRIEL ROSSETTI (1882)

. . . There should be an essential reform in the printing of Shakespeare's sonnets. After sonnet CXXV should occur the words *End of Part I.* The couplet-piece, numbered CXXVI, should be called *Epilogue to Part I.* Then, before CXXVII, should be printed *Part II. After* CLII, should be put *End of Part II* – and the last two sonnets should be called *Epilogue to part II.*

SOURCE: extract from *Recollections* (1882) p. 250.

SAMUEL BUTLER (1899)

. . . Fresh from the study of the other great work in which the love that passeth the love of women is portrayed as nowhere else save in the Sonnets, I cannot but be struck with the fact that it is in the two greatest of all poets that we find this subject treated with the greatest intensity of feeling. The marvel, however, is this, that whereas the love of Achilles for Patroclus depicted by the Greek poet is purely English, absolutely without taint or alloy of any kind, the love of the English poet for Mr W. H. was, though only for a short time, more Greek than English. I cannot explain this. . . .

SOURCE: extract from Introduction to *Shakespeare's Sonnets/ Reconsidered, and in part rearranged/with introductory chapters/ notes, and a reprint/of the original 1609 Edition* (1899).

LYTTON STRACHEY(1905)

He is a bold man who sets out in quest of the key which shall unlock the mystery of Shakespeare's sonnets. In that country the roads make heavy walking, and 'airy tongues that syllable men's names' lure the unwary traveller at every turn into paths already white with the bones of innumerable commentators. Yet the fascination of the search seems to outweigh its dangers, for each year adds to the number of these sanguine explorers, while it engulfs their predecessors in a deeper oblivion. Nor is it difficult to trace the sources from which the fascination of the sonnets springs. It is not only that the problem they present affords scope for the exercise of that sort of literary detective work which takes joy in tracking out, for instance, the author of the Junius Letters; there is another and more potent attraction in the mystery of the sonnets. For its solution seems to offer hopes of a prize of extraordinary value – nothing less than a true insight into the most secret recesses of the thoughts and feelings of perhaps the greatest man who ever lived. The belief that the sonnets contain the clue which leads straight into the hidden *penetralia* of Shakespeare's biography is at the root of most of the investigation that has been spent upon them . . . Whether the veil will ever be lifted which now shrouds the mysterious figure of 'Mr W.H.' is a question which Sir Thomas Browne would doubtless have pronounced to be 'above antiquarism'; but we may console ourselves with the thought that, after all, the identity of Shakespeare's friend is a matter of only secondary importance. It is Shakespeare's poetry which is the essential thing. Nor does the right method of interpreting his poetry – in spite of all the inkpots of all the commentators – lie open to any doubt. It is not in elaborate arguments, nor hazardous deductions, nor far-fetched comparisons that the truth about the sonnets is to be found, but in the sonnets themselves. Shakespeare's own words form the best motto for the reader beset with the snares and temptations of a seducing criticism:

> No! Let me be obsequious in thy heart;
> And take thou my oblation, poor but free,
> Which is not mix'd with seconds, knows no art,
> But mutual render, only me for thee.

No one who has read the sonnets in this spirit will ever believe that they are nothing more than literary exercises, or that they were merely written as propitiatory addresses to a patron. These theories belong to the artificialities of criticism, against which Canon Beeching, we are glad to find, makes a decided stand. For to accept them is to ignore what is patent to any reader of the sonnets whose feelings have not been 'mix'd with seconds' – the emotional tone which dominates the entire series.

Thus it has come about that the very poems which Mr Sidney Lee has declared to be devoid of any emotion whatever have been attacked by Hallam for the 'excessive and misplaced affection' which they display. For us it is, perhaps, sufficient to steer a middle course:

> O brother, speak with possibilities,
> And do not break into these deep extremes.

If we cannot recognize anything in Shakespeare's emotion for his friend which is either 'excessive' or 'misplaced', what need is there to be hurried into the opposite extreme, and to deny that the greatest of poets felt any emotion at all?

SOURCE: extracts from an article in the *Spectator* (1905) reviewing H. C. Beeching's edition of *The Sonnets of*

Shakespeare, and *Shakespeare Self-Revealed in His Sonnets, and Phoenix and Turtle,* by J. M., London; reprinted in *Spectatorial Essays by Lytton Strachey,* ed. James Strachey (1964) pp. 71, 74–5.

STEFAN GEORGE (1909)

. . . Among the reasons why Shakespeare's sonnets are still little esteemed by us, the most important, aside from the requirement of a very high understanding of verse, is an internal one: that our custom regards all poetry as entirely 'romantic', but these quatorzains, though supreme poetry, are entirely 'unromantic', the external (reason) concerns the subject. For a century editors and commentators fought fruitlessly: what was play and what emotion, who was the blond youth and who the black lady of the last section: they guessed, wrested, and erred, to the complete miscomprehension of spiritual tone. Not only in the procreation series (I–XVII), where indeed the spirit lies more hidden – no, throughout, the duller brains discovered stylistic exercises worked out to order; the baser (brains discovered) their own full loathsomeness: hardly one, however, understood the contents: the adoration before beauty and the glowing compulsion toward immortalization. In our day men and poets have spoken out plainly: at the centre of the sonnet sequence, in every situation and degree, stands the passionate devotion of the poet to his friend. One must accept this even where one does not understand; and it is likewise foolish to cast aspersions, either with reproaches or with justifications on what one of the greater mortals found good. Overmaterialistic and overintellectual ages especially have no right to bandy words on this point, since they cannot possibly suspect anything of the world-creating power of supersexual love . . .

SOURCE: extract from *Shakespeare Sonnette* (Berlin, 1909); anonymous translation reproduced in *A New Variorum Edition of Shakespeare: The Sonnets,* ed. H. E. Rollins, 2 vols (1944) vol. II, p. 408.

2. CRITICAL STUDIES

Sir Sidney Lee

THE CONCEITS OF THE SONNETS (1916)

At a first glance a far larger proportion of Shakespeare's sonnets give the reader the illusion of personal confessions than those of any contemporary, but when allowance has been made for the current conventions of Elizabethan sonnetteering, as well as for Shakespeare's unapproached affluence in dramatic instinct and invention – an affluence which enabled him to identify himself with every phase of human emotion – the autobiographic element, although it may not be dismissed altogether, is seen to shrink to slender proportions. As soon as the collection of Shakespeare's sonnets is studied comparatively with the many thousand poems of cognate theme and form that the printing-presses of England, France and Italy poured forth during the last years of the sixteenth century, a vast number of Shakespeare's performances prove to be little more than trials of skill, often of superlative merit, to which he deemed himself challenged by the poetic effort of his own or of past ages at home and abroad. Francis Meres, the critic of 1598, adduced not merely Shakespeare's 'Venus and Adonis' and his 'Lucrece' but also 'his sugared sonnets' as evidence that 'the sweet witty soul of Ovid lives in mellifluous and honey-tongued Shakespeare.' Much of the poet's thought in the sonnets bears obvious trace of Ovidian inspiration. But Ovid was only one of many nurturing forces. Echoes of Plato's ethereal message filled the air of Elizabethan poetry. Plato, Ovid, Petrarch, Ronsard, and Desportes (among foreign authors of earlier time), Sidney, Watson, Constable, and Daniel (among native contemporaries) seem to have quickened Shakespeare's sonnetteering energy in much the same fashion as

historical writings, romances or plays of older and contemporary
date ministered to his dramatic activities. Of Petrarch's and
Ronsard's sonnets scores were accessible to Shakespeare in
English renderings, but there are signs that to Ronsard and to
some of Ronsard's fellow-countrymen Shakespeare's debt was
often as direct as to tutors of his own race. Adapted or imitated
ideas or conceits are scattered over the whole of Shakespeare's
collection. The transference is usually manipulated with con-
summate skill. Shakespeare invariably gives more than he
receives, yet his primal indebtedness is rarely in doubt. It is just to
interpret somewhat literally Shakespeare's own modest criticism
of his sonnets (LXXVI 11 – 12):

> So all my best is dressing old words new,
> Spending again what is already spent.

The imitative or assimilative element in Shakespeare's
'sugared sonnets' is large enough to refute the assertion that in
them as a whole he sought to 'unlock his heart.'[1] Few of the poems
have an indisputable right to be regarded as untutored cries of
the soul. It is true that the sonnets in which the writer reproaches
himself with sin, or gives expression to a sense of melancholy, offer
at times a convincing illusion of autobiographic confessions. But
the energetic lines in which the poet appears to reveal his inmost
introspections are often adaptations of the less forcible and less
coherent utterances of contemporary poets, and the ethical or
emotional themes are common to almost all Elizabethan col-
lections of sonnets.[2] Shakespeare's noble sonnet on the ravages of
lust (CXXIX), for example, treats with marvellous force and
insight a stereotyped topic of sonnetteers, and it may have owed
its immediate cue to Sir Philip Sidney's sonnet on 'Desire.'[3]

Plato's ethereal conception of beauty which Petrarch first
wove into the sonnet web became under the influence of the
metaphysical speculation of the Renaissance a dominant element
of the love poetry of sixteenth century Italy and France. In
Shakespeare's England, Spenser was Plato's chief poetic apostle.
But Shakespeare often caught in his sonnets the Platonic note
with equal subtlety. Plato's disciples greatly elaborated their

master's conception of earthly beauty as a reflection or
'shadow' of a heavenly essence or 'pattern' which, though
immaterial, was the only true and perfect 'substance'. Platonic or
neo-Platonic 'ideas' are the source of Shakespeare's metaphysical
questionings (Sonnet LIII 1–4):

> What is your *substance*, whereof are you made
> That millions of strange *shadows* on you tend?
> Since every one hath, every one, one shade,
> And you, but one, can every *shadow* lend.[4]

Again, when Shakespeare identifies truth with beauty[5] and
represents both entities as independent of matter or time, he is
proving his loyalty to the mystical creed of the Graeco-Italian
Renaissance, which Keats subsequently summarised in the
familiar lines:

> Beauty is truth, truth beauty; that is all
> Ye know on earth, and all ye need to know.

Shakespeare's favourite classical poem, Ovid's 'Metamorphoses', which he and his generation knew well in Golding's
English version, is directly responsible for a more tangible thread
of philosophical speculation which, after the manner of other
contemporary poets, Shakespeare also wove dispersedly into the
texture of his sonnets.[6] In varied periphrases he confesses to a fear
that 'nothing' is 'new'; that 'that which is hath been before'; that
Time, being in a perpetual state of 'revolution', is for ever
reproducing natural phenomena in a regular rotation; that the
most impressive efforts of Time, which the untutored mind
regards as 'novel' or 'strange', 'are but dressings of a former
sight', merely the rehabilitations of a past experience, which
fades only to repeat itself at some future epoch.

The metaphysical argument has only a misty relevance to the
poet's plea of everlasting love for his friend. The poet fears that
Nature's rotatory processes rob his passion of the stamp of
originality. The reality and individuality of passionate experience appear to be prejudiced by the classical doctrine of

universal 'revolution'. With no very coherent logic he seeks
refuge from his depression in an arbitrary claim on behalf of his
friend and himself to personal exemption from Nature's and
Time's universal law which presumes an endless recurrence of
'growth' and 'waning'.

It is from the last book of Ovid's 'Metamorphoses' that
Shakespeare borrows his cosmic theory which, echoing Golding's
precise phrase, he defines in one place as 'the conceit of this
inconstant *stay*'[7] (xv 9), and which he christens elsewhere
'nature's changing course' (xviii 8), 'revolution' (lix 12),
'interchange of state' (lxiv 9), and 'the course of altering things'
(cxv 8). But even more notable is Shakespeare's literal con-
veyance from Ovid or from Ovid's English translator of the Latin
writer's physiographic illustrations of the working of the alleged
rotatory law. Ovid's graphic appeal to the witness of the sea
wave's motion –

> *As every wave* drives others forth, and *that that comes behind*
> *Both thrusteth and is thrust himself*; even so the times by kind
> Do fly and *follow* both at once and evermore renew –

is loyally adopted by Shakespeare in the fine lines:

> *Like as the waves* make towards the pebbled shore,
>   So do our minutes hasten to their end;
> *Each changing place with that which goes before,*
>   In *sequent* toil all forwards do contend. – Sonnet lx 1–4.

Similarly Shakespeare reproduces Ovid's vivid descriptions of
the encroachments of land on sea and sea on land which the Latin
poet adduces from professedly personal observation as further
evidence of matter's endless rotations. Golding's lines run:

> Even so have places oftentimes *exchanged their estate*,
> For *I have seen* it sea which was *substantial ground alate*:
> Again where sea was, *I have seen* the same become dry land.

This passage becomes, under Shakespeare's hand:

When *I have seen* the hungry ocean gain
   Advantage on the kingdom of the shore,
And *the firm soil* win of the watery main
   Increasing store with loss, and loss with store;
When *I have seen* such *interchange of state.* — (Sonnet LXIV)

Shakespeare has no scruple in claiming to 'have seen' with his
own eyes the phenomena of Ovid's narration. He presents Ovid's
doctrine less confidently than the Latin writer. In Sonnet LIX he
wonders whether 'five hundred courses of the sun' result in
progress or in retrogression, or whether they merely bring things
back to the precise point of departure (ll. 13–14). Yet, despite
his hesitation to identify himself categorically with the doctrine of
'revolution,' the fabric of his speculation is Ovid's gift.

In the same Ovidian quarry Shakespeare may have found
another pseudo-scientific theory on which he meditates in the
Sonnets — XLIV and XLV — the notion that man is an amalgam of
the four elements – earth, water, air, and fire; but that super-
stition was already a veteran theme of the sonnetteers at home
and abroad, and was accessible to him in many places outside
Ovid's pages.[8] In Sonnet CVI he argues that the splendid praises
of beauty which had been devised by poets of the past anticipated
the eulogies which his own idol inspired:

    So all their praises are but prophecies
      Of this our time, all you prefiguring;
    And, for they look'd but with divining eyes,
    They had not skill enough your worth to sing.

The conceit, which has Platonic or neo-Platonic affinities, may
well be accounted another gloss on Ovid's cosmic philosophy.
But Henry Constable, an English sonnetteer, who wrote directly
under continental guidance, would here seem to have given
Shakespeare an immediate cue:

    Miracle of the world, I never will deny
    That former poets praise the beauty of their days;

> *But all these beauties were but figures of thy praise,*
> *And all those poets did of thee but prophesy.*[9]

Another of Shakespeare's philosophic fancies – the nimble
triumphs of thought over space (XLIV 7–8) – is clothed in
language which was habitual to Tasso, Ronsard, and their
followers.[10]
The simpler conceits wherewith Shakespeare illustrates love's
working under the influence of spring or summer, night or sleep,
often appear to echo in deepened notes Petrarch, Ronsard, De
Baïf, and Desportes or English disciples of the Italian and French
masters.[11] In Sonnet XXIV Shakespeare develops the old-
fashioned fancy to which Ronsard gave a new lease of life – that
his love's portrait is painted on his heart; and in Sonnet CXXII he
repeats something of Ronsard's phraseology in describing how
his friend, who had just made him a gift of 'tables', is 'character'd'
in his brain.[12] Again Constable may be credited with suggesting
Shakespeare's Sonnet XCIX, where the flowers are reproached
with stealing their charms from the features of the poet's love.
Constable had published in 1592 an identically turned compliment in honour of his poetic mistress Diana (Sonnet XVII). Two
years later Drayton issued a sonnet in which he fancied that his
'fair Muse' added one more to 'the old nine.' Shakespeare
adopted the conceit (XXXVIII 9–10):

> Be thou the tenth Muse, ten times more in worth
> Than those old nine, which rhymers invoke.[13]

In two or three instances Shakespeare engaged in the literary
exercise of offering alternative renderings of the same conventional conceit. In Sonnets XLVI and XLVII he paraphrases
twice over – appropriating many of Watson's words – the un-
exhilarating notion that eye and heart are in perpetual dispute as
to which has the greater influence on lovers.[14] In the concluding
sonnets, CLIII and CLIV, he gives alternative versions of an
apologue illustrating the potency of love which first figured in the
Greek Anthology, had been translated into Latin, and sub-

sequently won the notice of English, French, and Italian sonnetteers.[15] . . .

SOURCE: from *A Life of William Shakespeare*, rewritten and enlarged version, 2nd ed. (London, 1916) pp. 177–85.

NOTES

1. Wordsworth in his sonnet on *The Sonnet* (1827) claimed that 'With this key Shakespeare unlocked his heart' -- a judgement which Robert Browning, no mean psychologist or literary scholar, strenuously attacked in the two poems *At the Mermaid* and *House* (1876). Browning cited in the latter poem Wordsworth's assertion, adding the gloss: 'Did Shakespeare? If so, the less Shakespeare he!'

2. The fine exordium of Sonnet CXIX:

> What potions have I drunk of Siren tears,
> Distill'd from limbecks foul as hell within,

adopts expressions in Barnabe Barnes's sonnet (No. XLIX), where, after denouncing his mistress as a 'siren,' that poet incoherently ejaculates:

> From my love's limbeck [*sc.* have I] still [di] stilled tears!

Almost every note in the scale of sadness or self-reproach is sounded from time to time in Petrarch's sonnets. Tasso in *Scelta delle Rime* (1582) part ii, p. 26, has a sonnet (beginning 'Vinca fortuna homai, se sotto il peso') which adumbrates Shakespeare's Sonnets XXIX ('When in disgrace with fortune and men's eyes') and LXVI ('Tired with all these, for restful death I cry'). Drummond of Hawthornden translated Tasso's sonnet in his sonnet (part I, No. XXXIII); while Drummond's Sonnets XXV ('What cruel star into this world was brought') and XXXII ('If crost with all mishaps be my poor life') are pitched in the identical key.

3. Sidney's *Certain Sonnets* (No. XIII) appended to *Astrophel and Stella* in the edition of 1598. In *Emaricdulfe: Sonnets written by E.C.*, 1595, Sonnet XXXVII beginning 'O lust, of sacred love the foul corrupter', even more closely resembles Shakespeare's sonnet in both phraseology and sentiment. E.C.'s rare volume is reprinted in the *Lamport Garland* (Roxburghe Club, 1881).

4. The main philosophic conceits of the Sonnets are easily traced to their sources. See J. S. Harrison, *Platonism in English Poetry* (New York, 1903); George Wyndham, *The Poems of Shakespeare* (London, 1898) pp. cxxiiff.; Lilian Winstanley, Introduction to Spenser's *Foure Hymnes* (Cambridge, 1907).

5. Cf.
'Thy end is truth and beauty's doom and date' (Sonnet XIV 14).
'Both truth and beauty on my love depend' (CI 3); cf. LIV 1, 2.

6. The debt of Shakespeare's sonnets to Ovid's *Metamorphoses* has been worked out in detail by the present writer in an article in the *Quarterly Review*, Apr 1909.

7. Golding, Ovid's Elizabethan translator, when he writes of the Ovidian theory of Nature's unending rotation, repeatedly employs a negative periphrasis, of which the word 'stay' is the central feature. Thus he asserts that 'in all the world there is not that that standeth at a *stay*', and that 'our bodies' and 'the elements *never stand at stay*'.

8. Cf. Spenser, LV; Barnes's *Parthenophil and Parthenophe*, LXXVII; Fulke Greville's *Cælica*, No. VII.

9. In his *Miscellaneous Sonnets* (No. VII) written about 1590 (see Hazlitt's edition, 1859, p. 27) – *not* in his *Diana*. Constable significantly headed his sonnet: 'To his Mistrisse, upon occasion of a Petrarch he gave her, showing her the reason why the Italian commentators dissent so much in the exposition thereof.'

10. Cf. Ronsard's *Amours*, I CLXVIII ('Ce fol penser, pour s'envoler trop haut'); Du Bellay's *Olive*, XLIII ('Penser, volage, et leger comme vent'); Amadis Jamyn, Sonnet XXI ('Penser, qui peux en un moment grande erre courir'); and Tasso's *Rime* (Venice, 1583) I, p. 33 ('Come s'human pensier di giunger tenta Al luogo').

11. Almost all sixteenth-century sonnets on spring in the absence of the poet's love (cf. Shakespeare's Sonnets XCVIII, XCIX) play variations on the sentiment and phraseology of Petrarch's well-known sonnet XLII, 'In morte di M. Laura', . . . See a translation by William Drummond of Hawthornden in Sonnets, part ii, No. IX. Similar sonnets and odes on April, spring, and summer abound in French and English (cf. Becq de Fouquières's *Œuvres choisies de J.-A. de Baïf, passim*, and *Œuvres choisies des Contemporains de Ronsard*, p. 108 (by Remy Belleau), p. 129 (by Amadis Jamyn) *et passim*). For descriptions of night and sleep see especially Ronsard's *Amours* (livre I CLXXXVI, livre II XXII; *Odes*, livre IV. No. IV., and his *Odes Retranchées* in *Œuvres*, edited by Blanchemain, II, 392–4). Cf. Barnes's *Parthenophil and Parthenophe*, LXXXIII, CV.

12. Cf. Ronsard's *Amours*, livre I CLXXVIII; *Sonnets pour Astrée*, VI. . . .

13. See Drayton's *Ideas Mirrovr* (1594) Amour 8. Drayton represents that his ladylove adds one to the nine angels and the nine worthies as well as to the nine muses. Sir John Davies severely castigated this extravagance in his Epigram *In Decium*. Cf. Jonson's *Conversations with Drummond* (Shakespeare Soc.) p. 15.

14. A similar conceit is the topic of Shakespeare's Sonnet xxiv. Ronsard's Ode (livre IV No. xx) consists of a like dialogue between the heart and the eye. The conceit is traceable to Petrarch, whose Sonnet lv or lxiii ('Occhi, piangete, accompagnate il core') is a dialogue between the poet and his eyes, while his Sonnet xcix or cxvii is a companion dialogue between the poet and his heart. Cf. Watson's *Tears of Fancie*, xix, xx (a pair of sonnets on the theme which closely resembles Shakespeare's pair); Drayton's *Idea*, xxxiii; Barnes's *Parthenophil and Parthenophe*, xx, and Constable's *Diana*, vi 7.

15. The Greek epigram is in *Palatine Anthology*, ix 627, and is translated into Latin in *Selecta Epigrammata* (Basel, 1529). The Greek lines relate, as in Shakespeare's sonnets, how a nymph who sought to quench love's torch in a fountain only succeeded in heating the water. An added detail Shakespeare borrowed from a very recent adaptation of the epigram in Giles Fletcher's *Licia* (1593) (Sonnet xxvii), where the poet's Love bathes in the fountain, with the result not only that 'she touched the water and it burnt with Love', but also

> Now by her means it purchased hath that bliss
> Which all diseases quickly can remove.

Similarly Shakespeare in Sonnet cliv states not merely that the 'cool well' into which Cupid's torch had fallen 'from Love's fire took heat perpetual', but also that it grew 'a bath and healthful remedy for men diseased'.

Robert Graves and Laura Riding

A STUDY IN ORIGINAL PUNCTUATION
AND SPELLING (1926)

. . . Shakespeare expressed, as accurately but in the common form of his time, what was peculiar to himself.

Here are two versions of a sonnet by Shakespeare: first, the version found in *The Oxford Book of English Verse* and other popular anthologies whose editors may be assumed to have chosen this sonnet from all the rest as being particularly easy to understand; next, the version printed in the 1609 edition of the *Sonnets* and apparently copied from Shakespeare's original manuscript, though Shakespeare is most unlikely to have seen the proofs. The alterations, it will be noticed in a comparison of the two versions, are with a few exceptions chiefly in the punctuation and spelling. By showing what a great difference to the sense the juggling of punctuation marks has made in the original sonnet, we shall perhaps be able to persuade the plain reader to sympathize with what seems typographical perversity in Mr. Cummings. The modernizing of the spelling is not quite so serious a matter, though we shall see that to change a word like *blouddy* to *bloody* makes a difference not only in the atmosphere of the word but in its sound as well.

I

Th' expense of Spirit in a waste of shame
Is lust in action; and till action, lust
Is perjured, murderous, bloody, full of blame,
Savage, extreme, rude, cruel, not to trust;
Enjoy'd no sooner but despisèd straight;
Past reason hunted; and, no sooner had,
Past reason hated, as a swallow'd bait

On purpose laid to make the taker mad:
Mad in pursuit, and in possession so;
Had, having, and in quest to have, extreme;
A bliss in proof, and proved, a very woe;
Before, a joy proposed; behind, a dream.
All this the world well knows; yet none knows well
To shun the heaven that leads men to this hell.

II

Th' expence of Spirit in a waste of shame
Is lust in action, and till action, lust
Is periurd, murdrous, blouddy full of blame,
Sauage, extreame, rude, cruell, not to trust,
Inioyd no sooner but dispised straight,
Past reason hunted, and no sooner had
Past reason hated as a swollowed bayt,
On purpose layd to make the taker mad.
Made In pursut and in possession so,
Had, hauing, and in quest, to haue extreame,
A blisse in proofe and proud and very wo,
Before a joy proposed behind a dreame,
All this the world well knowes yet none knowes well,
To shun the heauen that leads men to this hell.

First, to compare the spelling. As a matter of course the *u* in *proud* and *heauen* changes to *v*; the Elizabethans had no typographical *v*. There are other words in which the change of spelling does not seem to matter. *Expence, cruell, bayt, layd, pursut, blisse, proofe, wo* -- these words taken by themselves are not necessarily affected by modernization, though much of the original atmosphere of the poem is lost by changing them in the gross. Sheer facility in reading a poem is no gain when one tries to discover what the poem looked like to the poet who wrote it. But other changes designed to increase reading facility involve more than changes in spelling. *Periurd* to *perjured*, and *murdrous* to *murderous*, would have meant, to Shakespeare, the addition of another syllable. *Inioyd*, with the same number of syllables as *periurd*, is however

printed *Enjoy'd*; while *swollowed*, which must have been meant as
a three-syllabled word (Shakespeare used *ed* as a separate syllable
very strictly and frequently allowed himself an extra syllable in
his iambic foot) is printed *swallow'd*. When we come to *dispised*,
we find in the modern version an accent over the last syllable.
These liberties do not make the poem any easier; they only make
it less accurate. The sound of the poem suffers through re-spelling
as well as through alterations in the rhythm made by this use of
apostrophes and accents. *Blouddy* was pronounced more like *blue-
dy* than *bluddy*; the *ea* of *extreame* and *dreame* sounded like the *ea* in
great; and *periurd* was probably pronounced more like *peryurd* than
pergeurd.

But it is the changes in punctuation which do the most
damage: not only to the atmosphere of the poem but to its
meaning. In the second line a semicolon substituted for a comma
after the first *action* gives a longer rest than Shakespeare gave; it
also cuts the idea short at *action* instead of keeping *in action* and *till
action* together as well as the two *lust*'s. A comma after *blouddy*
makes this a separate characterization and thus reduces the
weight of the whole phrase as rhythmic relief to the string of
adjectives; it probably had the adverbial form of *blouddily*. Next,
several semicolons are substituted for commas; these introduce
pauses which break up the continuous interpenetration of
images. If Shakespeare had intended such pauses he would have
used semicolons, as he does elsewhere. Particularly serious is the
interpolation of a comma after *no sooner had*, which confines the
phrase to the special meaning 'lust no sooner had *past reason* is
hated past reason'. Shakespeare did not write in the syntax of
prose but in a sensitive poetic flow. The comma might as well
have been put between *reason* and *hated*; it would have limited the
meaning, but no more than has been done here. On the other
hand a comma is omitted where Shakespeare was careful to put
one, after *bayt*. With the comma, *On purpose layd* -- though it refers
to *bayt* – also looks back to the orginal idea of *lust*; without the
comma it merely continues the figure of *bayt*. In the orginal there
is a full stop at *mad*, closing the octave; in the emended version a
colon is used, making the next line run on and causing the
unpardonable change from *Made* to *Mad*. The capital 'I' of *in*

shows how carefully the printer copied the manuscript. Evidently, Shakespeare first wrote the line without *Made*, and then, deciding that such an irregular line was too dramatic, added *Made* without troubling to change the capital 'I' to a small one. In any case *Made* necessarily follows from *make* of the preceding line: 'to make the taker mad, made (mad)'; but it also enlarges the mad-making bayt to the generally extreame-making lust. The change from *Made* to *Mad* limits the final *so* of this line to *Mad* and provokes a change from comma to semicolon – 'Mad in pursuit and in possession so (mad)' – whereas *mad* is only vaguely echoed in this line from the preceding one. The meaning of the original line is: 'Made In pursut and in possession as follows', and also: 'Made In pursut and in possession as has been said'.

The comma between *in quest* and *to have extreame* has been moved forward to separate *have* from *extreame*. This line originally stood for a number of interwoven meanings:

1. The taker of the bait, the man in pursuit and in possession of lust, is made mad: is so made that he experiences both extremes at once. (What these extremes are the lines following show.)

2. The *Had, having and in quest*, might well have been written in parentheses. They explain, by way of interjection, that lust comprises all the stages of lust: the after-lust period (*Had*), the actual experience of lust (*having*), and the anticipation of lust (*in quest*); and that the extremes of lust are felt in all these stages (*to have extreame* – i.e. to have in extreme degree).

3. Further, one stage in lust is like the others, is as extreme as the others. All the distinctions made in the poem between *lust in action* and *till action lust*, between lust *In pursut* and lust *in possession* are made to show that in the end there are no real distinctions. *Had, having and in quest* is the summing up of this fact.

4. *Had* and *having* double the sense of *possession* to match the double sense of *action* implied by *Th' expence of Spirit in a waste of shame*; and *in quest* naturally refers to *In pursut*, which in turn recalls *till action*.

5. Throughout the poem it must be kept in mind that words qualifying the lust-interest refer interchangeably to the man who lusts, the object of lust and lust in the abstract. This in-

terchangeability accounts for the apparently ungrammatical effect of the line.

With the emended punctuation the line has only one narrow sense, and this not precisely Shakespeare's; the semicolon placed after *so* of the preceding line, cuts the close co-operation between them. The shifting of the comma not only removes a pause where Shakespeare put one, and thus changes the rhythm, but the line itself loses point and does not pull its weight. In this punctuation the *whole* line ought to be put into parentheses, as being a mere repetition. The *to have* linked with *in quest* is superfluous; *extreme* set off by itself is merely a descriptive adjective already used. Moreover, when the line is thus isolated between two semicolons, *Had, having,* etc., instead of effecting a harmony between the interchangeable senses, disjoints them and becomes ungrammatical. *Mad in pursuit, and in possession so* refers only to *the taker mad.* The next line, *A blisse in proofe and proud and very wo,* should explain *to have extreame*; it is not merely another parenthetical line as in the emended version. To fulfil the paradox implied in *extreame* it should mean that lust is a bliss during the proof and after the proof, and also *very wo* (truly woe) during and after the proof. The emended line, *A bliss in proof, and proved, a very woe,* which refers only to lust in the abstract, not equally to the man who lusts, means that lust is a bliss during the proof but a woe after the proof – and thus denies what Shakespeare has been at pains to show all along, that lust is all things at all times.

Once the editors began repunctuating the line they had to tamper with the words themselves. A comma after *proof* demanded a comma after *provd.* A comma after *provd* made it necessary to change *and very wo* so that it should apply to *provd* only. Another semicolon which they have put at the end of this line again breaks the continuity of the sense: the succeeding line becomes only another antithesis or rhetorical balance ('a joy in prospect, but a dream in retrospect,' to repeat the sense of 'a bliss during proof but woe after proof'), instead of carrying on the intricate and careful argument that runs without a stop through the whole sestet. The importance of the line is that it takes all the meanings in the poem one stage further. Lust in the extreme goes beyond both bliss and woe: it goes beyond reality. It is no longer lust *Had, having and in quest*; it is lust face to face with *love*. Even when consummated, lust still stands before an unconsummated joy, a proposed joy, and proposed not as a joy possible of consummation but as one only to be known through the dream by which lust leads itself on, the dream behind which this proposed joy, this love, seems to lie. This is the over-riding meaning of the line. It has other meanings, but they all defer to this. For example, it may also be read: 'Before a joy can be proposed, it must first be renounced as a real joy, it must be put behind as a dream'; or: 'Before the man in lust is a prospect of joy, yet he knows by experience that this is only a dream'; or: 'Beforehand he says that he proposed lust to be a joy, afterwards he says that it came as involuntarily as a dream'; or: 'Before (in face of) a joy proposed only as a consequence of a dream, with a dream impelling him from behind.' All these and even more readings of the line are possible and legitimate, and each reading could in turn be made to explain precisely why the taker is made mad, or how lust is *to have extreame*, or why it is both *a blisse* and *very wo*. The punctuated line in the emended version, cut off from what has gone before and from what follows, can mean only: 'In prospect, lust is a joy; in retrospect, a dream.' Though a possible contributory meaning, when made the *only* meaning it presents as the theme of the poem that lust is impossible of satisfaction, whereas the theme, as carried on by the next line, is that lust as lust *is* satisfiable but that satisfied lust is in conflict with itself.

The next line, if unpunctuated except for the comma Shakespeare put at the end, is a general statement of this conflict: the man in lust is torn between lust as he well knows it in common with the world and lust in his personal experience which crazes him to hope for more than lust from lust. The force of the second *well* is to deny the first *well*: no one really knows anything of lust except in personal experience, and only through personal experience can lust be known *well* rather than 'well-known'. But separate the second *well* from the first, as in the emended version, and the direct opposition between *world* and *none*, *well knowes* and *knowes well* is destroyed, as well as the word-play between *well knowes* and *knowes well*; for by the removal of the comma after the second *well*, this becomes an adverb modifying *To shun* in the

William Empson

AMBIGUITY OF GRAMMAR IN THE SONNETS (1930)

. . . Where there is a single main meaning (the case we are now considering) the device [ambiguity, not of word, but of grammar] is used, as in the following examples from Shakespeare's Sonnets, to give an interpenetrating and, as it were, fluid unity, in which phrases will go either with the sentence before or after and there is no break in the movement of the thought.

> But heaven in thy creation did decree
> That in thy face sweet love should ever dwell,
> Whate'er thy thoughts or thy heart's workings be,
> Thy looks should nothing thence, but sweetness tell.
>
> (XCIII)

You may put a full stop either before or after the third line.

> That tongue that tells the story of thy days
> (Making lascivious comments on thy sport)
> Cannot dispraise, but in a kind of praise,
> Naming thy name, blesses an ill report.   (XCV)

The subject of *blesses* is either *tongue* or *naming*, and *but in a kind of praise* qualifies either *blesses* or *dispraise*. These devices are particularly useful in managing the sonnet form because they help it to combine variety of argumentation and the close-knit rhythmical unity of a single thought.

There is in the following Sonnet one of those important and frequent subtleties of punctuation, which in general only convey rhythm, but here it amounts to a point of grammar.

> If thou survive my well contented daye
> When that churle death my bones with dust shall cover
> And shalt by fortune once more re-survey:
> These poor rude lines of thy deceased Lover;
> Compare them with the bettering of the time, . . .
>
> (XXXII)

Line 4 is isolated between colons, carries the whole weight of the pathos, and is a pivot round which the rest of the Sonnet turns. *Re-survey* might conceivably be thought of as intransitive, so that line 4 could go with line 5 in apposition to *them*, but the point is not that either line 3 or line 5 could stand without line 4, it is in fact next to both of them, and yet it stands out from either, as if the Sonnet had become more conscious of itself, or was making a quotation from a tombstone.

> Thou doost love her, because thou knowest I love her,
> And for my sake even so doth she abuse me,
> Suffering my friend for my sake to approve her,
> If I loose thee, my loss is my love's gaine,
> And loosing her, my friend hath found that losse. . . .
>
> (XLII)

According as line 3 goes backwards or forwards, the subject of *suffering* is either *she* or *I*. The device is not here merely a rhythmic one, but it carries no great depth of meaning; the Elizabethans were trained to use lines that went both ways, for example in those chains of Sonnets, such as the *Corona* of Donne, in which each began with the last line of the one before.

Donne, indeed, uses these methods with vehemence; I shall break this series from the Sonnets for a moment to quote an example from the *Epithalamion for Valentine's Day*.

> Thou mak'st a Taper see
> What the sunne never saw, and what the Arke
> (Which was of Soules, and beasts, the cage, and park)
> Did not containe, one bed containes, through thee,
> Two Phoenixes, whose joyned breasts . . .

'You make a taper see what the ark did not contain. Through you one bed contains two phoenixes.' 'You make a taper see what the sun never saw. Through you one bed contains what the ark did not contain, that is, two phoenixes.' The renewal of energy gained from starting a new sentence is continually obtained here without the effect of repose given by letting a sentence stop.

> Who lets so fair a house fall to decay,
> Which husbandry in honour might uphold
> Against the stormy gusts of winter's day
> And barren rage of death's eternal cold?
> O none but unthrifts, *dear my love you know*,
> You had a Father, let your Son say so.
>
> (XIII)

The phrase in italics is equally suited to the sentences before and after it; taking it as the former, a third meaning shows itself faintly, that *you know unthrifts*; 'the company you keep may be riotous or ascetic, but is not matrimonial.' Having quoted this for a comparatively trivial point of grammar, it seems worth pointing out that its beauty depends first on the puns, *house* and *husbandry*, and secondly on the shift of feeling from *winter's day*, winter is short, like its days; 'your child will grow up after you and your house will survive to see another summer,' to *death's eternal cold*; 'if the house does not survive this winter it falls for ever'; there is a contrast between these two opposite ideas and the two open, similarly vowelled, Marlowan lines that contain them, which claim by their structure to be merely repeating the same thought, so that the two notions are dissolved into both of them, and form a regress of echoes. . . .

SOURCE: extract from *Seven Types of Ambiguity* (1930; revised ed. 1935, reprinted 1953) pp. 50–2.

L. C. Knights

SHAKESPEARE'S SONNETS (1934)

I

That there is so little genuine criticism in the terrifying number of books and essays on Shakespeare's Sonnets can only be partly accounted for by the superior attractiveness of gossip. A more radical explanation is to be found in certain widespread, more or less unconscious assumptions. In the first place, although consciously we may not believe that the Sonnets – even the first hundred and twenty-six – form a continuous and ordered collection, we tend to assume that the collection is more homogeneous than in fact it is, and we tend, therefore, to make rather sweeping generalizations about 'The Sonnets' as a whole.[1] A second assumption was made amusingly explicit in the words that John Benson, the publisher of the 1640 edition – who had an eye on changing taste – addressed to the Reader: 'In your perusall you shall finde them SEREN, cleere and eligantly plaine, such gentle straines as shall recreate and not perplex your braine, no intricate or cloudy stuffe to puzzell intellect, but perfect eloquence.' Many of the Sonnets were written about the time of *A Midsummer Night's Dream* and *Romeo and Juliet*; the verse is therefore essentially unlike the verse of *King Lear* – it is incapable of subtleties; the meaning is on the surface. No doubt this is an exaggeration, but the effects of an assumption not very dissimilar to this can be seen in such essays as keep decently clear of William Hughes the sea cook, and the rest, and that attempt to approach the Sonnets directly, as poetry. George Wyndham, for example, in his essay on 'The Poems of Shakespeare' does not entirely confine himself to pointing out the more picturesque aspects of imagery and the melodic effect of certain lines; but his criticism encourages the belief not only that such things have an intrinsic importance, but that visual imagery, 'the music of vowel and consonant' and so on, have much the same function in the Sonnets as they have, say, in Spenser's stanzas on the Bower of Bliss. 'Apart from all else, it is the sheer beauty of diction in Shakespeare's Sonnets which has endeared them to poets.' Maybe (though they were endeared to Keats and Coleridge for other reasons, and Spenser, we remember, is the Poets' Poet); but the sentence illustrates the kind of limitation that the second assumption imposes: criticism is confined to a surface approach; it remains inappropriately and unnecessarily naïve. It is unfortunate that most readers are familiar with the Sonnets only in modern editions in which, as Laura Riding and Robert Graves pointed out, 'the perversely stupid reorganizing of lines and re-grouping of ideas' – all in the interests of 'clarity' – is achieved by the simple expedient of altering the original punctuation.[2] In the Arden Edition the majority of deviations of this kind are not even recorded in the textual notes. The assumption is thus imposed and perpetuated by the common text.

If we can rid ourselves of these two presuppositions we shall have gone some way towards a revaluation of the Sonnets. 'Shakespeare's Sonnets' is a miscellaneous collection of poems, written at different times, for different purposes, and with very different degrees of poetic intensity. (Gildon's edition had the appropriate title, *Poems on Several Occasions*.) The first necessity of criticism is to assess each poem independently, on its merits as poetry, and not to assume too easily that we are dealing with an ordered sequence. The second necessity is to know what kind of *development* to look for – which is a different matter.

I may as well say here that I believe all the Sonnets to be comparatively early in date – roughly from 1592 to 1597 or 1598; none of them is likely to have been written after the second part of *King Henry IV*.[3] We have no means of knowing how they came to be published by Thorpe in 1609 (J. M. Robertson made some attractive guesses), but the evidence suggests that the publication was unauthorized by Shakespeare, that the poems therefore had not been revised for publication, and that the arrangement adopted in the Quarto, except for the grouping of certain Sonnets that obviously go together, has no particular validity; although the printed sequence seems to represent a rough approximation to the time order in which they were composed. The possibility that some of the Sonnets – like *A Lover's Complaint*, which was published with them – are not by Shakespeare, is not likely to be disputed on *a priori* grounds by those who are familiar with the habits of contemporary publishers and the fortunes of authors' manuscripts in the sixteenth and seventeenth centuries. (The fate of the MS. of *Astrophel and Stella* is a common instance.) One can point to such things as the seventeenth-century poetical miscellanies with their haphazard assignment of authorship; and Cowley's Preface to the 1656 edition of his Poems begins with some interesting remarks in this connexion. But since there is no room for argument of this kind I assume a high degree of authenticity.

II

I do not of course propose to employ my slender resources in the long-standing Southampton – Pembroke controversy and its subtle ramifications; but the popular view that the Sonnets are in some way 'autobiographical' demands some notice. The eloquent chapters in which Frank Harris melts out Shakespeare's personal history from the poetic alloy ('The Sonnets give us the story, the whole terrible, sinful, magical story of Shakespeare's passion') are merely an exotic development of a kind of writing that is common among more eminent critics. 'No capable poet', says Dr. Bradley, 'much less a Shakespeare, intending to produce a merely "dramatic" series of poems, would dream of inventing *a story like that of the Sonnets*, or, even if he did, of treating it as they treat it.'[4] Now the first point that I wish to make against the common forms of biographical excursion (leaving aside for the moment more important considerations) is that the foundations on which they are built have not, to say the least, been the subject of any very discriminating attention. Those who are unwilling to accept the particular validity of Mr. Eliot's remark that 'the more perfect the artist, the more completely separate in him will be the man who suffers and the mind which creates; the more perfectly will the mind digest and transmute the passions which

are its material', backed though it is by the authority of Coleridge
(compare *Biographia Literaria*, xv, 2), have only to turn to the
Sonnets of supposedly highest biographical significance and
consider them as examples of personal poetry: that is, as
expressions by a powerful mind of reactions to a situation in
which the man himself is deeply concerned.

Sonnets xxxiii to xlii are headed by Sir Israel Gollancz,
'Love's First Disillusioning', the various sub-titles ending with
'Forgiveness'. Sonnet xlii runs:

> That thou hast her it is not all my griefe,
> And yet it may be said I lov'd her deerely,
> That she hath thee is cf my wayling cheefe,
> A losse in love that touches me more neerely.

Since the obvious is sometimes necessary, we may say that if
Shakespeare had suffered the experience indicated by a prose
paraphrase (for some of the biographical school the Sonnets
might as well have been in prose) it would have affected him very
differently from *this*. The banal movement, the loose texture of
the verse, the vague gestures that stand for emotion, are sufficient
index that his interests are not very deeply involved. (Contrast
the run and ring of the verse, even in minor sonnets, when
Shakespeare is absorbed by his subject – 'Devouring time blunt
thou the Lyons pawes . . .'.) His sole interest is in the display of
wit, the working out of the syllogism:

> Loving offendors thus I will excuse yee,
> Thou doost love her, because thou knowst I love her,
> And for my sake even so doth she abuse me,
> Suffering my friend for my sake to approove her, . . .
> But here's the joy, my friend and I are one,
> Sweete flattery, then she loves but me alone.

This, I admit, is a particularly glaring example, though it has
its parallels amongst the False Friend and Faithless Mistress
sonnets of 'Group B' (Numbers cxxvii – clii) to which the
notes commonly refer us at this point, and the complete insipidity

of one 'autobiographical' sonnet is enough to cause some honest
doubt. Sonnets LXXVIII to LXXXVI, dealing with the rival poets,
are superior as poetry, but here also it is plain that Shakespeare
derived a good deal of pleasure from the neatness of the
argument:

> I grant (sweet love) thy lovely argument
> Deserves the travaile of a worthier pen,
> Yet what of thee thy Poet doth invent,
> He robs thee of, and payes it thee againe.

Wyndham remarked that these nine sonnets are 'playful
throughout, suggesting no tragedy' – though 'playful' hardly
does them justice. They are rather fine examples of an unusual
mode of compliment and complaint, at once courtly and ironic.
Those who picture Shakespeare as completely enthralled by his
love for a particular friend or patron, and therefore deeply
wounded by neglect, can hardly have noticed the tone of critical,
and sometimes amused, detachment adopted towards himself
('Cleane starved for a looke'), the rival ('He of tall building and
of goodly pride'), and the recipient of his verses ('You to your
beautious blessings adde a curse, Being fond on praise, which
makes your praises worse').

Of course I do not mean to imply that Shakespeare had never
felt love or friendship or exasperation, or that his personal
experiences had no effect on his poetry. One can hardly say of the
Sonnets, as Johnson said of Cowley's *Mistress*, that the compositions are such as might have been written for penance by a
hermit, or for hire by a philosophical rhymer who had only heard
of another sex'. I am merely insisting that those who are attracted
by biographical speculation should be quite sure of what
Shakespeare is doing, of the direction and quality of his interests,
before they make a flat translation into terms of actual life: that is,
even the biographers must be literary critics. Some of the most
interesting and successful sonnets may well have had their
context in a personal relationship; but whenever we analyse their
interest (further illustration at this point would involve a good
deal of repetition later) we find that it lies, not in the general

theme or situation, which is all that is relevant to a biographical interpretation, but in various accretions of thought and feeling, in 'those frequent witty or profound reflexions, which the poet's ever active mind has deduced from, or connected with, the imagery and the incidents', in the exploration of a mood or discrimination of emotion. If this is so, the attempt to isolate the original stimulus (which in any case *may* have been an imagined situation – 'Emotions which the poet has never experienced will serve his turn as well as those familiar to him') is not only hazardous, it is irrelevant. After all, even if Shakespeare had assured us that the Sonnets were written under the stress of a friendship broken and restored and an intrigue with Mary Fitton, the only importance they could have for us would be as poetry, as something *made out of* experience.

With this criterion of importance we can see in proper perspective a second argument – commonly offered as the only alternative to the biographical theory – that the Sonnets are exercises on conventional themes, embellished with conventional ornaments. The argument has a place in criticism, and we should be grateful to Sir Sidney Lee for his exhaustive collection of parallels. When we read

> Not marble, nor the guilded monument,
> Of Princes shall out-live this powrefull rime

it is perhaps as well that we should know that the lines have an ancestry reaching back at least as far as Horace; it is as well that we should be familiar with the theme of mutability and the various forms of diluted Platonism that were common when Shakespeare wrote. But a convention is a general thought, a general attitude, or a general mode of presentation, and a discussion of Shakespeare's Sonnets in terms of the 'typical' Elizabethan sonnet sequence tells us no more about them than an account of the Revenge Play tells us about *Hamlet*.

III

The most profitable approach to the Sonnets is, it seems to me, to consider them in relation to the development of Shakespeare's blank verse. There are certain obvious difficulties: the Sonnets take their start from something that can, for convenience, be called the Spenserian mode, whereas the influence of Spenser on the early plays is both slighter and more indirect; and the dramatic verse naturally contains a good many elements that are not to be found in any of the Sonnets. But it is only by making what may seem an unnecessarily roundabout approach -- even then at the risk of over-simplification — that one can hope to shift the stress to those aspects of the Sonnets that it is most profitable to explore.

No account of the development of Shakespeare's blank verse in general terms can be very satisfactory. A comparison will help to point my necessary generalizations. Richard II's lament at Pomfret is a fairly typical example of the early set speeches:

> And here have I the daintiness of ear
> To check time broke in a disorder'd string:
> But for the concord of my state and time
> Had not an ear to hear my true time broke.
> I wasted time, and now doth time waste me;
> For now hath time made me his numbering clock:
> My thoughts are minutes; and with sighs they jar
> Their watches on unto mine eyes, the outward watch,
> Whereto my finger, like a dial's point,
> Is pointing still, in cleansing them from tears.
> Now sir, the sound that tells what hour it is
> Are clamorous groans, which strike upon my heart,
> Which is the bell: so sighs and tears and groans
> Show minutes, times, and hours: but my time
> Runs posting on in Bolingbroke's proud joy,
> While I stand fooling here, his Jack o' the clock.

The only line that could possibly be mistaken for an extract from a later play is the last, in which the concentrated bitterness ('Jack o' the clock' has a wide range of relevant associations, and the tone introduces a significant variation in the rhythm) serves to emphasize the previous diffuseness. It is not merely that the imagery is elaborated out of all proportion to any complexity of thought or feeling, the emotion is suspended whilst the conceit is developed, as it were, in its own right. Similarly the sound and movement of the verse, the alliteration, repetition and assonance, seem to exist as objects of attention in themselves rather than as the medium of a compulsive force working from within. Such emotion as is communicated is both vague and remote.

Set beside this the well-known speech of Ulysses:

> Time hath, my lord, a wallet at his back,
> Wherein he puts alms for oblivion,
> A great-siz'd monster of ingratitudes:
> Those scraps are good deeds past; which are devour'd
> As fast as they are made, forgot as soon
> As done: perseverance, dear my lord,
> Keeps honour bright: to have done is to hang
> Quite out of fashion, like a rusty mail
> In monumental mockery. Take the instant way;
> For honour travels in a strait so narrow
> Where one but goes abreast: keep then the path;
> For emulation hath a thousand sons
> That one by one pursue: if you give way,
> Or hedge aside from the direct forthright,
> Like to an enter'd tide they all rush by
> And leave you hindmost.

The verse of course is much more free, and the underlying speech movement gives a far greater range of rhythmic subtlety. The sound is more closely linked with — is, in fact, an intimate part of — the meaning. The imagery changes more swiftly. But these factors are only important as contributing to a major development: the main difference lies in the greater immediacy and concreteness of the verse. In reading the second passage more of the mind is involved, and it is involved in more ways. It does not contemplate a general emotion, it *lives* a particular experience. Crudely, the reader is not told that there is a constant need for action, he experiences a particular urgency.

This account could be substantiated in detail, but for my

purpose it may be sufficient to point to a few of the means by
which the reader is influenced in this way. Oblivion, at first a kind
of negative presence, becomes (via 'monster') an active, devouring force, following hard on the heels of time. ('Forgot',
balancing 'devoured', keeps the image in a proper degree of
subordination.) The perseverance that keeps honour bright
introduces a sense of effort, as in polishing metal, and (after a
particularly effective jibe at inactivity) the effort is felt as motion.
Moreover, 'Take the instant way' and 'keep then the path',
involving muscular tension, suggest the strain of keeping foremost. In the next two lines the roar and clatter of emulation's
thousand sons are audible, and immediately we feel the pressure
of pursuit ('hedge aside' is no dead metaphor) and – in the
movement of the verse, as though a dam had broken –
the overwhelming tide of pursuers. The short and exhausted line,
'And leave you hindmost', is the lull after the wave has passed.
   This line of development, continued in the plays of complete
maturity, is central. Primarily it is a matter of techinque – the
words have a higher potency, they release and control a far more
complex response than in the earlier plays – but it is much more
than that. The kind of immediacy that I have indicated allows
the greatest subtlety in particular presentment (The thing 'which
shackles accidents, and bolts up change' is *not* the same as 'The
deed which puts an end to human vicissitude'), whilst 'the quick
flow and the rapid change of the images', as Coleridge noted,
require a 'perpetual activity of attention on the part of the
reader', generate, we may say, a form of activity in which
thought and feeling are fused in a new mode of apprehension.
That is, the technical development implies – is dependent
on – the development and unification of sensibility. It is this kind
of development (in advance of the dramatic verse of the same
period in some respects and obviously behind it in others) that we
find in the Sonnets, and that makes it imperative that discussion
should start from considerations of technique.

Those aspects of technique that can to some extent be isolated as
showing 'the first and most obvious excellence . . . the sense of
musical delight' have been well illustrated by George Wyndham,

but his belief that 'Eloquent Discourse' is 'the staple of the Sonnets and their highest excellence' precludes the more important approach.

After 1579 the most pervasive influence on Elizabethan lyric poetry was that of Spenser. *Astrophel and Stella* may have been the immediate cause of the numerous sonnet cycles, but it was from Spenser that the sonneteers derived many of their common characteristics — the slow movement and melody, the use of imagery predominantly visual and decorative, the romantic glamour, the tendency towards a gently elegiac note. In the Spenserian mode no object is sharply forced upon the consciousness.

> Of mortall life the leafe, the bud, the floure,
> Ne more doth flourish after first decay,
> That earst was sought to decke both bed and bowre,
> Of manie a Ladie, and many a Paramoure:
> Gather therefore the Rose, whilest yet is prime . . .

As music this is perfect and one is forced to admire; but one is only mildly affected by the vision of the passage of time, and even the injunction to pluck the rose has no urgency. Now there is in Shakespeare's Sonnets a quality that, at a first reading, seems very near to this: Sonnets xcviii and cii, for example, are successful as fairly direct developments of the Spenserian mode. But if we turn to Sonnet xxxv we see the conjunction of that mode with something entirely new.

> No more bee greev'd at that which thou hast done,
> Roses have thornes, and silver fountaines mud,
> Cloudes and eclipses staine both Moone and Sunne,
> And loathsome canker lives in sweetest bud.
> All men make faults, and even I in this,
> Authorizing thy trespas with compare,
> My selfe corrupting salving thy amisse,
> Excusing thy sins more then thy sins are:
> For to thy sensuall fault I bring in sence,
> Thy adverse party is thy Advocate,

> And gainst my selfe a lawfull plea commence,
> Such civill war is in my love and hate,
> That I an accessary needs must be,
> To that sweet theefe which sourely robs from me.

The first four lines we may say, both in movement and imagery, are typically Spenserian and straightforward. The fifth line begins by continuing the excuses, 'All men make faults', but with an abrupt change of rhythm Shakespeare turns the generalization against himself: 'All men make faults, and even I in this', i.e. in wasting my time finding romantic parallels for your sins, as though intellectual analogies ('sence') were relevant to your sensual fault. The painful complexity of feeling (Shakespeare is at the same time tender towards the sinner and infuriated by his own tenderness) is evident in the seventh line which means both, 'I corrupt myself when I find excuses for you' (or 'when I comfort myself in this way'), and, 'I'm afraid I myself make you worse by excusing your faults'; and although there is a fresh change of tone towards the end (the twelfth line is virtually a sigh as he gives up hope of resolving the conflict), the equivocal 'needs must' and the sweet–sour opposition show the continued civil war of the emotions.

Some such comment as this was unavoidable, but it is upon the simplest and most obvious of technical devices that I wish to direct attention. In the first quatrain the play upon the letters *s* and *l* is mainly musical and decorative, but with the change of tone and direction the alliterative *s* becomes a hiss of half-impotent venom:

> All men make faults, and even I in thi*s*,
> Authori*z*ing thy trespa*s* with compare,
> My *s*elfe corrupting *s*alving thy ami*ss*e,
> E*x*cusing thy *s*ins more then thy *s*ins are:
> For to thy *s*en*s*uall fault I bring in *s*ence . . .

The scorn is moderated here, but it is still heard in the slightly rasping note of the last line,

To that sweet theefe which sourely robs from me.

From the fifth line, then, the alliteration is functional: by playing off against the comparative regularity of the rhythm it expresses an important part of the meaning, and helps to carry the experience alive into the mind of the reader. With Spenser or Tennyson in mind we should say that both alliteration and assonance were primarily musical devices, as indeed they are in many of the Sonnets:

> Noe longer mourne for me when I am dead,
> Than you shall heare the surly sullen bell
> Give warning to the world that I am fled
> From this vile world with vilest wormes to dwell.

Here, for example, the sound, if not independent of the meaning, usurps a kind of attention that is incompatible with a full and sharp awareness. But that which links the Sonnets, in this respect, with the later plays is the use of assonance and alliteration to secure a heightened awareness, an increase of life and power:

> Your love and pity doth the impression fill,
> Which vulgar scandall stampt upon my brow.

> Cheared and checkt even by the self-same skie.

> All this the world well knowes yet none knowes well . . .

> So shall I taste
> At first the very worst of fortune's might.

> And made myselfe a motley to the view.

In reading the last line the nose wrinkles in disgust, and we hear the rattle of the fool, – but I hope the reader will be inclined to look up the examples in their context (cxii, xv, cxxix, xc, and cx respectively).

A slight shift of attention brings into focus a second aspect of development connected with the first. If we open any of the great plays almost at random we find effects comparable in kind to this, from *Lear*:

> Crown'd with rank fumiter and furrow-weeds,
> With hor-docks, hemlocks, nettles, cuckoo-flowers,
> Darnel, and all the idle weeds that grow
> In our sustaining corn.

The rank and bristling profusion of the weeds is there, in the clogged movement of the first two lines, whilst the unimpeded sweep of the verse that follows contributes powerfully to the image of never-failing fertility. In many of the Sonnets we can see Shakespeare working towards this use of his medium, learning to use a subtly varied play of the speech rhythm and movement against the formal pattern of the verse:

> Ah yet doth beauty like a Dyall hand,
> Steale from his figure, and no pace perceiv'd.

> And on just proofe surmise, accumilate.

> Then hate me when thou wilt, if ever, now,
> Now while the world is bent my deeds to crosse . . .

> That it could so preposterouslie be stain'd . . .

In the steady movement of the first extract, in the slightly impeded progress of the second,[5] in the impetuous movement of the third, and the rising incredulity of the fourth, the verse (if I may borrow the phrase) 'enacts the meaning'. Perhaps one can hardly miss this kind of effect, but a development connected with it — the use of speech movement and idiom in the Sonnets to obtain a firmer command of tone (a matter of some importance in determining their meaning) — seems to have been fairly consistently overlooked. The sonnet form is a convention in which it is only too easy to adopt a special 'poetic' attitude, and to the four

'strong promises of the strength of Shakespeare's genius' which
Coleridge found in the early poems might well be added a fifth:
the way in which, in his Sonnets, he broke away from the formal
and incantatory mode (convention and precedent being what
they were) to make the verse a more flexible and transparent
medium. Sonnet VII has a typically stylized opening:

> Loe in the Orient when the gracious light,
> Lifts up his burning head, each under eye
> Doth homage to his new appearing sight,
> Serving with lookes his sacred majesty.

Contrast, say, Sonnet LXXXII:

> I grant thou wert not married to my Muse,
> And therefore maiest without attaint ore-looke
> The dedicated words which writers use
> Of their faire subject, blessing every booke.

In the first line we hear the inflexion of the speaking voice, and it
is the conversational movement that contributes the equivocal
note of amused irony, directed towards the fulsome dedications
and their – inevitably – fair subject. (Compare the 'precious
phrase by all the Muses filed' of Sonnet LXXXV.) Sometimes a
similar effect is used for deliberate contrast, as in

> Thus have I had thee as a dreame doth flatter,
> In sleepe a King, but waking no such matter, .

where after a line and a half of yearning the offhand col-
loquialism shows us Shakespeare detached and critical. It is of
course only by exploiting speech movement that any kind of
delicacy of statement is possible (reservation is an obvious case, as
in 'I found – or thought I found – you did exceed . . .'), but it is
the fairly frequent use of various ironic inflexions that it seems
particularly important to stress:

> He nor that affable familiar ghost
> Which nightly gulls him with intelligence . . .

> Farewell thou art too deare for my possessing,
> And like enough thou knowst thy estimate . . .

– and there are other examples more or less immediately
apparent.[6] To be alive to modulations of this kind is to
recognize – which is what one would expect – that the *intelligence* that created, say, *Troilus and Cressida*, is also at work in
the Sonnets.

I have already suggested that the critics who reconstruct a
Shakespeare hopelessly and uncritically subjugated by a particular experience must be quite deaf to variations of tone. It is the
same incapacity which causes them to read the Sonnets in which
the touch is lightest with portentous solemnity and to perform
various feats of legerdemain with the meaning. In Sonnet XCIV
the irony is serious and destructive.

> They that have powre to hurt, and will doe none,
> That doe not do the thing, they most do showe,
> Who moving others, are themselves as stone,
> Unmooved could, and to temptation slow:
> They rightly do inherit heavens graces,
> And husband natures ritches from expence,
> They are the Lords and owners of their faces,
> Others, but stewards of their excellence:
> The sommers flowre is to the sommer sweet,
> Though to itselfe, it onely live and die,
> But if that flowre with base infection meete,
> The basest weed out-braves his dignity:
>   For sweetest things turne sowrest by their deedes,
>   Lillies that fester, smell far worse then weeds.

This is commonly taken with Sonnet XCV and read as an
exhortation to chastity – ' 'Tis a sign of greatness to be self-
contained' is Gollancz's summary, and J. Q. Adams glosses: 'The
friend has fallen into a life of gross sensuality, and the poet finds it
necessary to rebuke him in the strongest language.' If nothing
else, 'Lillies that fester' (an image suggesting less the excesses of
sensuality than 'the distortions of ingrown virginity') might cast

some doubts on this simple interpretation. The opening is coldly analytic (I at least am unable to detect any symptoms of moral fervour), and the unprepossessing virtues of those 'who moving others, are themselves as stone' can hardly be held up for admiration; they remind us rather of Angelo, 'whose blood was very snow-broth'. If we remember Shakespeare's condemnation, in the early Sonnets, of those who husband their riches instead of acting as stewards of their excellence, we shall hardly be able to mistake the second quatrain for unambiguous praise; in any case the image suggested by 'They are the Lords and owners of their faces' is unobtrusively comic, and the comma after 'Others' suggests that Shakespeare is ironically repeating the opinion of the self-righteous. The Sonnet may have been intentionally equivocal, but there can be little doubt of Shakespeare's attitude – it is the attitude of *Measure for Measure* – and the poem (though not altogether successful) forms an interesting complement to the more famous Sonnet cxxix. Perhaps I had better add that I do not regard the earlier sonnet as an encouragement to incontinence.

The vivid and surprising 'Lillies that fester' has been commented upon as typically Shakespearean, and indeed the image, whether borrowed or not, is typical of the way in which contrasted sets of associations are fused in the verse of the later plays. But it is hardly representative of the imagery of the Sonnets. In the later plays a wide range of relevant associations, both of thought and feeling ('relevant' being clearly a matter for specific illustration), are compressed into a single image ('The bank and shoal of time'). Images of sight, touch, muscular adjustment and so on follow in rapid succession (no catalogue of 'visual', 'tactile', etc., is sufficient to cover the variety), and different modes may be combined in our response at any one point. And there are those unexpected and startling juxtapositions of contrasted images:

> The *crown* o' the earth doth *melt*.

> This sensible warm *motion* to become
> A kneaded *clod*.

Now in the Sonnets not all of these characteristic uses of imagery are developed: it is largely this which justifies us in assigning them a date earlier than *Troilus and Cressida* or *Measure for Measure*. With the exception of the striking line, 'Mine appetite I never more will grind On newer proof', we can find no parallels to 'Lillies that fester'. Such lines as

> Gor'd mine own thoughts . . .

and

> To bitter sawces did I frame my feeding

indicate an important line of development, but there is little of the intensely physical impact that we find in *Macbeth* ('The blanket of the dark', 'We'd jump the life to come'). Most of the images – even when finely effective – arouse only one set of vibrations in the mind:

> Full many a glorious morning have I seene,
> Flatter the mountaine tops with soveraine eie . . .

> My nature is subdu'd
> To what it workes in, like the Dyers hand.

If we place 'the dust and injury of age' (cviii) and ' . . . whose million'd accidents Creep in 'twixt vows . . .' (cxv) beside Macbeth's

> Tomorrow, and tomorrow, and tomorrow,
> Creeps in this petty pace from day to day . . .
> And all our yesterdays have lighted fools
> The way to dusty death

and ask ourselves exactly why 'creep' and 'dust' are used in each instance, we shall have a fair measure of the later development.

But even when we have made these qualifications the stress remains on the positive achievement; there is a clear advance on the early plays. In the Sonnets no image is *merely* decorative, as in Romeo's 'Two of the fairest stars in all the heaven . . .'. Few are excessively developed, as in the laments of Richard II or even as in the Bastard's 'Commodity, the bias of the world . . .'. There is indeed a constant succession of varied images, which, because they are concrete and because they are drawn from the world of familiar experience, give precise expression to emotion:

> Beated and chopt with tand antiquitie.
>
> Incertenties now crowne them-selves assur'de.
>
> But makes antiquitie for aye his page.
>
> And captive-good attending Captaine ill.

What it comes to is this: in the Sonnets, as in the later plays, the imagery gives immediacy and precision, and it demands and fosters an alert attention. But the range of emotions liberated by any one image is narrower, though not always less intense. We have not yet reached the stage in which 'the *maximum* amount of apparent incongruity is resolved simultaneously'.[7] That is, the creating mind has not yet achieved that co-ordination of widely diverse (and, in the ordinary mind, often conflicting) experiences, which is expressed in the imagery no less than in the total structure of the great tragedies. Put in this way the conclusion may seem obvious, but it is a point to which I shall have to return when I deal with Shakespeare's treatment of the Time theme in the Sonnets.

A complete account of technical development in the Sonnets would include a detailed discussion of ambiguity -- a technical device (if we may call it that) of which, since the publication of Mr. Empson's *Seven Types* and the Riding and Graves analysis of Sonnet cxxix, one can hardly fail to be aware; though the word seems to have caused some unnecessary critical shyness. But the argument would raise fundamental issues with which I do not feel competent to deal, and all that I have to offer − after a very

brief indication of the way in which the language of the Sonnets is
'charged' by means of overlaying meanings – is some caution.
There is a clear difference between the kind of compression
that we find in 'The steepe up heavenly hill' (VII), 'The world
without end houre' (LVII), or 'Th'imprison'd absence of your
libertie' (LVIII), and in such lines as 'So thou, thy selfe out-going
in thy noon' (VIII), or 'That I have frequent binne with unknown
mindes' (CXVII). The first three are forms of elliptical construction
requiring no unusual agility in the mind accustomed to English
idiom. In the last two the context demands that we shall keep two
or more meanings in mind simultaneously: 'thy selfe out-going'
means both 'over-reaching yourself' and 'you yourself going
further on'; 'unknown minds' are 'strangers', 'nonentities', and
perhaps 'such minds as I am ashamed to mention' (the Arden
Edition gives precedents for all these interpretations). In the
same way as two or more meanings are fused in one word,
different constructions may be run together, as in

> None else to me, nor I to none alive,
> That my steel'd sence or changes right or wrong.   (CXII)

or they may be overlaid:

> My selfe corrupting salving thy amisse   (XXXV)

There can, I think, be no doubt that Shakespeare deliberately
(though 'deliberately' may be too strong a word) avails himself of
the resources of the language in this way; I have chosen what
seem to be the most incontrovertible examples, and they are
clearly in line with his later development. In Sonnet XL and one
or two others we have something very like conscious experiment-
ing with simple forms of ambiguous statement.

Now the important point is this: that when ambiguity occurs in
successful verse it is valuable in much the same way as successful
imagery is valuable, as representing a heightened, more inclusive
and more unified form of consciousness. One need hardly say that
the mere presence of ambiguities is not necessarily an indication
of poetic value – they may equally represent unresolved con-

tradictions in the poet's mind — or that the estimate of success is a
more delicate matter (concerned with the whole poetic effect)
than the working-out of alternative meanings. There is no need
for me to praise Mr. Empson, though I may say that he is the only
critic I know of who has detected the equivocal attitude which
Shakespeare sometimes expresses towards his subject, and that
some of his analyses (of Sonnet LVIII, for example) seem to me
immediately convincing. But in perhaps the majority of cases (I
am confining my attention entirely to the pages he devotes to the
Sonnets)[8] his lists of meanings seem to me to be obtained by
focussing upon a part of the poem, almost one might say by
forgetting the poem, and considering the various grammatical
possibilities of the part so isolated. His analysis of Sonnet LXXXIII,
for example (pp. 168–75), is valuable as suggesting the conscious
and subliminal meanings that may well have been in
Shakespeare's mind at the time of writing, but only a few of them
are there, in the poem. It is very unfair to make this charge
without substantiating it in detail, but to do so would add many
pages to the already excessive length of this essay; I can only hope
that the reader will look up the analysis for himself – and my
account of Sonnet CXXIII, below, is relevant here. Mr. Eliot has
remarked that the Sonnets are 'full of some stuff that the writer
could not drag to light, contemplate, or manipulate into art'.[9]
The sentence might be taken by the biographers to refer to an
especially painful personal experience lying behind the Sonnets.
But it suggests more profitable speculation if we interpret it *in the
first place* as meaning that Shakespeare had not yet fully mastered
the technique of complex expression.

IV

These imperfect considerations of technique will perhaps have
been sufficient to establish the main point, that in the Sonnets,
within the limitations of the imposed form, Shakespeare is
working towards the maturity of expression of the great plays.
But having said this we need to remind ourselves of two things.
(The prevailing conception of technique as having something to
do with the place of the caesura and hypermetric feet may justify

the repetition.) The first is that the kind of technical development
that we have been discussing is in itself an attempt to become
more fully conscious (just as Spenser's technique is a method of
exclusion), and attempt to secure more delicate discrimination
and adjustment. The second is that technique does not function
in a vacuum, it can only develop as the servant of an inner
impulse. I shall conclude this essay by pointing to one or two of
the major interests that lie behind the Sonnets.

I have already said that I do not think 'The Sonnets' in any
sense an ordered collection; they vary from the most trivial of
occasional verses to poems in which a whole range of important
emotions is involved, and in the latter we find in embryo many of
the themes of the later plays; there is variety enough to make
discussion difficult. But it seems to me that two interests
predominate, making themselves felt, often, beneath the ostensible subject: they cannot be altogether disentangled from each
other or from other interests, and they are not quite the same in
kind; but the artificial grouping seems unavoidable. One is the
exploration, discrimination and judgment of modes of
being — attention consciously directed towards the kind of
integration of personality that is implied by the development of
technique. The second is an overwhelming concern with Time.

The first of these is not only expressed directly. Sonnet xxx is
one of those concerned with 'Friendship in Absence':

> When to the Sessions of sweet silent thought,
> I summon up remembrance of things past,
> I sigh the lack of many a thing I sought,
> And with old woes new waile my deare times waste;
> Then can I drowne an eye (un-us'd to flow)
> For precious friends hid in deaths dateles night,
> And weepe afresh loves long since canceld woe,
> And mone th' expence of many a vannisht sight. . . .
> But if the while I thinke on thee (deare friend)
> All losses are restored, and sorrowes end.

The Sonnet seems to be an early one, but even here beneath the
main current of elegiac emotion (the tribute to friendship is

gracefully conventional) there is a counter-current of irony directed by the poet towards himself. In the eighth line Shakespeare is conscious that the present moan, like the sighs [sights] previously expended, involves a fresh expense ('Every sigh shortens life'), so that the line means, 'I waste my time and energy regretting the time and energy wasted in regrets'; and the slight over-emphasis of the third quatrain adds to the irony. In other words, Shakespeare is aware of what he is doing (after all, 'sessions' implies judgment), and therefore achieves a more stable equilibrium. This is a minor example, but the implicit self-criticism is pervasive (we may compare the previous Sonnet: 'Yet in these thoughts myself almost despising'); and – although the poem quoted is far enough from anything by Donne or Marvell – the constant reference of the immediate emotion to a mature scale of values reminds us that Shakespeare – Nature's Darling – is not far removed from the Tradition of Wit.

In many of the Sonnets ostensibly concerned with a personal relationship we find there is something of far greater interest to Shakespeare than the compliments, complaints and pleas that provide the occasion of writing. Sonnet cx is in the form of a plea for the restoration of friendship:

> Alas 'tis true, I have gone here and there,
> And made my selfe a motley to the view,
> Gor'd mine owne thoughts, sold cheap what is most dear,
> Made old offences of affections new.
> Most true it is, that I have lookt on truth
> Asconce and strangely: But by all above,
> These blenches gave my heart an other youth,
> And worse essaies prov'd thee my best of love,
> Now all is done, have what shall have no end,
> Mine appetite I never more will grin'de
> On newer proofe, to trie an older friend,
> A God in love, to whom I am confin'd.
>   Then give me welcome, next my heaven the best,
>   Even to thy pure and most most loving brest.

There can be no doubt that here the most powerful lines are those

recording self-disgust,[10] and that there is a drop in intensity when
Shakespeare turns to address the friend directly, as in the final
couplet. The Sonnet is important as a direct approach to
sincerity — it records the examination and integration of character. Indeed in many of the Sonnets in which the friend is given
something more than perfunctory recognition it is hard to resist
the conclusion that Shakespeare is addressing his own conscience.

> You are my All the world, and I must strive,
> To know my shames and praises from your tounge,
> None else to me, nor I to none alive,
> That my steel'd sence or changes right or wrong,
> In so profound Abisme I throw all care
> Of others voyces, that my Adders sence,
> To cryttick and to flatterer stopped are . . .

— 'Like the deaf adder that stoppeth her ear; which will not
hearken to the voice of charmers, charming never so wisely.' The
reference is important; in the Sonnets Shakespeare is working out
a morality based on his own finest perceptions and deepest
impulses.[11] Sonnet CXXI, which has caused a good deal of
perplexity, seems to me mainly a protest against any rigidly
imposed moral scheme, a protest on behalf of a morality based on
the nature of the writer. But that morality can only be discussed
in terms that the poetry supplies.

An essay might well be written on the Time theme in Shakespeare. Starting from an examination of *King Henry IV, Troilus and
Cressida* and the Sonnets, it would illuminate some important
aspects of Shakespeare's genius and of the Elizabethan mind. But
before discussing Shakespeare's handling of this theme some
distinctions must be made.
    In the Sonnets Shakespeare's interest in the passage of time
and the allied themes of death and mutability is sufficiently
obvious. Not only does it provide the main theme of many of the
more important Sonnets, it continually encroaches on other
interests and overshadows them. And there is a clear difference in

intensity, tone and treatment between Shakespeare's 'Time' sonnets and other Elizabethan poems dealing with 'Time's thievish progress to eternity'; between

> When I consider everything that growes
> Holds in perfection but a little moment   (xv)

or

> Like as the waves make towards the pibled shore . . .
>
>   (lx)

and such typically Elizabethan things as

> In time the strong and stately turrets fall,
> In time the rose and silver lilies die,
> In time the monarchs captive are, and thrall,
> In time the sea and rivers are made dry

or

> Soon doth it fade that makes the fairest flourish,
> Short is the glory of the blushing rose

or anything to be found in Spenser's Mutability Cantos.

Now 'the problem of Time' is a metaphysical problem, and in various forms it is a preoccupation of some of the Metaphysical Poets. Moreover, between Shakespeare's mature verse and Donne's there are similarities which it is important to recognize – the immediacy, the images generating intense mental activity ('the intellect at the tip of the senses'), the exploiting of speech rhythm and idiom, and so on: a good deal of Mr. Eliot's account of Metaphysical Poetry applies equally – as he points out – to the blank verse of Shakespeare and other late Elizabethans. This being so, it is all the more important to stress that in the Sonnets 'the problem of Time' is not a metaphysical problem at all, – and the discussion of Platonic Forms and Ideal Beauty is irrelevant. Wherever we look, Shakespeare is concerned merely with the *effects* of time on animate and inanimate beings, on persons and personal relationships. As a poet, he reports and evaluates experiences, but he does not attempt to *explain* them, nor do they arouse speculation in his mind. So, too, the plays 'explain' nothing; they are experiences to be lived. Indeed if Time had presented itself to Shakespeare as a metaphysical problem it could not have been dealt with in the verse of the Sonnets. Mr. James Smith has made a necessary distinction.[12] He points out that 'verse properly called metaphysical is that to which the impulse is given by an overwhelming concern with metaphysical problems; with problems either deriving from, or closely resembling in the nature of their difficulty, the problem of the Many and the One', and that in Metaphysical Poetry it is the conflict arising out of the perception of such problems that is resolved by means of the metaphysical conceit, in which there is both unity and 'high strain or tension, due to the sharpness with which its elements are opposed'. Shakespeare's imagery in the Sonnets, as I have pointed out, rarely involves a high degree of tension; and when, in the later plays, we find images that not only possess richness of association but embrace conflicting elements, those elements are invariably drawn from experience and sensation, never from speculative thought: they make finer experience available for others, but they offer no resolution of metaphysical problems.

The temptation to look for the development of a metaphysical mode in the Sonnets is not perhaps very common. A second temptation has not proved so easy to resist, and most accounts of the Sonnets point to certain of them as showing 'Love's Triumph over Time', without bothering to explain what this may mean. Certainly, if we isolate those sonnets in which a reaction to the passage of time and the inevitability of death provides the main emotional drive it is permissible to look for a coherently developing attitude culminating in a solution that shall be at least emotionally satisfying. There is an obvious advance in maturity, an increasing delicacy in exposition, but unless we are prepared to accept assertion as poetry (that is, bare statement deliberately willed, instead of the communication in all its depth, fullness and complexity, of an experience that has been lived) we shall not find that solution in the Sonnets. An example may make my meaning clearer. Sonnet CXXIII is commonly taken to show that 'Love conquers Time':

> No! Time, thou shalt not bost that I doe change,
> Thy pyramyds buylt up with newer might
> To me are nothing novell, nothing strange,
> They are but dressings of a former sight:
> Our dates are breefe, and therefor we admire,
> What thou dost foyst upon us that is ould,
> And rather make them borne to our desire,
> Then thinke that we before have heard them tould:
> Thy registers and thee I both defie,
> Not wondring at the present, nor the past,
> For thy records, and what we see doth lye,
> Made more or les by thy continuall hast:
> This I doe vow and this shall ever be,
> I will be true dispight thy syeth and thee.

It is upon the ambiguity of the first two quatrains that I wish to direct attention. *Sense* 1: 'Time cannot make his boast that I change with his passage. The admired wonders of modern architecture are not novelties to me (since my conscious self is, in a sense, outside time); I have seen them all before, and I know that the modern examples are only variations on the old. Man's life is short; therefore he tends to wonder at things, foisted upon him by Time as novelties, which are really old, preferring to believe them newly created for his satisfaction [born to our desire] than to see them truly as repetitions of the old.' *Sense* 2 (Wyndham's interpretation): 'Time cannot boast that I change. The pyramids – built with a skill that was new compared with my age-old self [with newer might to me] – were, I saw, no novelties even in ancient Egypt, but merely dressings of a former sight. Man's life is short; therefore he tends to wonder at the antiquities foisted upon him by Time, preferring to accept as absolute the limitations imposed by birth and death [to make them (dates) the bourn to his desire] than to think that the years of his life have been counted [told] before.' A rough paraphrase of the last six lines is: 'I refuse to accept as ultimate truth either history (recording that time has passed) or the present passage of time; neither novelty not antiquity move me; the evidence of universal change given by history and the present time is false: only in appearance are past and present governed by time. I vow that I will be myself (and – perhaps – true to some person) in spite of death and time.'

The purpose of the Sonnet is clear: to affirm the continuous identity of the self in spite of the passage of time. But, though a remarkable achievement, its failure is indicated by the unresolved ambiguity. That *Sense* 1 is intended seems clear from line 10 – 'Not wondering *at the present*, nor the past' – as well as from the Elizabethan use of the word 'pyramids'; and even if we do away with the maladroit pun on 'borne' by interpreting it as 'bourn' in *Sense* 1 as well as in *Sense* 2 (and I find it impossible to exclude the meaning 'born to our desire') we are left with 'that is old' fitting awkwardly into the first interpretation. Moreover – and perhaps it is more important to notice this than the conflicting meanings which somehow refuse to resolve themselves into unity – the poem *asserts* rather than expresses a resolved state of mind: 'Thou shalt not boast', 'I defy', 'This I do vow', 'I will be true'.

In the manner of its assertion the Sonnet is in line with the more famous Sonnet CXVI ('Love's not time's fool') – a poem of which the difficulties have never, I think, been squarely faced – and with those sonnets promising some form of immortality. And, we may remark in conclusion, in all the Sonnets of this last type, it is the contemplation of change, not the boasting and defiance, that produces the finest poetry; they draw their value entirely from the evocation of that which is said to be defied or triumphed over. In the plays – from *Henry IV* to *The Tempest* – in which the theme of Time occurs, there is no defiance; the conflict is resolved by the more or less explicit acceptance of mutability.[13] I should like to give this remark precision in terms of literary criticism by examining the second part of *King Henry IV*, a play of which the prelude is spoken by the dying Hotspur towards the end of Part I:

But thought's the slave of life, and life time's fool . . . .

But perhaps enough has been said to show that, in this respect as in all others, the Sonnets yield their proper significance only when seen in the context of Shakespeare's development as a dramatist.

SOURCE: *Scrutiny*, III 2 (1934); reprinted in *Explorations* (1946) pp. 40–65, with additional notes.

NOTES

1. The tendency is encouraged by the fact that the Sonnets are printed in a numbered sequence, without titles. And remembering the part played by verbal habit in directing thought, we may consider the effect of the mere repetition of the phrase, 'The Sonnets'.

2. See their analysis of Sonnet CXXIX in *A Survey of Modernist Poetry*, pp. 63–81. [See above – Ed.] No one need suppose that, in complaining of wanton 'emendations', I am claiming complete infallibility for the Quarto.

3. 'The mortal moon hath her eclipse endur'd' (CVII) – the only 'external reference' of any difficulty – is more likely to refer to the ending of the Queen's climacterical year (1596) than to her death – as Dr. G. B. Harrison has pointed out.

4. I have italicized the phrase that forces the dilemma: *either* autobiographical or 'merely dramatic' and conventional.

5. 'Surmise' is object to the imperative 'accumilate'; the separating comma seems unnecessary.

6. Of course the tone is not determined solely by the movement; often, for example, the degree of seriousness with which Shakespeare is writing is indicated by the imagery. Consider the roses of Sonnet XCIX which 'fearfully on thornes did stand', or the poet's thousand groans, 'one on anothers necke', in Sonnet CXXXI.

7. The phrase is Edgell Rickword's (*Towards Standards of Criticism*, ed. F. R. Leavis, p. 120).

8. *Seven Types of Ambiguity*, pp. 65–73 and 168–75.

9. *Selected Essays*, p. 144.

10. To take the first three lines as referring merely to the profession of actor and playwright is too narrow an interpretation; the reference

seems to be to the way in which a sensitive intelligence has displayed its wares of wit and observation in common intercourse.

11. 'But we have to know ourselves pretty thoroughly before we can break the automatism of ideals and conventions. . . . Only through fine delicate knowledge can we recognize and release our impulses.' –D. H. Lawrence, *Fantasia of the Unconscious*, p. 60.

12. 'The Metaphysical Note in Poetry', in *Determinations*.

13. An acceptance, I should now (1944) add, that comes to be closely associated with the complementary recognition of new life and of values that are not subject to time. This has been admirably brought out by D. A. Traversi's *Approach to Shakespeare*, which also shows the essential continuity of development – a continuity of developing experience – between the Sonnets and the greater plays.

John Crowe Ransom

SHAKESPEARE AT SONNETS (1938)

. . . I begin with a most obvious feature: generally they are ill constructed.

They use the common English metrical pattern, and the metrical work is always admirable, but the logical pattern more often than not fails to fit it. If it be said that you do not need to have a correspondence between a poet's metrical pattern and his logical one, I am forced to observe that Shakespeare thought there was a propriety in it; often he must have gone to the pains of securing it, since it is there and, considering the extreme difficulty of the logical structure in the English sonnet, could not have got in by a happy accident. The metrical pattern of any sonnet is directive. If the English sonnet exhibits the rhyme-scheme ABAB CDCD EFEF GG, it imposes upon the poet the following require-ment: that he write three co-ordinate quatrains and then a couplet which will relate to the series collectively.

About a third of the sonnets of Shakespeare are fairly unexceptionable in having just such a logical structure. About half of them might be said to be tolerably workmanlike in this respect; and about half of them are seriously defective. . . . Possibly the commonest irregularity of logical arrangement with Shakespeare is in sonnets of the following type (LXIV):

> When I have seen by Time's fell hand defac'd
> The rich proud cost of outworn buried age;
> When sometime lofty towers I see down-raz'd,
> And brass eternal slave to mortal rage;
>
> When I have seen the hungry ocean gain
> Advantage on the kingdom of the shore,
> And the firm soil win of the watery main,
> Increasing store with loss and loss with store;

> When I have seen such interchange of state,
> Or state itself confounded to decay,
> Ruin hath taught me thus to ruminate,
> That Time will come and take my love away.
>
> This thought is as a death, which cannot choose,
> But weep to have that which it fears to lose.

Here the three quatrains look co-ordinate, but only the first two really are so. The third begins with the same form as the others, but presently shows that it is only summary of their content, and then actually begins to introduce the matter which will be the concern of the couplet. We must believe that Shakespeare found the couplet too small to hold its matter, so that at about line ten he had to begin anticipating it. But, as I said, this sonnet represents a pattern fairly common with him, and it is possible to argue that he developed it consciously as a neat variant on the ordinary English structure; just as Milton developed a variant from the Italian structure, by concluding the logical octet a little before or a little after the rhyme-ending of the eighth line.

Probably Shakespeare's usual structural difficulty consists about equally in having to pad out his quatrains, if three good co-ordinates do not offer themselves, and in having to squeeze the couplet too flat, or else extend its argument upward into the proper territory of the quatrains. But when both these things happen at once, the obvious remark is that the poet should have reverted to the Italian sonnet.

Structurally, Shakespeare is a careless workman. But probably, with respect to our attention to structure, we are careless readers. . . .

. . . The sonnets are mixed in effect. Not only the sequence as a whole but the individual sonnet is uneven in execution. But what to the critic is still more interesting than the up and the down in one style is the alternation of two very different styles: the one we have been considering, and the one which we are accustomed to define (following Doctor Johnson) as metaphysical. What is the metaphysical poetry doing there? Apparently at about the time of *Hamlet*, and perhaps recognizably in the plays but much more deliberately and on a more extended scale in the sonnets, Shakespeare goes metaphysical. Not consistently, of course.

So far as I know, Shakespeare has not ordinarily been credited with being one of the metaphysicals, nor have specimen sonnets been included in lists or anthologies of metaphysical poems. But many sonnets certainly belong there; early examples of that style. If it was not then widely practised, had no name, and could hardly yet have been recognized as a distinct style, then I would suppose that the sonnets as a performance represent Shakespeare seeking such effects as John Donne, a public if still unpublished wonder, by some curious method was achieving. But there was also, on a smaller scale, the example of a genuine pioneer in this field in the person of Sidney, if Shakespeare cared to look there; see his *Astrophel and Stella*, xciv, 'Grief, find the words, for thou hast made my brain.'

Certainly Shakespeare's lxxxvii, 'Farewell! thou art too dear for my possessing,' already quoted as an instance of good structure, is in the style. For its substance is furnished by developing the human relation (that of the renouncing lover) through a figure of speech; a legal one, in which an unequal bond is cancelled for cause. Three times, in as many quatrains, the lover makes an exploration within the field of the figure. The occasions are fairly distinct, though I should think their specifications are hardly respective enough to have satisfied Donne. But the thing which surprises us is to find no evidence anywhere that Shakespeare's imagination is equal to the peculiar and systematic exercises which Donne imposed habitually upon his. None, and it should not really surprise us, if we remember that Donne's skill is of the highest technical expertness in English poetry, and that Shakespeare had no university discipline, and developed poetically along lines of least resistance.

He is upon occasions metaphysical enough, but not so metaphysical as Donne; nor as later poets, Donne's followers, who were just as bold in intention as their master, though not usually so happy in act.

The impulse to metaphysical poetry, I shall assume, consists in committing the feelings in the case – those of unrequited love for example – to their determination within the elected figure. But

Shakespeare was rarely willing to abandon his feelings to this fate, which is another way of saying that he would not quite risk the consequences of his own imagination. He censored these consequences, to give them sweetness, to give them even dignity; he would go a little way with one figure, usually a reputable one, then anticipate the consequences, or the best of them, and take up another figure. . . .

. . . Lovers (and other persons too) often have feelings which cannot take, and do not seek, their natural outlet in physical actions. The feelings may be too complex anyhow, and too persistent, to be satisfied with simple actions, they overrun the mark; or perhaps the lovers have to go upon an absence, and the feelings get dammed up. Then they find appropriate actions through imagination, in intellectual constructions. These lovers at their best are poets. These poets at their best perform complete actions, very likely by means of metaphysical poems. So, on the one hand, there is an associationist poetry, a half-way action providing many charming resting-places for the feelings to agitate themselves; and, on the other hand, there is a metaphysical poetry, which elects its line of action and goes straight through to the completion of the cycle and extinction of the feelings.

This gives us associationist poetry *versus*, I think, behavioristic. For our discussion seems to have turned psychological. If romantic poets are not fully aware of what they are doing, metaphysical poets are self-conscious and deliberate, and in fact they are very like technical psychologists. They start with feelings, they objectify these imaginatively into external actions. They think that poetry, just as behavioristic psychologists think that psychology, can make nothing out of feelings as they stand. . . .

. . . But Shakespeare honestly realizes the metaphysical image, and I shall cite, with some remark, the sonnets in which he seems to me to have the most conspicuous success.

I begin with xxx, 'When to the sessions of sweet silent thought'; it is smart work, but only half the sharpness belongs to the strict object; the rest is accidental or mechanical, because it is oral or verbal; it is word-play, and word-play, including punning, belongs to the loose poetry of association. Technically perfect and altogether admirable in its careful modulation is LVII, 'Being your slave, what should I do but tend'; and so faithfully does it stick to the object, which is the behavior suitable to the slave kept waiting, that not till the couplet is there any direct expression of the feelings of the actual outraged lover.

Sonnet LX, 'Like as the waves make toward the pebbled shore', is ambitious and imperfect. The first quatrain says that our minutes are always toiling forward, like waves. The second quatrain introduces a different and pretentious image of this tendency, and shows its fatal consequence:

> Nativity, once in the main of light,
> Crawls to maturity, wherewith being crown'd,
> Crooked eclipses 'gainst his glory fight,
> And Time that gave doth now his gift confound.

The lines will be impressive to that kind of receptivity whose critical defences are helpless against great words in musical phrases. Nativity means the new-born infant, but maturity seems only an object in his path, or at the goal of his path, evidently a crown which he puts on. Thereupon the astrological influences turn against nativity, and Time enters the story to destroy his own gift; this must be the crown that nativity has picked up. We are confused about all these entities. In the third quatrain Shakespeare declines to a trite topic, the destructiveness of Time, and represents him successively as transfixing the flourish set on youth (however he may do that), delving the parallels in beauty's brow (as a small demon with a digging instrument?), feeding on the rareties of nature's truth (as gluttonous monster), and mowing everything with his scythe (as grim reaper). A field of imagery in which the explorer has performed too prodigiously, and lost his chart.

And now LXXIII, with its opening quatrain:

> That time of year thou mayst in me behold
> When yellow leaves, or none, or few, do hang

Upon those boughs which shake against the cold,
Bare ruin'd choirs, where late the sweet birds sang.

The structure is good, the three quatrains offering distinct yet equivalent figures for the time of life of the unsuccessful and to-be-pitied lover. But the first quatrain is the boldest, and the effect of the whole is slightly anti-climactic. Within this quatrain I think I detect a thing which often characterizes Shakespeare's work within the metaphysical style: he is unwilling to renounce the benefit of his earlier style, which consisted in the breadth of the associations; that is, he will not quite risk the power of a single figure but compounds the figures. I refer to the two images about the boughs. It is one thing to have the boughs shaking against the cold, and in that capacity they carry very well the fact of the old rejected lover; it is another thing to represent them as ruined choirs where the birds no longer sing. The latter is a just representation of the lover too, and indeed a subtler and richer one, but the two images cannot, in logical rigor, co-exist. Therefore I deprecate *shake against the cold*. And I believe everybody will deprecate *sweet*. This term is not an objective image at all, but a term to be located at the subjective pole of the experience; it expects to satisfy a feeling by naming it (that is, by just having it) and is a pure sentimentalism. . . .

SOURCE: extracts from *The World's Body* (1938) pp. 273, 277–8, 285–7, 291–2, 295–8.

PART FOUR
Recent Studies
1952 – 76

Winifred M. T. Nowottny

FORMAL ELEMENTS IN SHAKESPEARE'S SONNETS: SONNETS I – VI (1952)

Despite Shakespeare's own description of his sonnets as being
'far from variation or quick change', they have proved to be
remarkably resistant to generalizations. It is, however, the
purpose of this article to suggest that there is one generalization
that can be made about them; one, moreover, that affords a point
of view from which it is always helpful to regard them: namely,
that the *Sonnets* reveal Shakespeare's strong sense of form, and
that it is with respect to their form that the peculiar features or
striking effects of individual sonnets may best be understood.
There are in the *Sonnets* so many experiments with form that it
would be difficult to lay down at the outset a definition of 'form'
at once comprehensive and precise, but the meaning of the term
as it is used here will be sufficiently indicated by describing 'form'
as 'that in virtue of which the parts are related one to another', or
indeed as 'that which manifests itself in the relationships of the
parts'. What is important for the purposes of this article is not the
precise definition of form, but rather the indication of elements
which commonly contribute to the manifestation of form. At the
present day, the most illuminating criticism of individual sonnets
is characterized by its concentration on imagery, and though it is
true that imagery in the *Sonnets* is of great importance, it is not of
exclusive or even of paramount importance. In this article I shall
try to show that in Shakespeare's sonnets imagery is subordinated
to the creation of the form of the whole and that imagery itself is
at its most effective when it supports or is supported by the action
of formal elements of a different kind.

Sonnets I–VI of the 1609 Quarto afford illustration. Shakespeare is often praised for his power of using imagery as an
integrating element, yet in these sonnets it is evident that he has

sacrificed the integration of the imagery of the individual sonnet to larger considerations of form; this sacrifice has features which show that it is in fact a sacrifice and not the ineptitude of a novice in sonnet-writing. In Sonnet I, the degree to which the images assist the organization of the poem is slight indeed. Almost every line has a separate image, and these images are heterogeneous (for instance: 'Beauty's rose' – 'heir' – 'contracted' – 'flame' – 'famine' – 'foe' – 'herald' – 'buriest' – 'glutton'). The relation between the images is, for the most part, a relation via the subject they illustrate; it is not by their relations to one another that the poem is organized. This, however, is not ineptitude. The separateness, the repetitiveness (in that there is no increasing penetration of the object, but only an ever-renewed allegorization), and the regularity (a single new image in each of the first twelve lines) give this sonnet the character of a litany. If Sonnet I is indeed in its rightful place, there would seem to be here a recognizable decorum of form in the poet's electing to open by a litany of images[1] a sonnet sequence which makes extended use of each. Further, the hypothesis that in Sonnet I there is a decorum of form which to the poet seemed more important than the congruity of images within the individual sonnet is borne out by some features of Sonnets II – IV. The imagery of Sonnet II falls into two distinct parts connected by a modulation. In the first quatrain there is a group of images all referring to the beauty of the face; in the third quatrain a very different group, not visual like the first, but moral or prudential, relating to beauty considered as treasure, inheritance, and a matter for the rendering of accounts; the intervening quatrain is entirely devoted to a modulation from one type to the other:

> Then, being ask'd where all thy beauty lies,
> Where all the treasure of thy lusty days,
> To say, within thine own deep-sunken eyes,
> Were an all-eating shame and thriftless praise.

(In this modulation the visual and the prudential – 'beauty' and 'treasure' – are formally balanced, and the 'deep-sunken' unites the eyes and the treasure in a single imaging epithet.) This careful four-line modulation suggests that Shakespeare was well aware of the virtue of relating images one to another as well as to the object they convey; yet the very necessity for a modulation here derives from the remoteness from one another of the two types of imagery. Here again the discrepancy finds its justification in larger considerations of form: namely, in the relation of Sonnet II to Sonnets III and IV. Sonnet III takes up and expands the first quatrain of Sonnet II, turning as it does upon the beauty of the face ('Look in thy glass, and tell the face thou viewest . . .'), and Sonnet IV takes up and expands the third quatrain of Sonnet II, turning as it does entirely upon beauty as treasure, inheritance, and a matter for the rendering of accounts. It is further to be observed that Sonnets V and VI repeat this pattern, V dealing with visual beauty in visual terms, and VI dealing with 'beauty's treasure' in a long-sustained conceit drawn from usury. Would it be fanciful to suggest that the infelicity of the usury conceit in Sonnet VI reflects the difficulty the poet found in bringing this little sequence to a formally symmetrical conclusion?

In each of these six sonnets, features of the individual sonnet are illuminated by a consideration of the design of the whole group. But since we have no external warrant of the correctness of the 1609 order, the case for Shakespeare's sense of form must further be argued on grounds affording independent corroboration. This is found in Sonnet IV where, though the imagery chosen relates the sonnet to its fellows, the development of that imagery within the sonnet is a self-contained exercise in abstract form. The sonnet must be quoted and discussed in full.

> Unthrifty loveliness, why dost thou spend
> Upon thyself thy beauty's legacy?
> Nature's bequest gives nothing, but doth lend,
> And, being frank, she lends to those are free.
> Then, beauteous niggard, why dost thou abuse
> The bounteous largess given thee to give?
> Profitless usurer, why dost thou use
> So great a sum of sums, yet canst not live?
> For, having traffic with thyself alone,
> Thou of thyself thy sweet self dost deceive.

Then how when nature calls thee to be gone?
What acceptable audit canst thou leave?
Thy unus'd beauty must be tomb'd with thee,
Which, used, lives, th'executor to be.

Here we have a sonnet in which, patently, there is a high degree
of organization. Firstly, the imagery of financial matters is
sustained throughout. Secondly, there is within this integrated
scheme a number of strongly marked subsidiary systems. The
most immediately striking, which may therefore be cited first, is
the ringing of the changes in lines 5–8 on 'abuse' – 'usurer' –
'use', which is taken up in the couplet by 'unus'd', 'used'.
Another marked system is that of the reflexive constructions
associated with 'thee': 'spend upon thyself' – 'traffic with
thyself' – 'thou of thyself thy sweet self dost deceive', taken up in
the couplet by 'thy . . . beauty . . . tomb'd with thee'. That these
are deliberate systems, not inept repetitions, is proved by the way
in which they interlock in the couplet: 'unus'd' is, in the first line
of the couplet, linked with 'thy beauty . . . tomb'd with thee',
and this contrasts with the second line of the couplet, where there
is a linking of 'used', 'executor', and 'lives', to produce the
complete formal balance in thought, diction and syntax, of

Thy unus'd beauty must be tomb'd with thee,
Which, used, lives, th'executor to be.

This formal balance is of course closely related to the thought of
the sonnet: Nature, which lends beauty in order that it may be
given, is contrasted with the youth, whose self-regarding results
in a usurious living on capital alone, which is a negation of
Nature and of life; these paradoxes of the thought make possible
the correspondences and contrasts of the verbal systems. What is
remarkable is the way in which the poet evolves from this
material an intricate and beautiful form which is very close to the
art of fugue. Like the fugue, its effect resides in the interaction of
the parts; critical analysis, which cannot reproduce the simul-
taneousness of the original, must labor heavily behind, discussing

first the development of each part and then their interaction. We may note, then, that 'Unthrifty loveliness', with which the sonnet opens, is, as it were, a first blending of those two distinct voices, 'why dost thou spend upon thyself' and 'Nature's bequest'. The second quatrain blends them again in 'beauteous niggard', which is itself an inversion, formally complete, of 'unthrifty loveliness', and moreover an inversion which leads on to the extreme of 'profitless usurer'; further, the movement toward the judgment represented by 'profitless usurer' has all the while been less obtrusively going on in the verbs as well as in the vocatives ('spend' – 'abuse' – 'yet canst not live'). Then, with 'yet canst not live', the sonnet brings out the second voice, that reflexive (and self-destructive) action announced in 'spend upon thyself', but kept low in the first eight lines, maintaining itself there only by the formal parallels of 'why dost thou spend' – 'why dost thou abuse' – 'why dost thou use'. This voice now emerges predominant in 'For, having traffic with thyself alone', and this voice in turn reaches its extreme of formal development in the line 'Thou of thyself thy sweet self dost deceive'. The remaining lines bring the two voices to a sharp contrast with 'nature calls thee to be gone' (where 'nature' and 'thee' achieve a syntactical nearness embodying a conflict of opposed concepts, and this conflict-in-nearness is fully stated in the complete formal balance of the couplet). In this rough analysis of the blending of the voices in this sonnet, much has had to be passed over, but now we may go back and point to the incidental contrast and harmony of 'beauteous niggard' with 'bounteous largess'; to the transition, in the pun of 'canst not live', from usury to death (which leads on to the contrast in the couplet); to the felicity of 'audit' in line 12, which is relevant not only to all the financial imagery that has gone before, but also to the rendering of an account when life is at an end; to the subtle conceptual sequence of 'unthrifty loveliness' (the fact of beauty), 'beauteous niggard' (the poet's reproof), 'profitless usurer' (the youth's own loss), and finally, 'unus'd beauty' (the whole tragedy – of beauty, of the poet, and of the youth – in the hour of death). Thus this sonnet, which in its absence of visual imagery has little attraction for the hasty reader, reveals itself to analysis as having an intricate beauty of form to which it would be hard to find a parallel in the work of any other poet.

Though Sonnet IV is a *tour de force* in the handling of form, Sonnet V is even more important to the critic who would make much of formal elements, in that it has a quality which sets it apart from the preceding four: a quality the average reader might call seriousness or sincerity. Here Shakespeare deals with Time and Beauty (and for the application of these to the particular case of the youth requires Sonnet VI, linked to V by 'Then let not . . . '). The evident artifice of Sonnets I–IV (emblematic imagery, conceits, punning and patterned word play) gives place in Sonnet V to language which, though it is of course figurative, derives its figures from that realm of common experience in which processes conceived philosophically by the mind have in fact their manifestations to the senses: from the seasons which figure Time, from the flower and its fragrance which figure Beauty and Evanescence. In short, the poem appeals to us in that realm of experience where we are all, already, half poets. Yet despite this change from the 'artificial' to the 'sincere', this poem too derives much of its strength from its formal design. This design is simple but perfect. The easy continuous process of Time is stated in lines themselves easy and continuous:

> Those hours that with gentle work did frame
> The lovely gaze where every eye doth dwell,

and in the next two lines, which suggest that this process implies a coming reversal, the reversal is still a thing of the future and is indicated not by any change in the movement but only by the verbal contrasts between 'gentle' and 'will play the tyrant' and between 'fairly' and 'unfair'. So the continuous movement flows uninterrupted through these lines and on into the fifth: 'For never-resting time leads summer on'. But in the sixth line, 'To hideous winter and confounds him there', the reversal so casually foretold in the first quatrain becomes, by the violence of 'hideous winter' and 'confounds' and by the change of tense, a present catastrophe, and the movement of the fifth and sixth lines taken together perfectly corresponds to the sense: the running-on movement of summer is checked by 'hideous winter' and again by the heavy pause at 'there'. The next two lines embody perfectly, by sound and imagery as well as by sense, this checking and reversal:

> Sap check'd with frost and lusty leaves quite gone,
> Beauty o'ersnow'd and bareness everywhere.

(Particularly subtle is the way in which the alliteration of 'lusty leaves' gives place to that of 'beauty' with 'bareness'.) Now in the remaining six lines the poet in his turn attempts a reversal, and the beauty of the form is to be seen in the way in which he now uses the two kinds of movement already laid down in the sonnet (the one of flowing, the other of checking). What he does is to *transfer to Beauty* the flowing movement of Time, and then to *arrest* Beauty in a state of permanent *perfection*; this he does by the long flowing movement, ending in arrest and permanence, of the line, 'Then, were not summer's distillation left . . . .'.

This triumphant transfer to Beauty of the movement formerly associated with Time, is of a piece with the imagery of the next line ('A liquid prisoner pent in walls of glass'), where Beauty's distillation is at once arrested ('prisoner', 'pent') yet free ('liquid') and visible ('glass'); this image of course reverses the implications of the earlier images of winter, where the sap was checked with frost and beauty was o'ersnow'd. Thus the movement of the first eight lines proves to have been designed not merely to make the sound repeat the sense, but rather to lay down formal elements whose reversal enables the poet to reverse the reversal implicit in Time. Similarly, the image of distillation is seen to be not merely an illustration of the concept of preserving Beauty, but also an answer to the image of winter's freezing of the sap and obliteration of Beauty. Clearly, the formal elements of Sonnet v are part of the poetic logic: the movement, as much as the imagery, is a means of poetic power. It is because of this that the study of formal elements in the *Sonnets* is not an arid academic exercise. Such a study can help one to arrive at a fuller understanding of Shakespeare's means of communication and a fuller possession of those poetic experiences with which the *Sonnets* deal.

This article has dealt only with the first six sonnets of the 1609 Quarto. These six sonnets are not exceptional in their successful handling of form; from the whole range of the *Sonnets* many examples more subtle and more striking might have been chosen but it seemed to me best, in order to argue the case for Shakespeare's interest in form, to make no arbitrary selection, but simply to begin at the beginning and scrutinize what is to be found there. The findings warrant a much greater attention to formal aspects of the *Sonnets* than is at present customary. The result of such an attentiveness to Shakespeare's handling of form is the discovery that the greater the immediate effect of a sonnet, the more surely does it prove, upon examination, that the effects rest no less upon the form than upon the appeal of the sentiments or of the imagery (as, for instance, in the famous Sonnet CXVI, 'Let me not to the marriage of true minds . . .'). Again, it will be found that many of the sonnets which are not commonly held to be of the finest, reveal an unsuspected depth and strength when they are, after scrutiny of their form, revalued. It is upon this last point that particular stress may well be laid, for it is here that one becomes aware of new possibilities for the interpretation of Shakespeare's language, not only in the poems but also in the plays. A close study of the language of the *Sonnets* makes it clear that, great as was Shakespeare's ability to use imagery not only for its beauty but also for its integrating power, he possessed in even greater measure the power to make the formal elements of language express the nature of the experience with which the language deals. No doubt a knowledge of rhetoric, which must direct attention to verbal patterns, did something to develop this power. Of the early plays it may be true to say that sometimes the rhetorical forms are empty, that they have little virtue beyond that of providing a ready-made mold for the flow of what is thought and felt. But Shakespeare's rejection of rhetorical forms of the overelaborate and merely self-regarding type was coupled with an increasing awareness of the expressiveness of those forms he did retain. Thus in the language of the great plays the recurrence of a marked form is not fortuitous, nor is it, in cases where a recurring form is associated with a particular speaker, merely a device for adding body to a character; that is to say, these features of the style are rarely, if ever, designed to contribute merely to the creation of a 'character part'; they are almost always an expression of something essential in the speaker himself considered in his relation to the play as a whole. Pope in his preface to his edition of Shakespeare commented on the highly individualized styles of the characters. It still remains for the interpreters of Shakespeare in our own time to discover to what extent these styles are expressive as well as characteristic. And further it may be said that the expressiveness of formal organizations in Shakespeare's language is matched by the expressiveness of form in all his dramatic structures. Every age rediscovers the genius of Shakespeare. It is open to ours to discover and to show the working of his genius in the realm of forms.

SOURCE: *Essays in Criticism*, II (January 1952) 76–84.

NOTE

1. The litany of images is at the same time a litany of considerations or arguments, for in these sonnets the image is often an emblem of an argument.

G. K. Hunter

THE DRAMATIC TECHNIQUE OF SHAKESPEARE'S SONNETS (1953)

Though most modern critics would accept the fact that Shakespeare's sonnet-sequence has a pervasive poetry with an excellence recognizably Shakespearean, the peculiar quality of this excellence remains undefined. This may be because criticism of the sonnets has been overshadowed by biographical speculation. There have been few aesthetic critics and these have confined themselves to *minutiae*, and have disregarded or noticed only with condemnation the reactions of their biographically-minded fellows. No one seems to have attempted to explain by what means Shakespeare presents traditional materials so that an overwhelmingly biographical reaction is set up in the reader. Neither the accepted categories of lyric or narrative nor the contemporary verse-fashions – Petrarchan, Anti-Petrarchan, Metaphysical, etc. – will account for this unique flavour in the sequence as a whole and for the concentratedly 'Shakespearean' effect of such sonnets as XV, XVIII, XXX, CXXIX. It is not perhaps a coincidence that the critics who accept these categories tend to find Shakespeare's sonnet-technique in some way misdirected, from Keats with his 'full of fine things said unintentionally – in the intensity of working out conceits' to John Crowe Ransom, 'Shakespeare had no University discipline and developed poetically along lines of least resistance'.[1]

I wish to suggest here that it is rather the approach to the Sonnets as lyric, narrative, or metaphysical exercises that is misdirected. Critics who ignore the biographical approach miss a valuable clue to the bias of Shakespeare's technique – bias which twists the normal Petrarchan line towards the characteristically Shakespearean flavour of

When not to be receives reproach of being . . .

Oh that our nights of woe might have remembered . . .
Never believe that in my nature reigneth . . ..

I contend that when Shakespeare writes like this he is not misdirecting his talent, not being a quaint and elaborate lyrist, a failed and soured Petrarchan, a Metaphysical *manqué*, or a passionate autobiographical poet whose confessions are cut short by his conceits, so much as – what one would expect – a *dramatist*.

Let us consider in this light two sonnets which, without being masterpieces, seem to me to sound the authentic Shakespearean note:

Say that thou didst forsake me for some fault,
And I will comment upon that offence:
Speak of my lameness, and I straight will halt,
Against thy reasons making no defence.
Thou canst not, love, disgrace me half so ill,
To set a form upon desired change,
As I'll myself disgrace; knowing thy will,
I will acquaintance strangle and look strange;
Be absent from thy walks; and in my tongue
Thy sweet beloved name no more shall dwell,
Lest I, too much profane, should do it wrong,
And haply of our old acquaintance tell.
   For thee, against myself I'll vow debate,
   For I must ne'er love him whom thou dost hate.

(LXXXIX)

Was it the proud full sail of his great verse,
Bound for the prize of all too precious you,
That did my ripe thoughts in my brain inhearse,
Making their tomb the womb wherein they grew?
Was it his spirit, by spirits taught to write
Above a mortal pitch, that struck me dead?
No, neither he, nor his compeers by night
Giving him aid, my verse astonished. [etc.]

(LXXXVI)

The power of these poems does not reside in lyrical utterance; the vision they present is an individual's, and to that extent like lyric, but in them the reader is not concerned with solitary imaginings presented as of universal significance (as in the Odes of Keats and Shelley), but with the relation of one human heart to others. By setting up a system of tensions between forces presented as persons Shakespeare's sonnets engage the reader's interest in a manner akin to the dramatic. Sonnet LXXXIX is presented as a 'still' from a love-drama, a picture in which the gestures not only make up a present harmony, but hint (with subtle economy of means, which reveals the dramatist) at a psychological background, so that a powerful reaction is built up, as if to a history of love. In Sonnet LXXXVI the number of the characters involved is greater, but the technique is the same. An emotional state (estrangement) is expressed by means of a pattern of human figures; as a result of the hints at characterization we become involved as if with personalities, and so experience the dramatic impact. The reaction of the commentator who finds in the 'lameness' of LXXXIX proof of a physical defect in the author is an indication of the force of this impact, and the number of 'keys' to the 'sonnet-story' would seem to show that it is fairly constant throughout the sequence.

At this point the reader might object that the dramatic vividness in Shakespeare's sonnets is only a heightened form of a commonplace Elizabethan quality and that the biographical reaction is not produced by technique so much as by natural curiosity about the greatest and most enigmatic of our poets. Comparisons with other Elizabethan poets show, however, that the Sonnets are not only supreme in dramatic effectiveness, but almost unique in the methods by which this effect is obtained. Many of the sonneteers in Sir Sidney Lee's collection are good dramatic 'plotters' i.e. they can organize a set scene so that the figures contrast effectively and carry well the emotional charge that the author has imparted to them. For example:

> Oft with true sighs, oft with uncalled tears,
> Now with slow words, now with dumb eloquence;
> I Stella's eyes assailed, invade her ears:

But this, at last, is her sweet breathed defence.
'That who indeed infelt affection bears,
So captivates to his saint both soul and sense;
That wholly hers, all selfness he forbears: [etc.]
                    (Sidney, *Astrophel and Stella*, LXI)

But such scenes are set at a middle-distance from the reader; the effect that is almost unique in Shakespeare is that of immediate contact with the suffering mind. We learn what it felt like to be the lover in such-and-such a situation, and the figures are arranged to increase the poignant immediacy of our apprehension – so that if the beloved is young the lover is represented as old, if the lover is poor the beloved must be high-born, etc. The brilliance of the language makes the context of these emotions so vivid that the reader naturally supplies from his imagination a complete dramatic situation.

Shakespeare's 'plots' differ from those of contemporary sonneteers in that we are seldom given visual descriptions of the persons involved. This difference does not involve him in a modern 'psychological' presentation: when the lover appears before the reader there is no self-dramatization in the sense that he is presented as a significant and interesting individual. When we hear of him

Beated and chopped with tanned antiquity   (LXII)

Desiring this man's art and that man's scope   (XXIX)

As an unperfect actor on the stage   (XXIII)

we are no nearer any conception of his personality. The dramatic power of conveying personal tensions is achieved by patterning the persons, not by analysing them.

Shakespeare uses the conventions of the sonnet *genre* in such a way that he conjures before us the tone and accent of the traditional personages. Thus like other sonnet-heroes Shakespeare's lover suffers from the tyranny of the beloved while welcoming this slavery as a blessed condition:

Being your slave, what should I do but tend
Upon the hours and times of your desire?
I have no precious time at all to spend,
Nor services to do, till you require.
Nor dare I chide the world-without-end hour
Whilst I, my sovereign, watch the clock for you, [etc.]

                                                   (LVII)

The verse is charged here with that heartfelt simplicity which
gives the utterance of Shakespeare's greatest dramatic creations
their full force. We fully share the feelings of this slave, seeing the
objects described as coloured by his predominating emotion.
Sidney, whose treatment of the Petrarchan situations can often
be compared with Shakespeare's in artistic worth, gives charm to
a parallel description:

          . . . now, like slave-born Muscovite,
        I call it praise to suffer tyranny:
          And now employ the remnant of my wit
        To make myself believe that all is well;
        While with a feeling skill, I paint my hell.   (II)

But the effect here is different in kind from Shakespeare's; the
intellect is more analytical, and the simile has the objective
quality of a rational self-criticism, which Shakespeare's lacks. In
Sidney there seems to be a greater distance between speaker and
reader and consequently the reader tends to take a less impli-
cated and so less biographical view of the situation.[2]
    The tradition in which the Sonnets are written did not always
provide material entirely suitable for Shakespeare's dramatic
technique; but even in his treatments of the more mechanically
ingenious themes something of the same quality of imagination
emerges. Sonnet XLVI deals with the traditional theme of a war
between the heart and eye; a more commonplace treatment of
the same theme may be seen in Thomas Watson's *Tears of Fancy*:

        My hart accus'd mine eies and was offended,
        Vowing the cause was in mine eies aspiring:

Mine eies affirmd my hart might well amend it,
If he at first had banisht loues desiring.
Hart said that loue did enter at the eies,
And from the eies descended to the hart:
Eies said that in the hart did sparkes arise,
Which kindled flame that wrought the inward smart,
Hart said eies tears might soone haue quencht that fl[ame]
Eies said . . . [etc.]   (xx)

Compare Shakespeare:

Mine eye and heart are at a mortal war,
How to divide the conquest of thy sight;
Mine eye my heart thy picture's sight would bar,
My heart mine eye the freedom of that right.
My heart doth plead that thou in him dost lie,
A closet never pierced with crystal eyes,
But the defendant doth that plea deny,
And says in him thy fair appearance lies.
To 'cide this title is impanneled
A quest of thoughts, all tenants to the heart;
And by their verdict is determined
The clear eye's moiety and the dear heart's part:
    As thus; mine eye's due is thine outward part,
    And my heart's right thine inward love of heart.
                                                        (xlvi)

Shakespeare's poem is not simply a better example of a conceited
sonnet, it is a more affecting poem, and this is because he makes
the conceit serve a felt human situation. Watson concentrates on
the antithetical litigants to such an extent that he loses sight of the
human 'I' and 'thou'. Shakespeare, in spite of the frigidity of
many of the images ('conquest', 'picture', 'closet'), manages to
animate the legal imagery with a sense of the lover's craving. He
never forgets that the poem is a lover's confession, and accordingly it is directed throughout towards the figure of the beloved.

The same pressure of desire in the speaking voice shapes
Shakespeare's treatment of another stock theme – the vision of

the beloved in a dream – in such a way that the conceits
employed are subordinated to the expression of personal
emotion:

> When most I wink, then do mine eyes best see,
> For all the day they view things unrespected;
> But when I sleep, in dreams they look on thee,
> And, darkly bright, are bright in dark directed.
> Then thou, whose shadow shadows doth make bright,
> How would thy shadow's form form happy show
> To the clear day with thy much clearer light,
> When to unseeing eyes thy shade shines so! [etc.]
>
> (XLIII)

Here 'darkly bright, are bright in dark directed' is not merely a
piece of wordplay but also a triumphant dance of words
expressing the lover's delight. The emphatic 'thee' in line three
and 'thou' in line five impress on us the fact that the poem, for all
its conceits, is a love poem directed towards a beloved object. The
contrasts between the radiance of dream and the drabness of
reality, the brightness of the beloved and the brightness of the
sun, remain expressive of an emotional situation. Shakespeare
does not pursue the paradox into areas where it is liberated from
this dramatic use and acquires the 'metaphysical' interest of
seeming to comment on the nature of experience in general. This
is the effect of Sidney's treatment of the same theme:

> I start! look! hark! but what in closed up sense
> Was held, in open sense it flies away;
> Leaving me nought but wailing eloquence.
>   I, seeing better sights in sight's decay;
> Called it anew, and wooed sleep again:
> But him her host, that unkind guest had slain.
>
> (XXXVIII)

Here the subsidiary antitheses between closed sleep and open
sight, between sight and eloquence, between sleep and Stella as
host and guest seem concerned to pursue the mystery in the

experience rather than to convey the emotional tension involved. The last line has a degree of detachment common in Sidney but rare in Shakespeare. Other treatments of this theme further sharpen our sense of Shakespeare's individual bias. Linche's version (*Diella*, xxiv) and Griffin's (*Fidessa*, xiv) are dramatically 'plotted', but raise no emotion. These poets are content to bombast out their fourteen lines with vapid repetitions, whereas Shakespeare's words are for ever creating in the mind of the reader *new* relationships.

At the same time he avoids the enlargement of intellectual interest, the refinement of perception, which accompanies the elaboration of similar material in the poems of Donne. Some critics have claimed that 'the . . . sonnets as a performance represent Shakespeare seeking such effects as John Donne . . . was achieving'.[3] I think this is an error. Donne's poem 'The Dreame' (though not Petrarchan and not a sonnet) obviously springs from the convention we have discussed above. Here however we find not the stock contrast between the cruelty of the real lady and the kindness of the phantom, but a more philosophical distinction: the phantom is banished by the coming of the real mistress, but her going again makes the lover question the nature of that reality (in a way not found in any of the previous treatments). The subsidiary antitheses reason/ phantasy, fable/history, etc., show us that Donne is not concerned to build up a poignant image of a loving mind; the figure of the beloved in Donne is not the goal of the whole poem, but rather a symbol for the deeper mystery of the things that lovers experience:

> Coming and staying show'd thee, thee,
> But rising makes me doubt, that now,
>   Thou art not thou.

It is the whole problem of identity that is raised by lines like these.[4]

The bias of Shakespeare's style is no less evident in his handling of details of technique than in the general effect of his treatment of stock themes. He uses the rhetorical tricks which were the

common property of the sonneteers but in a way which is mainly
expressive of an individual's emotion. For example, the paradoxes in the Sonnets are used less to present the piquantly
paradoxical quality of the objective Petrarchan situation and
more to communicate a paradoxical quality in the lover's
emotion. Of course, lines like 'Still losing when I saw myself to
win' (CXIX) can easily be paralleled from other
sonneteers – e.g. Drayton's 'Where most I lost, there most of all I
wan' (*Idea*, 62). But where Drayton and others tend to use such
paradoxes to pattern a situation, Shakespeare's are usually
expressive – we feel what it is to endure such situations:

> Thou blind fool, Love, what dost thou to mine eyes,
> That they behold, and see not what they see?
> They know what beauty is, see where it lies,
> Yet what the best is take the worst to be.
>
> > (CXXXVII)

> My love is as a fever, longing still
> For that which longer nurseth the disease;
> Feeding on that which doth preserve the ill,
> The uncertain sickly appetite to please.
>
> > (CXLVII)

> O, from what power hast thou this powerful might
> With insuffciency my heart to sway?
> To make me give the lie to my true sight,
> And swear that brightness doth not grace the day?
>
> > (CL)

In such cases it is not the situation that is paradoxical; it is the
condition of the lover's being.

Again, this does not mean that the figure has become
'Metaphysical' in Shakespeare, i.e. that it has become a speculative comment on the human condition. When Donne says

> I must confesse, it could not chuse but bee
> Prophane, to think thee any thing but thee.
>
> (*The Dreame*)

or

> Since thou and I sigh one anothers breath,
> Who e'r sighes most, is cruellest, and hastes the others death.
>
> (*A Valediction: of Weeping*)

he uses a paradoxical playfulness to indicate a state of loving but detached emotion; any difficulty in understanding the meaning seems to mirror the intellectual effort of the poet to bring into focus (and almost within comprehension) a truly human but hitherto undescribed situation. Donne's analysis of the state of loving enlarges our appreciation of human richness by its bizarre re-association of elements plucked out of their normal contexts; here, we feel, is a mind thinking its way through an emotional situation; Shakespeare's world is still recognizably a world of 'normal contexts'; the vision is unhackneyed only because he records the intense immediacy of individuals caught in the stock situation:

> Only my plague thus far I count my gain,
> That she that makes me sin awards me pain.
>
> (CXLI)

Here, as in the dramas, the individual voice transcends and transforms the convention Shakespeare accepted.

In simile, as in paradox, Shakespeare's bias is towards expressiveness. In most of the Sonnets in Sir Sidney Lee's collection the simile is a device either to describe the physical charms of the beloved or to indicate general conditions in the Petrarchan situation:

> Like as a ship, that through the ocean wide,
> By conduct of some star, doth make her way . . .
> So I, whose star, that wont with her bright ray

Me to direct, with clouds is over-cast,
Do wander now, in darkness and dismay . . .

(Spenser, XXXIV)

As in some countries, far remote from hence,
The wretched creature destined to die;
Having the judgment due to his offence
By Surgeons begged, their Art on him to try . . .
Even so my Mistress works upon my ill . . .

(Drayton, 50)

These (and the many like them) give clarity and force to the
poems they adorn, but do not impart that sense of immediate
emotional contact which a majority of Shakespeare's similes,
drawn from the familiar experience of simple humanity, do give:

Lo, as a careful housewife runs to catch
One of her feather'd creatures broke away,
Sets down her babe, and makes all swift dispatch . . .
So runn'st thou after that which flies from thee,
Whilst I thy babe chase thee afar behind . . .

(CXLIII)

So am I as the rich, whose blessed key
Can bring him to his sweet up-locked treasure . . .

(LII)

In CXLIII the emotional relationships are defined and made
immediate by the simile; in LII it is the human emotion implicit in
the comparison which makes the chief effect.

Treatments of the same theme – absence – in poems of merit
which use simile as the main feature of their construction may be
compared, to show in an extended fashion Shakespeare's individual use of this figure.

How like a winter hath my absence been
From thee, the pleasure of the fleeting year!
What freezings have I felt, what dark days seen!

What old December's bareness every where!
And yet this time removed was summer's time;
The teeming autumn, big with rich increase,
Bearing the wanton burthen of the prime,
Like widowed wombs after their lords' decease:
Yet this abundant issue seem'd to me
But hope of orphans and unfather'd fruit;
For summer and his pleasures wait on thee,
And, thou away, the very birds are mute;
  Or, if they sing, 'tis with so dull a cheer
  That leaves look pale, dreading the winter's near.

                                      (XCVII)

Like as the Culver, on the bared bough,
Sits mourning for the absence of her mate;
And, in her songs, sends many a wishful vow
For his return that seems to linger late:
So I alone, now left disconsolate,
Mourn to myself the absence of my love;
And, wandering here and there all desolate,
Seek with my plaints to match that mournful dove.
No joy of aught that under heaven doth hove
Can comfort me, but her own joyous sight:
Whose sweet aspect both God and man can move,
In her unspotted pleasance to delight.
  Dark is my day, while her fair light I miss,
  And dead my life that wants such lively bliss.

                            (Spenser, LXXXVIII)

Spenser's simile is a graceful one and conveys the gentle melancholy of the poem, but it does not make the lover's feelings vivid by conveying them in images universally charged with these emotions. Shakespeare's 'December's bareness' and 'dark days' are stripped back to their bare function as objective correlatives of the emotion between lover and beloved; they do not intrude at all between the reader and this emotion. Spenser's culver on the other hand is intruded deliberately as a symbol to indicate the mood of the poem (rather than the mood of the persons in the poem). Accordingly, Spenser's image has the charm of an idyll; Shakespeare's generates in the reader a reaction more proper to drama.

Further details of Shakespeare's subject-matter and style could be analysed, but enough has no doubt been said to show how far from the fashions of which they were born Shakespeare's sonnets are taken by his dramatically expressive way of writing. The subject-matter and the rhetoric may be that of the Petrarchan tradition, the effect may sometimes seem Metaphysical, but the uniquely Shakespearean quality of the sequence is not to be explained by either of these labels. We have here what we might expect: a dramatist describes a series of emotional situations between persons (real or fictitious) in a series of separate short poems; the Petrarchan instruments turn in his hands into means of expressing and concentrating the great human emotions, desire, jealousy, fear, hope and despair, and of raising in the reader the dramatic reactions of pity and terror by his implication in the lives and fates of the persons depicted.

Source: *Essays in Criticism*, III 2 (April 1953) 152–64.

NOTES

1. 'Shakespeare at Sonnets', in *The World's Body* (1938) p. 286. [See part Three above – Ed.]

2. The difference here illustrated between Sidney and Shakespeare the sonneteer is exactly the same difference as we find between *Astrophel and Stella*, XXXIX and *1 Henry IV*, III i 5–31.

3. 'Shakespeare at Sonnets', p. 285.

4. Mr. J. B. Leishman in his *The Monarch of Wit* speaks of Metaphysical poetry as 'the dialectical expression of personal drama'. I accept this definition, but it should be understood that in Donne the personal drama is used as the starting-point for an individual exploration of sensibility, whereas in Shakespeare the whole function of the poem is to convey the emotional quality of the drama. In Donne the language aspires towards intellectual clarity, though not without the glow of passion, but Shakespeare's language aims to give maximum

impact to his figures without making their precise function clear. I presume that this is what Leishman refers to when he says of Donne's love-poetry, 'we do not feel that it is in any way symbolic of something else as so often when reading Shakespeare's Sonnets' (p. 224).

G. Wilson Knight

SYMBOLISM (1955)

. . . certain supposed 'conceits' or 'fancies' may be in reality attempts to grapple with some super-thought which baffles expression. The most usual medium for such intuitions is poetic symbolism, and the Sonnets show a rich use of it. Indeed, the weighty realisation of these imaginative solidities sets them apart from the poetry of Donne and Marvell. True, both Donne and Marvell have their imagery and symbols, and some of Donne's recall Shakespeare's. But with the more metaphysical poets the symbol is, as it were, subdued to – in Donne it is often there to be mocked by – the thinking; it grows from a matrix of metaphysical speculation and intellectual gymnastics. In the best Sonnets the thinking is put at the service of the symbol, and sometimes appears, as we shall see, to lag behind it. The result is that whatever 'eternity' Shakespeare succeeds in establishing is far more than a concept, or web of concepts: it flowers from close physical perception, and holds all the colour and perfume of spring.[1]

One feels that it is only with the greatest reluctance, and perhaps even a sense of guilt, that the poet is forced to admit, if he ever does admit, that it is the distilled truth of the boy, the eternal 'idea', in Plato's sense, that he loves rather than the boy himself; and in so far as he writes of the 'idea' rather than of the thing itself, his writing becomes philosophic rather than strictly poetic; at the best, 'metaphysical poetry', as with Donne and Marvell. Those are concerned with, and brilliantly transmit, their own experience of love, but they have nothing much to say of the loved-one: in Marvell's *Definition of Love* we cannot even be sure of his or her sex. Since they never realise a personality outside themselves, we are not forced to join with them in adoration. But when in Shakespeare we read:

> Why should poor beauty indirectly seek
> Roses of shadow, since his rose is true? (LXVII)

we cannot avoid being half-in-love with the youth ourselves. There is a more vivid realisation of the loved person in that one little word 'his', which might well be italicised, than in all Donne's love-poetry. Nor does Shakespeare confine himself, as, on the whole, you might say that Michelangelo does, to a few archetypal thoughts. Such thoughts he has, but they are part only of a closely realised drama, showing all the variety, and hinting the physical detail, of an actual experience. Sense-perception is vivid. We enjoy a rich physical apprehension, the flush and bloom of a young life, with all the perfumes of spring in company, rather as when we read Chaucer's description of his young Squire. We are aware of nature before we proceed to metaphysics: if 'this composed wonder of your frame' (LIX) is a miracle, it is a miracle born less from our minds than from the 'great creating Nature' of *The Winter's Tale* (IV iii 88). At their greatest moments the Sonnets are, indeed, less love-poetry than an almost religious adoration before one of 'the rarities of Nature's truth' (LX); that is, one of the splendours of human creation. So, though nothing but poetry can meet his problem, yet Shakespeare's move from love to the great poetry of the plays might yet be called, paradoxically, a fall, a second-best: 'for these dead birds sigh a prayer'.

We shall now list the main associations used by the poet to establish verbal contact with the miracle which is his theme. About these there is nothing very abstruse or learned. They are, on the natural plane, flowers, especially the rose; on the human plane, kingship, with gold; on the universal, the Sun, with gold; on the spiritual, jewels. Rose, King, Sun, Gold, Jewels. Our examination need pay slight regard to the Sonnets' order: we shall use our usual practice of 'spatial' analysis, seeing the symbols as existent powers in their own right irrespective of, though of course never contradicting, their particular contexts.

Our first sonnet has 'beauty's rose' (I). One of our finest end-couplets runs:

> For nothing this wide universe I call
> Save thou, my rose; in it thou art my all.   (CIX)

The rose as truth is contrasted with shams and vices. The youth's 'true' rose of beauty, in the exquisite passage recently quoted, is contrasted with the false beautifyings of society (LXVII). If faults be present in him, 'roses have thorns, and silver fountains mud' (XXXV). His beauty encloses 'sins' as the rose contains a 'canker' (XCV). But 'canker' may also mean wild roses, as when 'canker-blooms' are said to have colour without 'the perfumed tincture' of 'sweet roses', which survive death in distillation, even as the inmost truth of the boy's beauty is distilled by poetry (LIV). With the rose we may group the lily: 'Lilies that fester smell far worse than weeds' (XCIV). The youth is the 'pattern' of both 'the lily's white' and 'the deep vermilion in the rose' (XCVIII). In one sonnet the poet relates, point by point, violet, lily, marjoram and roses, red and white, together with the 'vengeful canker' of destruction, to the separate excellences of his love's beauty (XCIX). In contrast his mistress' cheeks have nothing of 'roses damask'd, red and white' in them (CXXX). It is easy to understand the intense poetic appeal made by the Wars of the Roses to Shakespeare in the three parts of *Henry VI*, so rich in impressions of human loveliness and pathos caught in the shambles of meaningless destruction, all summed by the line, 'The red rose and the white are on his face' (*3 Henry VI*, II v 97).

Next, kingship. Royal images recur, as in the love-poetry of Donne, some of them holding similar connotations. The poet addresses the youth as 'lord of my love', to whom he sends a 'written ambassage' (XXVI); he is 'my sovereign' and the poet his 'servant' or 'slave' (LVII). Love-passages in the dramas offer parallels. There is Bassanio's

> There is such confusion in my powers,
> As, after some oration fairly spoke
> By a beloved prince, there doth appear
> Among the buzzing pleased multitude . . .
>   (*The Merchant of Venice*, III ii 178)

> My heart beats thicker than a fev'rous pulse;
> And all my powers do their bestowing lose,
> Like vassalage at unawares encountering
> The eye of majesty.
>
> (*Troilus and Cressida*, III ii 36)

The lover is abased before a blazing power. The loved one is royal, and so compared to 'a throned queen' (XCVI). He is 'crowned' with various gifts of nature and fortune (XXXVII), especially 'all those beauties whereof now he's king' (LXIII). Like a sovereign, he radiates worth, his eyes lending 'a double majesty' to the rival poets' 'grace' (LXXVIII); if it were not for certain suspicions, he would be owning 'kingdoms of hearts' (LXX). This royalty is somehow shared by the lover; having found his own king, he regards all other, more commonplace, grandeurs as poor stuff in comparison. His astronomy, learned from those 'constant stars', his love's eyes, cannot, and clearly has no desire to, busy itself with the fortunes of 'princes'; it is a different 'art', prophesying 'truth and beauty' (XIV). After all, 'great princes' favourites' enjoy an insecure glory in comparison (XXV); time changes the 'decrees of kings', but his love is lasting (CXV); it is in no sense 'the child of state', and is independent of 'smiling pomp' (CXXIV); bearing 'the canopy' means nothing to him, nor does any such external 'honouring' (CXXV). The result is that the poet, through accepted love, becomes himself royal. His mind is 'crown'd' with the wondrous youth, and is accordingly 'kingly' (CXIV); when he is sure of him, he is a 'king', but when disillusioned, 'no such matter' (LXXXVII). However depressed he may be in other ways, in so far as his love is assured, it brings such wealth, well-being and power, 'that then I scorn to change my state with kings' (XXIX).

Such symbols act variously as contrasts or comparisons, and apply to either partner of the love-association. Our final impression is of love itself as king, of some super-personality, the Sun of Sonnet XXIV . . ., made of, or liberated by, the love of two human beings, as when Donne in *The Ecstasy* writes 'else a great Prince in prison lies'. Love liberates this mysterious sovereign, allows him to realise himself in human terms. This sovereign reality it is which is indicated by the word 'love' of our phrase 'in love with', Nerissa's 'lord love' of *The Merchant of Venice* (II ix 101). It is something, or someone, experienced immediately, 'crowning the present' (CXV); either that, or known beyond death, as in Romeo's 'I reviv'd and was an emperor' in *Romeo and Juliet* (v i 9), and Cleopatra's 'I dream'd there was an emperor Antony', in *Antony and Cleopatra* (v ii 76). The associations are just, since the king, properly understood, holds within society precisely this super-personal and supernal function. In more obviously religious terms we have Henry VI's:

> My crown is in my heart, not on my head;
> Not deck'd with diamonds and Indian stones,
> Nor to be seen.   (*3 Henry VI*, III i 62)

But the Sonnets never engage too far in mysticism, and perhaps our finest example of all, warm with meanings both physical and heraldic, is the line, 'Then in the blazon of sweet beauty's best' (CVI), where kings are not specifically mentioned at all.

Kingship is naturally golden, and golden impressions recur with similar variations in use. 'Gilded honour' may be 'shamefully misplac'd' (LXVI); poets flatter the youth with 'golden quill' (LXXXV); his hair is contrasted with false 'golden tresses' (LXVIII); Shakespeare's poetry can make him outlive 'a gilded tomb' (CI). More important is his eye 'gilding' the object on which it gazes (XX) — eyes in Shakespeare's are active powers, not just passive reflections — and the lovely phrase characterising youth as 'this thy golden time' (III). Stars are 'gold candles' (XXI).

The Sun is nature's king, and also pre-eminently golden. Throughout Shakespeare king and sun are compared. The Dark Lady's eyes are 'nothing like the Sun' (CXXX); they are 'mourning', because dark, eyes, and may at the best be compared to the 'morning sun' in a grey dawn, or the evening star (CXXXII). With the Fair Youth, the association ' that sun, thine eye' (XLIX) comes easily enough. The successful lover compares himself to the morning 'lark' singing 'hymns at Heaven's gate' (XXIX), though, when things go wrong, 'basest clouds' obscure the Sun, who now rides 'with ugly rack on his celestial face', and steals to the west disfigured (XXXIII); for 'clouds and eclipses stain both Moon and Sun' (XXXV). In our 'transparency' sonnet (XXIV) the Sun functions as the supernal love corresponding to Donne's prince. The Sun, 'daily new and old' (LXXVI), is visualised in all positions of his diurnal course, with close reference to age. Youth is a 'day' ready to decline (XV), and the poet's age just such an hour 'as after sunset fadeth in the west' (LXXIII).

We have various clusters of king, gold, and sun. King and gold come together in 'the gilded monuments of princes' (LV); and sun and gold, when the Sun's 'gold complexion' is dimmed in the sonnet, 'Shall I compare thee to a summer's day?' (XVIII), or the young man graces 'the day' and 'gilds' the evening in place of stars (XXVIII). We may have all three. So 'great princes' favourites' are compared to the mari*gold* opening to the Sun's 'eye' (XXV). Man's life resembles the diurnal progress of the Sun, who first 'lifts up his burning head' from the orient, everything beneath him doing 'homage' to his 'sacred majesty' as he makes his 'golden pilgrimage', till finally he 'reeleth' to his setting (VII). Love resembles a 'glorious morning' seen to 'flatter the mountain tops with sovereign eye', kissing meadows with his 'golden face', and 'gilding' streams with his 'heavenly alchemy' (XXXIII).

These impressions are not just decoration. They are attempts to realize in 'black ink' (LXV) the wonder of youthful beauty at 'this thy golden time' (III); and beyond that, to make real and visible, without relying on abstract terms, that supernal and authoritative Love of which lovers are part only, expressions, voices.

Nor is all this so simple and obvious as it sounds. The Sun is not a necessary, nor even a natural, accompaniment to Shakespearian romance: the Moon is more usual. Shakespeare's heterosexual love-themes are usually moonlit, as with the Balcony scene of *Romeo and Juliet*, the central scenes of *A Midsummer Night's Dream*, and the fifth act of *The Merchant of Venice*, though Portia has 'sunny' locks (I i 170). Much of *As You Like It* shows us a shadowed, dappled, world, and in *Twelfth Night* the Sun never dominates until Sebastian's, 'This is the air, that is the glorious sun' (IV iii 1). *Antony and Cleopatra* has 'gaudy' *nights* (III xi 182) and Enobarbus's moonlit death, the Sun itself acting rather as a background power than as a present witness, until Cleopatra's dream. Certainly in *Love's Labour's Lost* the Sun is lyrically vivid as a love-accompaniment. But this early play is made on a pattern of its own; it ends with winter; it is full of sonnet-material; and it is exactly this sort of love-poetry that is not repeated. Our first really convincingly sun-impregnated love-scene is the sheep-shearing festival of *The Winter's Tale*.

The Sun is male, the Moon female; the one suggests the intellectual consciousness, the other emotion, the twilit world of romance. When Shelley's Hermaphrodite (= poetry) in *The Witch of Atlas* is fully *awakened*, then we may expect the Sun. When sensual love, whose natural medium, as D. H. Lawrence insisted, is the dark world below consciousness, is our theme, the Sun may, as in Donne's *The Sun Rising*, be an intruder, though, in so far as such a love is vividly and directly lived by day, with a strong physical awareness fully accepted, as in *The Winter's Tale*, it may be in place. Normally, we can say that it is far from easy to blend it with a heterosexual love. As an extreme example of a natural tendency, we have the 'woman wailing for her demon-lover' under a 'waning moon' in *Kubla Khan*; and we must remember Lorenzo's and Jessica's list of famous moonlit love-incidents in their 'In such a night . . . ' duet (*The Merchant of Venice*, V i 1–22). That last act is, in its way, a recovery and a retreat – yet how wonderful a retreat – from the stern compulsions of the greater action.

But it is precisely among those 'stern compulsions' that the Sun is likely to assume poetic centrality. . . .

The various natural and cosmic symbolisms of the Sonnets grow from a soil of normal Shakespearian imagery: flowers, crops, and seasons; moon and stars; effects of winter, cloud, storm and tempests; inundation (LXIV); and wrecks (LXXX). The love-quest is a sea-voyage (LXXX, LXXXVI), as in *Troilus and Cressida* (see *The Shakespearian Tempest*, II, 72; IV, 172–4). Stars may be important, sometimes holding astrological significance (XIV, XV, XXVI, CXVI); they may be more directly descriptive or symbolic (XXI, CXXXII); they are symbols of constancy (XIV, CXVI).

We have already reviewed certain impressions of 'gold'. 'Gold' naturally accompanies 'sun' and 'king'; the king's crown, and indeed gold in general, might be called 'solid sunlight'. Gold has for centuries exerted magical radiations and its value, worth and power, its 'virtue' in the old sense, need no emphasis. These properties make it an apt symbol for any high value, or worth.

Love is such a value, and it is regularly in Shakespeare compared to rich metals or merchandise (*The Shakespearian Tempest*, ii, 65–9). Throughout poetry precious stones symbolise what may be called 'spiritual value' (*Christ and Nietzsche*, v, 193–5; and see pp. 137, 141, 159). All this is powerful in the Sonnets.

The 'rich gems' of 'earth and sea' are regarded as a natural love-comparison (xxi); though cruel, the Dark Lady is 'the fairest and most precious jewel' (cxxxi); and the youth's image by night hangs 'like a jewel' before the poet's soul (xxvii), recalling Romeo's 'It seems she hangs upon the cheek of night like a rich jewel in an Ethiop's ear' (*Romeo and Juliet*, iv 49). Compared with 'a prize so dear', the poet's 'jewels' are as 'trifles' (lxviii); even the youth's faults are to be prized as a poor 'jewel' may be on the figure of 'a throned queen' (xcvi); his tears are as 'pearl', and called 'rich' (xxxiv); he is himself costly, a matter of 'riches' (lxxxvii). One sonnet is packed with suggestions of 'rich', 'treasure', 'stones of worth', 'chest', and 'robe', and contains the grand line, 'captain jewels in the carcanet' (lii). Most striking of all is:

> Where, alack,
> Shall Time's best jewel from Time's chest lie hid?
>
> (lxv)

As elsewhere throughout Shakespeare, such symbols blend with rich merchandise and sea-voyages. Love, it is true, is too rich to be 'merchandis'd' (cii), but symbolically the thought may act serenely enough:

> Was it the proud full sail of his great verse
> Bound for the prize of all too precious you . . . (lxxxvi)

Poetry is itself a quest. Apart from all flattery and advantage, it is a spiritual penetration and achievement, in some deep sense a possession, of the mysterious splendour. But the poet is, of course, jealous in a human fashion too: he is like a 'miser' so intent on 'the prize of you', that he varies between pride of possession and horrible doubts lest 'the filching age' may 'steal his treasure' (LXXV).

Shakespeare's bitter comments on the youth's risking 'infection' from a sinful society (LXVII), with the cutting conclusion 'thou dost common grow' (LXIX), may indeed derive from a questionable jealousy and possessiveness. We need not assume that the young man, who is once specifically said to have survived the temptations of youth victoriously (LXX), was naturally vicious. In certain moods Shakespeare would, clearly, regard all society as too base for a youth of so infinite and mysterious a worth. His love was to him the inmost centre and furthest aim of all things, its value lying beyond human assessment:

It is the star to every wandering bark,
Whose worth's unknown although his height be taken.

(CXVI)

It was the crowning glory of creation, and more than that. 'Jewels', as we have said, suggest spiritual values, and this love is also religious.

Our theme (XXXI) is 'dear, religious, love' ('dear' meaning 'of highest value'). It is not 'idolatry' (CV) – compare Hector's aspersions on idolatry at *Troilus and Cressida*, II ii 56 – because it and its object are constant (CV). Even though faults be found, even though there be no objective 'image', to quote Hector, 'of the affected merit' (*Troilus and Cressida*, II ii 60), 'Heaven' has somehow decreed in the youth's 'creation' that only 'sweet love' can dwell in his 'face'; he cannot *look* faithless or bad (XCIII). Such beauty, with its 'heavenly touches' (XVII), exists in its own right; it is itself 'sacred' (CXV); and the poet complains that, since artifice became the fashion, 'sweet beauty' has no 'holy bower' (CXXVII). As it is, the youth's presence is said to 'grace impiety' when he mixes with sinful people (LXVII). Shakespeare's love-poetry, his

own 'better part', is 'consecrate to thee' (LXXIV); he has
'hallow'd' his 'fair name' in verses which are as 'prayers divine'
(CVIII); and his own love is offered as an 'oblation' (CXXV). The
idealised boy is even called 'a god in love', and 'next my heaven
the best' (CX). He is the poet's 'better angel'. Adoration can go no
further.

Such is the experience, or phenomenon, straining the sweetest
and grandest symbols, natural, human, and divine, to do justice
to 'this composed wonder of your frame' (LIX). It is pre-eminently
an incarnate mystery or miracle, not unlike that symbolised by
Dante's Gryphon in the *Purgatorio* (XXXI). The poetry gives us a
close-up of the thing itself, not merely, as does Donne, of the
supervening and enclosing experience. It is a marvel here and
now, 'crowning the present', even though leaving us 'doubting of
the rest' (CXV). For there can be no permanence. That is our
problem: the problem of *Troilus and Cressida, Hamlet, Othello,
Timon of Athens, Antony and Cleopatra*. And yet, somehow, we feel
that it should, indeed must, be permanent. The poet must say,
and we applaud him for saying it, 'Love's not Time's fool' (CXVI),
but he fears, and so do we, that it may be. He starts a sonnet with
'To me, fair friend, you never can be old', but continues:

Ah, yet doth beauty, like a dial-hand,
Steal from his figure and no pace perceiv'd. (CIV)

Can both be true? One way or another, we shall surely come up
against the agony of Troilus: 'This is, and is not, Cressid' (*Troilus
and Cressida*, V ii 143). On this torturing antithesis, the greatest
passages of the Sonnets converge.

SOURCE: extracts from *The Mutual Flame* (1955) pp.
58–64, 65–8.

NOTE

1. For a similar judgement see G. K. Hunter's 'Dramatic Technique
of Shakespeare's Sonnets', *Essays in Criticism*, III 2 (Apr 1953).
[Preceding essay in this volume – Ed.]

M. M. Mahood

SHAKESPEARE'S WORDPLAY: THE SONNETS (1957)

. . . The interplay of mixed feelings in the sonnets on the woman, on time and poetry, and on the rival poet, are conflicts understood and expressed with a confident wit. But the complex relationship of the poet and the youth is further involved with other relationships: that of player to rich patron and, since the youth represents many things Shakespeare lacks and craves in his own personality, Shakespeare's quarrel with himself. When Shakespeare thus unlocks his heart, it is to reveal its stores in disarray. In only a few of the poems addressed to the youth are these stored experiences ordered into a work of art.

The difficulty confronting us at this point is that any separation of the successful from the unsuccessful sonnets is bound to seem, at worst, an arbitrary and very personal choice and, at the best, to be based on criteria which are not universally acceptable. Thus John Crowe Ransom distinguishes as goats among the sonnets the 'associationist' ones which provide 'many charming resting-places for the feelings to agitate themselves', and, as sheep, the 'metaphysical' sonnets which go 'straight through to the completion of the cycle and extinction of the feelings'. [See Part Three above.] For Mr Ransom, wordplay belongs to the poetry of association, and so the punning sonnets are among the unsuccessful ones. This view is, of course, based on a strictly kathartic theory of poetry; but probably the poetic theory more generally acceptable today is nearer to that of the seventeenth-century Aristotelians: the belief that poetry should communicate feeling, but feeling purified by being fully and finally comprehended – in fact, all that is summed up in Herbert's definition of prayer as 'The land of spices; something understood'. If this is our criterion, we shall look first in a sonnet, not for the kind of logic which could be reduced to a prose syllogism, but for a satisfying organisation of sound and sense that conveys the ordered movement of thought into which the emotion has been shaped.

The Shakespearean sonnet is not an easy form to handle. In an Italian form of sonnet, even one which, like Milton's 'On his Blindness', does not keep strictly to the divisions of octave and sestet, there is a marked ebb and flow of thought corresponding to two emotional impulses: in that case, despair and resignation. But the final couplet of the English sonnet is too brief to contain the entire counter-statement to the first three quatrains without giving the impression that the poet is trying to wrench the poem back on its course. If, however, the poet too anxiously anticipates the final turn of thought throughout the first twelve lines, the couplet loses its epigrammatic spring. A subdued sort of word-play is a useful device to the poet in these circumstances. It allows him to introduce the counter-movement of thought before the reader is aware of its presence, so that the final couplet satisfies both by conscious surprise and by its fulfilment of a subconscious expectation. This is what happens in Sonnet: LXIII

> Against my loue shall be as I am now
> With times iniurious *hand* chrusht and ore-worne,
> When houres haue dreind his blood and fild his brow
> With *lines* and wrincles, when his youthfull morne
> Hath *trauaild* on to Ages steepie night,
> And all those beauties whereof now he's King
> Are vanishing, or vanisht out of sight,
> Stealing away the treasure of his Spring.
> For such a time do I now fortifie
> Against confounding Ages cruell knife,
> That he shall neuer *cut* from memory
> My sweet loues beauty, though my louers life.
>> His beautie shall in these blacke lines be seene,
>> And they shall liue, and he in them still greene.

The turn accomplished by the couplet from the theme of time

destroying the youth's beauty to that of its preservation through
poetry is skilfully prepared, throughout the preceding quatrains,
by an oblique image of Time (or Time–Age, a composite figure)
and the poet working in competition one with the other. Time
defaces the young man's beauty by scribbling upon it or
overscoring it, at the same time as the poet is making of it a
speaking picture for posterity. This theme of writing or engraving
is implicit in the subsidiary meanings of *hand* in line two, *lines* in
line four, and *cut*, which can mean engrave ('This figure that thou
here seest put, It was for gentle Shakespeare cut'). *Trauaild*, one
of Shakespeare's favourite portmanteau words, packed with the
two meanings 'travelled' and 'travailed', helps here by introduc-
ing the ideas of effort; the poet's toil undoes the result of life's
weary journey through time.

In Sonnet LXV, the couplet's counter-statement is again
carefully prepared in the preceding lines:

> Since brasse, nor stone, nor earth, nor boundlesse sea,
> But sad mortallity ore-swaies their power,
> How with this rage shall beautie hold a plea,
> Whose *action* is no stronger then a flower?
> O how shall summers hunny breath hold out,
> Against the wrackfull siedge of battring dayes,
> When rocks impregnable are not so stoute,
> Nor gates of steele so strong but time decayes?
> O fearefull meditation, where alack,
> Shall times best Iewell *from* times chest lie hid?
> Or what strong hånd can hold his swift foot back,
> Or who his *spoile* of¹ beautie can forbid?
> O none, vnlesse this miracle haue might,
> That in black inck my loue may still shine bright.

The first four lines of this would be a strong rhetorical question,
compelling our assent, were its compulsion not weakened by the
double meaning of *action*; for while the action of beauty, taking
the word in the sense of 'physical force', cannot compare with the
resistance of brass and stone, the legal meaning of 'a process',
induced by *plea* in the preceding line, hints that physical strength

cannot deflect the course of justice and of the justicers above. There is a sense in which both flowers and summer are stronger than rocks, because they are endlessly renewed while rocks are continually eroded away; and with this in mind, we can read both lines three to four and lines five to eight as exclamations, rather than as rhetorical questions compelling a negative answer. The second quatrain can then be paraphrased: 'How successfully the renewing vitality of summer resists the assaults of time! Unassailable rocks and gates of steel are not as strong as it; on the contrary, time itself wears away.' And once our consent to these rhetorical questions has been weakened in this way, without our being aware of it, there may be some hesitation about our response to the next question:

> O fearefull meditation, where alack,
> Shall times best Iewell *from* times chest lie hid?

The ambiguity of *from* imparts two meanings to this: either 'Where can the best jewel that Time has produced out of his casket be hidden?' or 'Where can Time's jewel be hidden away so that it may not be put back into Time's chest, the grave?' Put in this second form, the question produces the inevitable answer that the youth's soul and body will be preserved by their immortality from Time – 'the womb of all things and perhaps their grave'. This undertone is sustained by the quasi-religious language of 'fearful meditation' and 'miracle', by the harrowing-of-hell notion in 'gates of steel' and by the opening lines' Apocalyptic imagery. Herbert would have developed this undertone into the poem's counter-statement, but Shakespeare is concerned with the immortality bestowed by art, and uses the religious theme only to make the reader receptive to his final claim. The ambiguity of *spoil* helps. It may mean 'spoiling', the ruination of time; but it suggests also precious plunder – gold and jewels – which is indestructible and in safe keeping. So the whole sonnet subtly prepares us for the claim made in the last couplet.

Another formally satisfying sonnet, the thirtieth, also uses an elaborate play of meaning to anticipate its confident end:

When to the Sessions of sweet silent thought
I sommon vp remembrance of things past,
I sigh the lacke of many a thing I sought,
And with old woes new waile my *deare* times waste:
Then can I drowne an eye (vn-vs'd to flow)
For *precious* friends hid in deaths dateles night,
And weepe a fresh loues long since *canceld* woe,
And mone th'*expence* of many a vannisht sight.
Then can I greeue at greeuances *fore-gon*,
And heauily from woe to woe *tell* ore
The sad *account* of fore-bemoned mone,
Which I new *pay* as if not *payd* before.
   But if the while I thinke on thee (*deare* friend)
   All losses are restord, and sorrowes end.

Sweet sets the tone of this in the first line. Shakespeare's
melancholy is well-savoured. 'Summon' suggests that he is too
judiciously detached from his memories for them to be painful to
him, and this detachment is implicit in *dear, precious, cancelled,
expense, tell, account, pay*. Besides their strongly felt meanings, these
words all have neutral meanings which are as impersonal as
book-keeping entries; *expense*, for example, means primarily 'the
price paid', whereas in 'Th'expence of spirit' this meaning is
subordinate to the emotive one. Even when an emotion is stated,
the tone of the verse dissipates the force of the statement. 'Then
can I greeue at greeuances fore-gon' has the suggestion of 'I could
upset myself – if I tried'; the verbal jingle robs the line of any
solemnity, and grievances *forgone* are repudiated and forgotten as
well as simply past. This is not the anguish of a Francesca over
past happiness in days of misery, but the contemplation of old
misfortunes in a happy time. Shakespeare's eye, in fact, is kept on
the credit side of the ledger all through the poem, and when the
dear friend is produced at the last we understand why this reverie
over disaster has been far more sweet than bitter.

   The sonnets in which Shakespeare's conflict of feelings is most
clearly understood and so most poetically organised are the ones
about the rival poet and these addressed to the dark woman. The
poet is clearly an adversary whose skill Shakespeare respects at

the same time as he is convinced of the superior strength and sincerity of his own verse, and these counterpoised feelings dance an ironic set of changes in a sonnet such as the eighty-fifth, which begins:

> My toung-tide Muse in manners holds her *still*,
> While comments of your praise richly compil'd
> Reserue their Character with goulden quill,
> And *precious* phrase by all the Muses fil'd.

According to the meanings we give *still* and *precious*, this says either: 'My Muse keeps silent as becomes her when other poets write so exquisitely well in your praise', or: 'My Muse, by her reticence, remains well-mannered whatever excesses of affectation other poets may commit in their praise of you.' Irony is pushed a stage further in the sonnets to the woman. Whereas the equivoques addressed to the youth are veiled by tact and compassion, those to the mistress are brutally obvious. She is 'rich in *Will*', 'the wide worlds *common* place', 'the *baye* where all men ride'. The only satisfying thing for Shakespeare about this infatuation with a light woman who has not even acknowledged beauty to commend her, is that each perfectly understands and accepts the other's deception and self-deception. The theme of Sonnet cxxxviii might be summed up in the refrain of a recent poet as 'You know I know you know I know you know'.[2] Its insight not only makes it a more coherent poem than most of those addressed to the youth but also, if we allow love poetry more scope than the posy to a ring, one of the finest love poems:

> When my loue sweares that she is made of truth,
> I do beleeue her though I know she lyes,
> That she might think me some vntuterd youth
> Vnlearned in the worlds false subtilties.
> Thus *vainely* thinking that she thinkes me young,
> Although she knowes my dayes are past the best,
> *Simply* I credit her false speaking tongue,
> On both sides thus is *simple* truth supprest:
> But wherefore sayes she not she is vniust?

And wherefore say not I that I am old?
O loues best *habit* is in seeming trust,
And age in loue, loues not t'haue yeares *told*.
Therefore I lye with her, and she with me,
And in our *faults* by *lyes* we flattered be.

Faults has a double meaning to enforce the wordplay on *lie*; it means both the lovers' adultery and their deception of each other. As Patrick Cruttwell says: 'Of this climactic poem the last couplet, with its pun on "lye" is the very apex; the pun forces together the physical union and its context, as it were, its whole surrounding universe, of moral defilement and falsehood.'[3] Yet the total impression of the sonnet is not one of bitterness, but of acceptance. The lovers need one another in their common weakness.

Only a few of the sonnets to the youth show an irony as fully realised and as moving as this. Sonnet LXXXVII, which concludes the Rival Poet sequence, allows a pensive understanding of the youth's calculating temper to show through its seeming self-abasement:

Farewell thou art too *deare* for my possessing,
And like enough thou knowst thy *estimate*,
The Charter of thy *worth* giues thee releasing:
My *bonds* in thee are all determinate.

Here the play of meaning between 'valuable' and 'beloved' for *dear*, 'your valuation of yourself' and 'the amount of my esteem' for *estimate*, 'value' and 'worthiness' for *worth*, and 'claim' and 'shackle' for *bond*, offers distinct and conflicting readings of the whole passage. Either Shakespeare is saying: 'You are so good and great that you may well end our friendship on the ground that there is no corresponding worth in me', or he means: 'Because of your social advantage over me, you exact too high a price for our friendship, so I have decided to break free.' In addition, there is a strong hint of the meaning: 'I have lavished affection on a creature who is just not worth it.' Shakespeare is in fact recording the terrible moment of apprehension when he means all these at once. A tone of guarded compliment masks his feelings in the following lines of the sonnet, but this profound disillusionment breaks through in the final couplet:

> Thus haue I had thee as a dreame doth flatter,
> In sleepe a King, but waking no such matter.

The irony here is grave and steady; in Sonnet LVIII, where a compliment is likewise framed in two ironic statements, the tone is one of exasperation: 'That God forbid, that made me first your slaue' evokes the natural protest that the speaker was not created any man's slave, and this sting remains even when we have grasped the fact that this god is Cupid. Its smart is still felt in the final couplet, which may be the voice of a man prostrate with adoration or of one querulous with impatience — 'You think this is what I am made for, do you?'

> I am to waite though waiting so be hell,
> Not blame your pleasure be it ill or well.

The hectic tone of this suggests a strong tension of feelings. There is more calmness and deliberation in the preceding sonnet, the fifty-seventh, which will serve as a final example of Shakespeare's verbal precision in defining the interplay of mixed feelings:

> Being your slaue what should I doe but tend,
> Vpon the *houres*, and times of your desire?
> I haue no precious time at al to *spend*;
> Nor *seruices* to doe til you require.
> Nor dare I chide the world without end houre,
> Whilst I (my soueraine) watch the clock for you,
> Nor thinke the bitternesse of absence sowre,
> When you have bid your seruant once adieue.
> Nor dare I question with my iealious thought,
> Where you may be, or your affaires suppose,
> But like a sad slaue stay and thinke of nought
> Saue where you are, how happy you make those.
>   So *true* a foole is loue, that in your *Will*
>   (Though you doe any thing) he thinkes no ill.

Lines three and four are a little obscure. We might paraphrase: 'I have no strong claims on my time and attention except yours'. But *spend* can have a more forceful meaning of 'expend' or even 'waste' and this insinuates an unexpected note of protest: 'Time is too valuable for me to waste it in this fashion'. The ecclesiastical senses of *hours* and *services* and the echo of the doxology in 'world without end' serve to buttress the counterstress set up by this protest; Shakespeare resents the time he has squandered upon a false devotion. And once this note of resentment has been struck, its reverberations are heard in the over-strong protestations of 'Nor dare I chide . . .' and 'Nor dare I question'. The extent to which Shakespeare does chide and question is shown in the last two lines of the sonnet which appear to say:'Love is so foolishly faithful in your Will Shakespeare that he cannot think ill of you, whatever you do'; but which also say: 'Love is so utterly foolish that, however wilful and perverse you are, it cannot see the wrongness of your behaviour.' In depicting this blend of adulation and contempt, and in all those sonnets where verbal ambiguity is thus used as a deliberate dramatic device, Shakespeare shows that superb insight into states of strangely mixed feelings which enabled him to bring to life a Coriolanus or an Enobarbus. Like Freud, he found the causes of quibbling by studying his own quibbles; and the detachment which such an analysis implies imparts to the best of the Sonnets that objectivity we look for in the finest dramatic poetry.

Source: *Shakespeare's Wordplay* (1957) pp. 102–10.

NOTES

1. For 1609 *or*.
2. Thom Gunn, 'Carnal Knowledge'.
3. Patrick Cruttwell, 'A Reading of the Sonnets', *Hudson Review*, v (1952) 563–4.

Yvor Winters

POETIC STYLES, OLD AND NEW (1959)

. . . There are few of the sonnets of Shakespeare . . . which do
not show traces of genius of an unusually beguiling kind; and in a
fair number we have more than traces. Yet in the past ten years or
so I have found them more and more disappointing. In the first
place there is in a large number of the poems an attitude of servile
weakness on the part of the poet in the face of the person
addressed; this attitude is commonly so marked as to render a
sympathetic approach to the subject all but impossible, in spite of
any fragmentary brilliance which may be exhibited. It will not
do to reply that this is a convention of the courtly style and should
not be taken seriously. If it is a convention of the courtly style,
then it is a weakness in that style. But it is not an invariable
quality of the courtly poets, it occurs very seldom in poets of the
plain style, and Shakespeare seems to mean it seriously. In the
second place, Shakespeare seldom takes the sonnet form with any
real seriousness. The sonnets are almost invariably conceived in
very simple terms and are developed through simple repetition or
antithesis, so that they never achieve the closely organized
treatment of the subject which we find in the best of Jonson and
Donne. This weakness is often aggravated by the fact that
Shakespeare frequently poses his problem and then solves it by an
evasion or an irrelevant cliché: this is more or less the method of
the courtly style at its weakest, but the element of genius which
goes into many of these sonnets raises one's expectations to the
point that one cannot take this sort of triviality with good grace.
In the third place, Shakespeare often allows his sensitivity to the
connotative power of language to blind him to the necessity for
sharp denotation, with the result that a line or passage or even a
whole poem may disappear behind a veil of uncertainty: in this
last weakness he is even farther from his major contemporaries

than in any of the others. I shall endeavor to illustrate these
weaknesses as they occur in poems which I shall discuss.
I will begin with LXVI:

> Tir'd with all these, for restful death I cry
> As to behold desert a beggar born,
> And needy nothing trimm'd in jollity,
> And purest faith unhappily forsworn,
> And gilded honor shamefully misplac'd,
> And maiden virtue rudely strumpeted,
> And right perfection wrongfully disgrac'd,
> And strength by limping sway disabled,
> And art made tongue-tied by authority,
> And folly – doctor-like – controlling skill,
> And simple truth miscalled simplicity,
> And captive good attending captain ill:
> > Tir'd with all these, from these I would be gone,
> > Save that, to die, I leave my love alone.

This is one of a number of Elizabethan poems dealing with
disillusionment with the world. Others are Gascoigne's
Woodmanship, *The Lie* by Raleigh, and *False world, goodnight*, by
Ben Jonson. But whereas Gascoigne, Raleigh, and Jonson offer
the best solution that they can, Raleigh with righteous defiance,
Gascoigne and Jonson with a combination of scorn for corruption
and Christian acceptance of the individual fate, Shakespeare
(like Arnold after him in *Dover Beach*) turns aside from the issues
he has raised to a kind of despairing sentimentality, and the effect
is one of weakness, poetic and personal. The same thing occurs in
many sonnets: for examples XXIX (*When in disgrace with fortune and
men's eyes*) and XXX (*When to the sessions of sweet silent thought*). I do
not wish to deny the many felicities in these poems, for they are
real; but the poems do not rise to the occasions which they invoke.
The poem which I have just quoted would be a fine example of
the plain style, except for the couplet, which represents sentimental degeneration of the courtly rhetoric.

It would be easy to make a list of inept phrases from the
sonnets. The clichés, for example, are numerous and well-known,

and so are the bad plays on words ('When first your eye I eyed'). But most poets sin in this fashion much of the time, or in some comparable fashion. There is another kind of weak phrasing in Shakespeare, however, which is prevalent in his work and more serious than the cliché or the bad pun; it is characteristic of later ages rather than his own, and it sets him apart from his great contemporaries. This is his use of words for some vague connotative value, with little regard for exact denotation. An interesting example occurs in cxvi:

Let me not to the marriage of true minds
Admit impediments. Love is not love
Which alters when it alteration finds,
Or bends with the remover to remove:
O no! it is an ever-fixed mark,
That looks on tempests and is never shaken;
It is the star to every wandering bark,
Whose worth's unknown, although his height be taken.
Love's not Time's fool, though rosy lips and cheeks
Within his bending sickle's compass come;
Love alters not with his brief hours and weeks,
But bears it out even to the edge of doom.
If this be error, and upon me proved,
I never writ, nor no man ever loved.

The difficulty here resides in the word *worth*. The fixed star, which guides the mariner, is compared to true love, which guides the lover. The mariner, by taking the height of the star, can estimate his position at sea, despite the fact that he knows nothing of the star's 'worth'. Worth, with reference to the star, probably means astrological influence, though it might mean something else. The lover, by fixing his mind on the concept of true love, similarly can guide himself in his personal life. But what does *worth*, as distinct from *height*, mean in this second connection? For the lover can scarcely guide himself by a concept of true love, he can scarcely indeed have a concept of true love, unless he has some idea of the worth of true love. The comparison blurs at this point, and with it the meaning. One may perhaps push the astrological influence

here and say that the lover, although he has a general knowledge
of the nature and virtue (if virtue can be separated from worth) of
true love, yet does not know precisely the effect upon him that
true love will have. But this will not do: he obviously knows
something of the effect, for the rest of the poem says that he does.
There is simply no such separation between the two functions of
true love as there is between the two functions of the star, yet the
comparison is made in such a way as to indicate a separation.

This kind of thing does not occur in Greville or Donne or
Jonson. Even in the more ornate Sidney — for example in the
clumsy figurative language of *Leave me, O love* — it is usually
possible to follow the thought even though the figure may be
mishandled. But here one loses the thought. Greville, in *Down in
the depth*, employs the language of theology; Donne employs the
language of astrology (and other technical language) in the
Valediction of my Name in a Window. Nothing is lost by this
precision, but on the contrary there is a gain, for the emotion
cannot have force when its nature and origin are obscure.
Shakespeare contents himself here with a vague feeling of the
mysterious and the supernatural, and the feeling is very vague
indeed.

The sonnet is characteristic in other respects. The successive
quatrains do not really develop the theme; each restates it. This
makes, perhaps, for easy absorption on the part of the more or less
quiescent reader, but it makes also for a somewhat simple and
uninteresting poetry. The sonnet form is short, and the great poet
should endeavor to use it more efficiently, to say as much as can
be said of his subject within its limits; such efficiency is never
characteristic of Shakespeare. Lines nine and ten are clichés,
which are barely rescued by an habitual grace, and the
concluding couplet is a mere tag, which has no dignity or purpose
in relationship to the sonnet or within itself. Yet the first four lines
have precision, dignity, and simplicity, which are very moving,
and the twelfth line has subdued grandeur, due in part to the
heavy inversion of the third foot and to the heavy anapest and
iamb following. The high reputation of the sonnet is due about
equally, I suspect, to its virtues and its faults.

One of the most perplexing of the sonnets is CVIII:

> Not mine own fears, nor the prophetic soul
> Of the wide world, dreaming on things to come,
> Can yet the lease of my true love control,
> Suppos'd as forfeit to a confin'd doom.
> The mortal moon hath her eclipse endur'd,
> And the sad augurs mock their own presage;
> Incertainties now crown themselves assur'd,
> And peace proclaims olives of endless age.
> Now with the drops of this most balmy time
> My love looks fresh, and death to me subscribes,
> Since, spite of him, I'll live in this poor rime,
> While he insults o'er dull and speechless tribes:
>   And thou in this shalt find thy monument
>   When tyrants' crests and tombs of brass are spent.

The sonnet has given rise to a great deal of scholarly speculation, most of which the reader can find summarized in Rollins's variorum edition of the sonnets. One of the commonest interpretations is that which identifies the mortal moon with Elizabeth and the eclipse with her death. The friend, then, is Southampton, who was released from prison upon the accession of James, and lines six, seven, eight, nine, and ten refer to the general fears that there would be civil disorder upon the death of Elizabeth and to the fact that James was nevertheless crowned with no disorder. The interpretation is fairly plausible, though by no means certain; but it involves two difficulties which, I think, have never been met. The tone of the poem is scarcely explained by this interpretation: the tone is sombre and mysterious, as if supernatural forces were under consideration – this tone is most obvious in the first quatrain, but it persists throughout. Furthermore, in line eleven we have a monstrous *non sequitur*, for there is not the remotest connection between Southampton's release from prison or the events leading up to it and Shakespeare's making himself and Southampton immortal in verse. To this objection the reader may reply that the concluding lines are merely in a Petrarchan convention and should not be taken too seriously. They may represent such a convention, but they have to be taken seriously, for the tone of seriousness and mystery, the

magnificence of the language, are such that we are not prepared
for triviality at this point. If this interpretation (or I think any
other in the variorum editions) is accepted, then the poem stands
as one of the most striking examples of Shakespeare's inability to
control his language, of his tendency to indulge vague emotion
with no respect for meaning. And the poem may, in fact, be such
an example.

Leslie Hotson, however, has come forward with another
theory. He believes that the mortal moon (mortal: deadly, death-
dealing) is the Spanish Armada, of which the line of battle was
moon-shaped, and which attacked England and was defeated in
1588, a year of which there had been dire predictions for
generations, some of the prophets having thought it the year in
which the world would end. Hotson is an irritating writer, as
everybody who has read him carefully must know. But whatever
objections one may have to Hotson's theory, there is no denying
the fact that he documents it fully and impressively.
Furthermore and this is a point which Hotson fails to
mention – this interpretation explains the mysterious tone of the
poem (for in these terms we are dealing literally with supernatural forces, as well as with the most terrifying of natural
forces), and it eliminates the *non sequitur* (for the lives of both the
poet and the friend had been threatened, and both have
survived). Hotson's theory clarifies the poem at every point, in
spite of the conventional elements in the poem and the obscurely
allusive manner of writing.

One can make certain obvious objections to Hotson's theory.
For example, Hotson claims that the entire sequence was done by
1588; this in spite of the facts that Shakespeare repeatedly refers
to himself as an aging man and that there are many parallels in
phrasing between the sonnets and the later plays. Furthermore,
Hotson bases this claim on the explication of only one sonnet
other than the sonnet just discussed. But in favor of Hotson's
view would be the very weaknesses which I have been
describing – weaknesses which might well be those of a young
man -- although Hotson appears to be unaware of them. However, these weaknesses might easily be those of an older man,
more at home in the dramatic form, writing carelessly for a

private audience, and working in a style which in the course of his mature life became obsolete. Even with Hotson's explanation, however, or with another as good, the poem is faulty. No poem is wholly self-contained, but most poems work within frames of reference which are widely understood. This poem appears to have a very particular frame of reference, about which it will always be impossible to be sure. The poem is almost all connotation, with almost no denotation; it is almost purely vehicle, with almost no tenor; it is almost wholly ornament, with almost nothing to which the ornament can be attached. It would be easy to say that such a poem is a kind of forerunner of some of the deliberately obscure work of the past hundred years; but this work is all based on closely related theories – those of Mallarmé or of Pound, for examples – and Shakespeare had no such theories. Shakespeare's ideas about the nature of poetry were those of his age, but he was often unable to write in accordance with them. Such a poem as this must have been the result of inadvertence.

Whatever the faults of the sonnets as wholes, their incidental beauties are numerous. These beauties are often of the most elusive kind, and they are probably felt by many readers without ever being identified. Consider, for example, line six of Sonnet XIX: 'And do whate'er thou wilt, swift-footed Time'. There is a plaintive desperation in the line which it is impossible to describe but which any sensitive reader can feel. In what is being said there is a stereotyped but real and timeless fear, and this is expressed in part by the helplessness of the imperative and in part by the archaic cliché *swift-footed*. It is expressed also in the emphases of the rhythmical pattern: the first three feet are all heavily accented, but each succeeding foot more heavily than the one preceding, so that we reach a climax on *wilt*, followed by the long pause of the comma, the pause in turn followed by a foot lighter and more evenly stressed, and this by a very heavily stressed foot. This is not an original line nor a great one; it is derivative and minor -- but it is moving.

More obvious are the moral perceptions in the second quatrain of XXIX:

When in disgrace with fortune and men's eyes
I all alone beweep my outcast state,
And trouble deaf heaven with my bootless cries,
And look upon myself, and curse my fate,
Wishing me like to one more rich in hope,
Featur'd like him, like him with friends possess'd,
Desiring this man's art, and that man's scope,
With what I most enjoy contented least;
Yet in these thoughts myself almost despising,
Haply I think on thee, – and then my state,
Like to the lark at break of day arising
From sullen earth, sings hymns at heaven's gate;
    For thy sweet love remember'd such wealth brings
    That then I scorn to change my state with kings.

The first quatrain of this sonnet is a passable example of what the French would call *la poésie larmoyante*; it is facile melancholy at its worst. And yet the next four lines are precise and admirable; they are a fine example of the plain style. In the third quatrain we have the lark which has made the sonnet famous. The lark is an ornament, in the same way as Donne's compasses. In the last six lines we are told, of course, that the poet's state of mind has changed; and we are told why – he has thought of the friend or lady, whichever it may be. But this is a sentimental, an almost automatic, change, and it is hard to understand after the four lines preceding. It is what I have previously called an evasion of the issue posed. And the lark is a sentimental lark: at the descriptive level, *sullen, sings hymns,* and *heaven's gate* are all inaccurate. The lark is burdened with the unexplained emotions of the poet. But the lark is not representative of any explanatory idea. The lark suffers in these ways from comparison with the pigeons of Wallace Stevens, of which I shall write briefly later in this book. We have more lark than understanding in these lines, and more easy sentiment than lark.

    One of the most fascinating passages is the description of the imperceptible but continuous action of Time in CIV:

        Ah! yet doth beauty, like a dial hand,
        Steal from his figure, and no pace perceived;

So your sweet hue, which methinks still doth stand,
Hath motion, and mine eye may be deceived.

And yet even here we are in grammatical difficulty, for it is the
dial hand (or its shadow) which should steal from the figure; it is
not beauty. Or if we take *figure* to mean the human form or face,
then the dial hand is left with no reference, and there is no basis
for the second half of the comparison. We understand the
passage, of course, but the statement is careless.

One can find good poems among the sonnets which do not
achieve at any point the greatness of certain lines from sonnets
which fail. Such, for examples, are XXIII, CXXIX, and CXLVI. The
first of these is correct but minor; the second (*The expense of spirit*)
is powerful in phrasing, but repetitious in structure – as Douglas
Peterson has shown (*Shakespeare Quarterly*, V 4), it derives its
structure and much of its matter from a passage in Wilson's *Art of
Rhetorique* – and appears to be a forceful exercise on a limited
topic; the third is somewhat commonplace when compared with
the best of Donne's *Holy Sonnets*.

The most impressive sonnet of all, I suspect, is LXXVII, in which
the peculiarly Shakespearian qualities are put to good use, in
which the peculiar faults are somehow transformed into virtues.
Jonson, Donne, and Greville – indeed most of the great poets of
the Renaissance – tend to deal with the experiential import of
explicit definitions and sometimes to offer explicit and figurative
excursions from definitions. In the plain style at its plainest, the
passion with which the human significance of the definitions is felt
is communicated by the emotional content of the language in
which they are stated: that is, we do not have definition here and
emotion there, but meaning and emotion coexist at every
moment; in the relatively ornate style, the excursions are
controlled in a general but clear way by the definitions. But
Shakespeare's approach to his subject is indirect and evasive. In
LXXVII the explicit subject is not very important: it provides the
occasion for the entry into the poem of certain perceptions which
appear to be almost accidental but which are really
Shakespeare's obsessive themes.

LXXVII appears to have been written to accompany the gift of a blank book:

> Thy glass will show thee how thy beauties wear;
> Thy dial how thy precious minutes waste;
> The vacant leaves thy mind's imprint will bear,
> And of this book this learning may'st thou taste.
> The wrinkles which thy glass will truly show
> Of mouthed graves will give thee memory;
> Thou by thy dial's shady stealth mayst know
> Time's thievish progress to eternity.
> Look! what thy memory cannot contain
> Commit to these waste blanks, and thou shalt find
> Those children nursed, delivered from thy brain
> To take a new acquaintance of thy mind.
>   These offices, so oft as thou wilt look,
>   Shall profit thee and much enrich thy book.

The first quatrain states the ostensible theme of the poem: time passes and we age, yet by writing down our thoughts, we take a new acquaintance of our mind, acquire a new learning. The second quatrain enlarges upon the passage of time; the last six lines revert to the moralizing.

But something very strange occurs along the way. The imperceptible coming of wrinkles displays the physical invasion of the enemy, just as the imperceptible movement of the dial's shadow displays the constant movement of the enemy. In the ninth line, however, the enemy invades the mind, the center of being; it was the figure of the book which enabled the poet to extend the poem to this brilliant and terrifying suggestion, yet so far as the development of the theme is concerned, the extension occurs almost by the way, as if it were a casual and merely incidental feeling.

> Look! What thy memory cannot contain
> Commit to these waste blanks. . . .

This command, in isolation, is merely a command to make

good use of the book, and the remainder of the passage deals wholly with the advantages of doing so; yet the command follows the lines in which we have observed the destruction of the physical being by time, and in this position it suggests the destruction of the mind itself. This terrifying subject, the loss of identity before the uncontrollable invasion of the impersonal, is no sooner suggested than it is dropped.

There is a related but more curious employment of pure suggestion in the word *waste* in the same passage. The word is obviously a pun, with the emphasis on the secondary meaning. It means not only *unused* or *blank* (this is the primary meaning, and it gives us a tautology), but it means *desert* or *uninhabited* or *uninhabitable*, a sense reinforced by the verb *waste* in the second line; but rationally considered, the pages are not waste in this second sense, but are instruments offered for actually checking the invasion of the waste. A feeling, in other words, is carried over from its proper motive to something irrelevant to it, and the dominant feeling is thus reinforced at the expense of the lesser; this dominant feeling, one should add, arises not from the ostensible theme of the poem – the book and its use – but from the incidental theme which has slipped into the poem. In order to express the invasion of confusion, the poem for a moment actually enters the realm of confusion instead of describing it. The poem, I think, succeeds; but after having examined the unsuccessful confusion of other sonnets, I cannot decide whether the success is due to skill or to accident. . . .

SOURCE: extract from *Four Poets on Poetry*, ed. Don Cameron Allen (1959); reproduced in Yvor Winters, *Forms of Discovery* (1967) pp. 52–63.

F. T. Prince

THE SONNET FROM WYATT
TO SHAKESPEARE (1960)

The sum total of sonnets in English from the sixteenth century to
the present day, including those in 'Shakespearian' form or
otherwise irregular, would be but a fraction of those in Italian or
French. Sonnets in the strict Italian form would be but a small
proportion of the English total, a fraction of a fraction; and of
these some of the most remarkable, those of Milton and Hopkins,
rely on great freedom of modulation. It is clear that the extreme
facility of the form in Italian is only equalled by its difficulty in
English.

Rhyme in Italian is so abundant, the genius of the language is
so musical and expressive, that this intricate form proved capable
of almost endless employment from its invention in the thirteenth
century. By the late sixteenth century, there existed an enormous
mass of Italian sonnets of all kinds, amorous, didactic, satiric,
occasional. Minor poets or personalities with little artistic power
had found the form convenient for dozens of purposes. Occasionally an original talent would give it a new twist: Burchiello
would invent the nonsense sonnet, Della Casa would develop the
'heroic'; Campanella would render it metaphysical, Marino
lascivious. English poets would not know of many of these
experiments, and would not be capable of evaluating them if they
did. But their own experiments would be helped, later in the
century, by the glowing successes of the sonnet-form in France;
the poetry of the Pléiade is as much a part of the background of
Sidney, Daniel, and Shakespeare, as the sonnet in Italy.

The Petrarchan tradition to which such invidious references
are often made by English critics was thus only one stream in the
great flow of sonnets in Italy. We may admit that it was also the
most important, being that part of the sonnet tradition which had

most literary purpose and most interest of content. Is it necessary
to say plainly that Petrarch was a very great poet? It may be
stated, whether necessary or not, since no one would come to this
conclusion from a reading of most English critics and literary
historians.

The sonnet had emerged as a new poetic force in the *dolce stil
novo* of the thirteenth century. Cavalcanti and Dante had
revealed in it a magic of the intellect and the senses, but in very
brief compass. Petrarch completed its evolution with 300 sonnets
of sustained and deeply felt beauty; in their kind they have never
been equalled. The sixteenth-century Italians, led by Bembo,
took up the literary effort where Petrarch had left off; they strove
to enrich and elevate the form, loading their verses with
reminiscences, not only of Petrarch, but of Horace and Virgil.
The minor poets might continue to turn out their sentiments and
fancies; the dangers of the form for the Italians lay in its facility;
but the most sensitive and original poets recognized this, and
sought to avoid it.

Such discriminations were of necessity excluded in England.
The problem was to write a sonnet at all, not to explore the finer
potentialities. It is doubtful whether the first experimenters could
have realized this, though the movement of Wyatt's thought in
his sonnets shows a remarkable awareness of the problems. Even
the generation of Spenser and Sidney were blind to many
dangers. The English were struggling to fit a vigorous and
recalcitrant language to the exigencies of a form they did not
wholly understand. Instinctively and rightly, they tended to
strike out versions of it more suited to the genius of their language.

Wyatt's sonnets have been the subject of controversy and of some
oversubtle conjecture. The chief puzzle is, of course, that the poet
of the exquisitely modulated songs should write such apparently
rough and unmetrical verses in his sonnets, whether in his
adaptations from the Italian or his less numerous originals.

Some scholars have attempted to prove that the irregularities
of the sonnets are carefully contrived. Others have attributed
them to Wyatt's use of the 'pausing line' of medieval poetry,

while acknowledging that this interpretation does not cover all the difficulties.

A flaw liable to appear in all such conjectures is the assumption that Wyatt was as fully aware of the possibilities of the English decasyllabic line as we are, and that he must have consciously chosen not to develop them, preferring some more unusual effect. The older, relatively less well-informed, view that Wyatt was a tentative innovator seems more sensible, even if it failed to do justice to the rare achievement of the greater part of his work.

The basis of any interpretation must be the acknowledgement that Wyatt was not wholly an innovator, for his songs continued a long and flourishing tradition. But his sonnets are indeed an attempt to do something new in English, and something particularly difficult to do with the techniques then available.

Thus the only English metre which could be thought akin to the Italian hendecasyllable was the 'pausing line' of the fifteenth century, handed down to Skelton and the other poets immediately preceding Wyatt. Its commonest use was in the seven-line stanza descended from Chaucer, and favoured by Skelton both in *Magnificence* and in elegiac or descriptive pieces. Some lines from a speech by Cloaked Collusion will show the movement of the metre:

> Two faces in a hood / covertly I bear,
>   Water in the one hand, / and fire in the other;
> I can feed forth a fool, / and lead him by the ear:
> Falsehood-in-Fellowship / is my sworn brother.
> By Cloaked Collusion, / I say, and none other,
> Cumberance and trouble / in England first began. . . .
>   (*Magnificence*, Stage 2, Sc. ii)

If the pausing line is used for poems in which the statement is unfolded through several lines, it becomes plain that it is a rhythmical unit which tends to check the flow of the thought. The natural effect of trying to write sonnets in this metre is to smooth it and give it greater continuity of movement. The closely-argued sonnet dialectic — 'the sense variously drawn out from one verse to another' – pulls at the broken, swaying rhythm and tries to absorb the segments of the line into a larger unity.

If we look at Wyatt's adaptations or translations from the Italian we may see the pressure of the form upon the native rhythm of the 'pausing line'. In all his sonnets there are more or less self-contained, antithetically-balanced lines, in which a marriage is effected between the pausing rhythm and the pattern of the original. The following show something of this pattern: Nos. xii, xxviii, xxix (sextet), xxx, xxxiii, xcv (octet). Wyatt's choice of sonnets to translate may have been affected by his perception that the pausing line (as we may see from the extract from Skelton) lends itself to such a 'method of discourse'. One, at least, of his choices is a poem composed of such antitheses (here paradoxes and epigrams) from beginning to end:

> I fynde no peace / and all my warr is done;
> I fere and hope, / I burne and freise like yse;
> I fley above the wynde / yet can I not arrise;
> And noght I have / and all the worold I seson [seize on];
> That loseth nor locketh / holdeth me in prison
> And holdeth me not, / yet can I scape nowise;
> Not letteth me lyve / nor dye at my devise,
> And yet of deth / it gyveth none occasion.
> Withoute Iyen, I se; / and withoute tong I plain;
> I desire to perisshe, / and yet I aske helthe;
> I love an othre, / and thus I hate my self;
> I fede me in sorrowe / and laughe in all my pain;
> Likewise displeaseth me / boeth deth and lyffe;
> And my delite / is causer of this stryff.

This poem (No. xxvi) shows at least two things: Wyatt's appreciation of the Italian 'methods of discourse' (i.e. unfolding or patterning of statements by parallelism and contrast); and the effect of these on his metre. The nature of the pausing line is to hobble, and occasionally to lunge or swing; a sustained inevitability, such as the sonnet requires, is therefore beyond its proper reach. Yet in Wyatt's hands something is happening to the line; it is moving towards the English 'heroic pentameter', with its greater smoothness and flexibility. Thus in the above poem the pauses within the line tend to lose their importance, and in some lines hardly operate (ll. 8, 14). Four lines can be scanned as 'iambic pentameter' (ll. 1, 2, 3, 14). Others approach the same rhythm, if one or two syllables are slurred (ll. 5, 6, 7, 11, 12). One factor stands out as holding back the more sustained rhythm which is seeking to emerge, and that is Wyatt's addiction to such rhymes as *done, seson, occasion.* . . .

If this theory is sound, we might expect to see the pressure on the pausing line even more clearly in sonnets where the argument is more complex and the statement is unfolded continuously instead of being built up by a series of self-contained lines. In fact many of Wyatt's sonnets keep the hobbling movement of the 'pausing line', even in elaborate argument. (Nos. XXVII, XXXI, XXXII, among others. The effect of the rhymes already mentioned is very evident here.) Some, however, arrive at a more regular movement: such is no. LXXIX (I have marked only those lines which cannot be read except with a pausing cadence):

> Unstable dreme according to the place,
>> Be stedfast ons; or els at leist be true:
>> By tasted swetenes make me not to rew
> The sudden losse of thy fals fayned grace.
> By goode respect in such a daungerous case
>> Thou broughtes not her into this tossing mew,
>> But madest my sprite lyve / my care to renew,
>> My body in tempest / her succour to enbrace.
> The body dede, the spryt had his desire;
>> Paynles was th' one, / th' othre in delight:
>> Why then, Alas, did it not kepe it right,
> Retorning to lepe / into the fire,
>> And where it was at wysshe / it could not remain?
>> Such mockes of dremes they torne to dedly pain.

The tendency to 'iambic pentameter' is plainer here, though here, as elsewhere, we find lines which a skilled writer like Wyatt could have brought closer to this pattern, had he wished. Perhaps he set himself this task, as one experiment among others, in the following sonnet, No. CXLV, where no trace of the pausing line remains:

> Dyvers dothe use as I have hard and know,
>   When that to chaunge ther ladies do beginne,
>   To morne and waile, and never for to lynne,
>   Hoping therbye to pease ther painefull woo.
> And some ther be, that when it chanseth soo
>   That women change and hate where love hath bene,
>   Thei call them fals, and think with woordes to wynne
>   The hartes of them wich otherwhere dothe gro.
> But as for me, though that by chaunse indede
>   Change hath outworne the favor that I had,
>   I will not wayle, lament, nor yet be sad;
> Nor call her fals that falsley ded me fede:
>   But let it passe and think it is of kinde,
>   That often chaunge doth plese a womans minde.

Wyatt himself may have attached no special importance to the emergence of the new rhythm; in his sonnets, as in his satires, epigrams, and translations of the Psalms, he continues to write pausing lines. But the new line was seized upon by his earliest disciple, Surrey, who devoted himself to it with almost brutal determination. And through Surrey it became the predominant purpose of the poets of the next generation, those represented in *Tottel's Miscellany*, to beat out regular verses in this metre and in 'Poulter's measure' – an unattractive form whose popularity at this time can only be explained because it was practically impossible to write it without a regular thumping beat.

The *inevitability* which is one of the chief aims of all sonnets, but particularly of the Italian form, thus played a decisive part in Wyatt's experiments, and in doing so forwarded the rise of the most important of modern English metres. (Perhaps my account does not stress sufficiently the influence as a model of the Italian hendecasyllable; but this has been acknowledged, while the pressure of the sonnet-dialectic has not.) English poets promptly concentrated on exploiting the new metre, and this for the time being diverted their interest from the sonnet in its stricter form.

The English or Shakespearian sonnet had been foreshadowed by
Wyatt in one poem printed in *Tottel*, as well as in his frequent use
of a concluding couplet within the Italian pattern. Surrey invents
the Shakespearian form proper. He only once attempts the
Italian form, and then imperfectly, and moves from three
imitations of Wyatt's poem in *Tottel* to the full freedom of the
Shakespearian type, the advantages of which are obvious to the
poet wishing to develop strong regular rhythms. Surrey as a love-
poet lacks the intensity of realization which we find in most of
Wyatt's love-poetry (though hampered in the sonnets by technical experiment). The following sonnet will serve to show how far
Surrey travels from Wyatt in devising a new type of verse and in
adopting a more external rhetoric:

> Set me wheras the sunne doth parche the grene,
> Or where his beames do not dissolve the yse:
> In temperate heate where he is felt and sene:
> In presence prest of people madde or wise.
> Set me in hye, or yet in lowe degree:
> In longest night, or in the shortest daye:
> In clearest skye, or where clowdes thickest be:
> In lusty youth, or when my heeres are graye.
> Set me in heaven, in earth, or els in hell,
> In hyll, or dale, or in the fomyng flood:
> Thrall, or at large, alive where so I dwell:
> Sicke, or in health: in evil fame, or good.
> Hers will I be, and only with this thought
> Content my self, although my chaunce be nought.

The poem is as conventional in expression and sentiment as
Petrarch is often supposed to be, but is not; it anticipates the
'correctness' of some eighteenth-century poets, and probably
derives from the same sources in Latin poetry.

The poets of *Tottel's Miscellany* follow Surrey in abandoning
Petrarch as a model for sonnets. In so far as they write sonnets at
all they tend to write in the Shakespearian form, and to think of it
as a useful epigrammatic pattern for all purposes. Only two
sonnets in the collection, after Wyatt and Surrey, recur to

Petrarch, and these companion pieces both breathe of the discouragement which English poets had come to feel, in comparing their resources with his:

> O Petrarke hed and prince of Poets all,
> Whose luvely gift of flowyng eloquence,
> Wel may we seke, but finde not how or whence
> So rare a gift with thee did rise and fall . . .

> With petrarke to compare there may no wight,
> Nor yet attain unto so high a stile . . .

The decline in the formal influence of Italian verse is accompanied by an increase in the number of poems which look to the most familiar classical poets, Horace, Martial, or Ovid.

The great outburst of Elizabethan sonneteering was almost confined to the 1590s. *Astrophel and Stella*, printed in 1591, and the signal setting many of the minor poets to work, of course belongs to the earlier 1580s; Shakespeare's Sonnets, the greatest poetry produced by the whole *furore*, though not printed until 1609, have been felt to belong for the most part to the preceding decade. The concentration of most of the Elizabethan sonnet-writing into a space of ten years gave it something of the air of a poetical debauch, and may have contributed to the disfavour into which the form soon fell.

There were also, however, underlying reasons of a more permanent kind which account for the change of opinion, the sudden lapse of enthusiasm. Some had been foreshadowed in the first wave of English sonneteering, and they should have been glimpsed, at least, in the account I have given.

It is important to note that there was an interval of about twenty-five years in which, if we cannot say that no sonnets were written, we can assert that the form had been more or less put aside. And when the revival of the sonnet began in the early 1580s, on Sidney's initiative and under his influence, it is remarkable to see that the pattern of its introduction and wider application parallels what had happened two generations before.

Once more a single personality of genius turns to the love-poetry of Petrarch, and re-creates it in his own image. Once more his disciples and successors move further and further away from this starting-point, until the native Elizabethan form prevails over Petrarch. While this pattern is observable in the total view offered by such a collection as Sidney Lee's, it is repeated within the limits of a single writer's work, as with a dying fall, if we look at the body of sonnets built up by Drayton, in his *Idea*, between 1594 and 1619.

Sidney's return to Petrarch is plain, though its importance may be less so. He excludes the Shakespearian form from *Astrophel and Stella*. His leisurely travels abroad, his personal knowledge of French and Italian poetry, and his adherence as a critic to Renaissance ideas of decorum, seem to have convinced him that a 'real' sonnet must be in the Italian form, however difficult this might be in English. He deserves all honour for this appreciation of the value of formal strictness. However, his practical application of the decision shows some lack of perception. Thus for the sestet he almost always uses the pattern: CDCDEE. This is a step away from Wyatt's CDDCEE, and a step in the wrong direction. One of the chief unwritten rules of the Italian form is that the sestet is composed of two tercets, and that it must not therefore be allowed to turn into a quatrain followed by a couplet. If it does, the subtle symmetry (in inequality) of two fours, followed by two threes, is lost, and the unity of the whole is affected. It is true that a scrutiny of Sidney's sonnets reveals that he deliberately pauses, if possible, at the end of the first tercet; yet the pull of the final couplet is so strong, and the arrangement of rhymes, CDCD, so plainly asks for independence, that the sestet more often than not fails to give the effect of two tercets. Sidney's sonnets tend to be extended epigrams, in which the ring of the closing couplet is emphasized by the manner in which Stella is introduced, somewhat obviously, to produce a full close. It cannot be denied that Sidney justifies this last device, for it is found in some of the best pieces. One of these may be quoted as illustrating, not only this, but many other things which contribute to the potency of *Astrophel and Stella*:

> Having this day, my horse, my hand, my lance
>   Guided so well; that I obtained the prize:
>   Both by the judgement of the English eyes;
> And of some sent by that sweet enemy, France!
> Horsemen, my skill in horsemanship advance;
>   Townsfolk, my strength; a daintier judge applies
>   His praise to sleight, which from good use doth rise;
> Some lucky wits impute it but to chance;
> Others, because, of both sides, I do take
>   My blood from them who did excel in this;
>   Think Nature me a man-at-arms did make.
> How far they shot awry! the true cause is,
>   Stella lookt on, and from her heavenly face
>   Sent forth the beams which made so fair my race.

Here we have an example, not only of the features already mentioned, but of Sidney's habitual care in working out what he has to say; he is direct, concise, exact. There is an efficiency in his language and syntax which reveals an active intelligence and an unusual sense of reality, qualities which remind us that Sidney was more than a poet: the man of affairs, and of the greatest affairs, the aristocrat who cultivated his mind for action, the courtier who could write as he did to Queen Elizabeth on her proposed marriage to the Duc d'Alençon, formed habits of expression which did not fail to affect his verse.

Sidney's adherence to the strict sonnet-form goes together with his acute awareness of himself, his needs and his environment; he has a greater sense of reality than any other Elizabethan sonneteer except Shakespeare, and Shakespeare's awareness is chiefly of different things. Throughout *Astrophel and Stella* we feel the pressure, direct or indirect, of complex actual circumstances, of a day-to-day life in which the poet and his love are enmeshed. If there is a touch of play-acting about the young courtier going through the motions of the tournament, it is an added grace, rather than a false note. The court was like this, and no one should underestimate the importance of its apparent trivialities. There is the core of fact, and within that a core of truth. Sidney's horsemanship, his noble blood, his standing with all sorts of

people, his discreet but firm ostentation of himself and his gifts: all
these are conveyed. And at the heart of his poem, as of his life,
Sidney puts a secret passion which gives it the indispensable
further dimension.

   The psychology of Sidney's love for Penelope Devereux has
been thought strange; but the strangeness is of a kind which
springs from reality. *Astrophel and Stella* records a troubled
passion, and one which would have been guilty if Sidney had had
his way. Sidney was a young man, and in spite of his self-
discipline and the habitual sweetness of his temper, there was a
darker, more violent side to his nature, which gives strength to
many poems:

> Reason, in faith thou art well serv'd, that still
> Wouldst brabbling be with Sense and Love in me... (x)

> No more, my dear, no more these counsels try:
> O give my passions leave to run their race...   (LXIV)

> But ah! Desire still cries, 'Give me some food!'   (LXXI)

Sidney's characteristic as a lover is a wilful assertion of passion, in
the face of all the barriers that deny him satisfaction. And among
these barriers is his own reason and conscience. It is not surprising
that, in spite of its relative immaturity and its not infrequent
faults of taste, *Astrophel and Stella* dazzled its contemporaries, and
can still persuade us of its essential truth. This is what the sonnet
can do, this is what it is for: to express a conflict in the lover. Every
sonnet is a compressed drama, and every sonnet-sequence is a
greater drama built up of such dramatic moments. The struggle
is not only, as it often seems to be in the followers of Petrarch,
between the lover and the loved, the faithful adorer and the
ungrateful mistress; this, which is so common as to be almost
universal, is nevertheless only a part of the deeper struggle
between dream and reality, between thought and passion, which
is inescapable in all but the crudest love-experience. The
Petrarchan love-sonnet sprang from one historical effort to
interpret sexual love, the *dolce stil novo*; it has never been used

successfully since, even in a modified form, except by poets who lived through a comparable effort to interpret human passion. Sidney's love for Stella may have been no more than an episode, a chapter in a young man's development. But many things conspired to make the young man and the episode unique -- his temperament, his mind, his position, the environment, his gift for poetry.

In precisely the same degree in which Sidney himself was unique – and we know in what degree he was felt to be so by his contemporaries – his sonnet-sequence was unique; and it takes very little perception now to see that no other sonnet-writer of the period, who aimed at producing a similar result, would have found himself able to attain it.

The publication of *Astrophel and Stella* in 1591 set off a frenzy of sonneteering which soon wore itself out. What does criticism, as opposed to literary history, have to say about *The Tears of Fancie*, *Parthenophil and Parthenophe*, *Phillis*, *Licia*, *Zepheria*, *Diella*, and the rest of these melodious doodlings? The first point to make is that a generous proportion of all this is not in sonnet-form at all. Barnabe Barnes in *Parthenophil and Parthenophe* (1593) writes many so-called sonnets of fifteen lines, in addition to a mass of so-called madrigals, elegies, canzons, and odes; Robert Tofte in *Laura* (1597) writes mostly in twelve lines made up of two stanzas of six. Subtracting such inventions, we find the bulk of the sonnets to be 'Shakespearian'. The only determined effort to write in the Italian form is made by Henry Constable in *Diana* (1594?). Samuel Daniel and Michael Drayton both seem to have begun with it, but to have moved fairly soon away from it. Spenser takes up a variation of the Shakespearian form which he makes entirely his own.

The movement away from Italian form is a sign of life, but for the most part of a bubbling or frothing kind of life, which develops melody, prettiness, smoothness, gaiety, or mere silly fancy at the expense of all else. These writers are the inheritors of Surrey's somewhat boyish delight in the 'correct' use of verse, mythology, and conventional sentiments. The results of such 'correctness', unredeemed by social or personal distinction, are so

facile and artificial as to seem imbecile. Perhaps we can condone
them if we think of them as forms of automatic writing, in which
the English language is exploring its potentialities in certain
limited directions. *Diella* (1596) offers a concentration of such
poems:

> When Flora vaunts her in her proud array,
>   Clothing fair Tellus in a spangled gown;
> When Boreas' fury is exiled away,
>   And all the welkin cleared from angry frown:
> At that same time, all Nature's children joy;
>   Trees leave, flowers bud, plants spring, and beasts
> Only my soul, surcharged with deep annoy,   increase.
>   Cannot rejoice, nor sighs nor tears can cease:
> Only the grafts of sorrow seem to grow;
>   Set in my heart, no other spring I find.
> Delights and pleasures are o'ergrown with woe,
>   Laments and sobs possess my weeping mind.
> The frost of grief so nips Delight at root:
> No sun but She can do it any boot.

After 1591 the history of the sonnet becomes the history of the
'Shakespearian' sonnet: vitality passes out of the Italian form and
does not return until the seventeenth century, in the sonnets of
Donne and Milton. Sidney and Daniel prepare the way for
Shakespeare's Sonnets; they provide the two strains which meet
and are raised to a new pitch of intensity in Shakespeare, the
passionate and the richly rhetorical. Spenser is only a part of the
background to Shakespeare. Drayton takes up only the literary
or rhetorical strain from Sidney and Daniel; he continues it while
Shakespeare is writing, and seeks to assimilate also the Shakespeare revelation; but even at his best, which is remarkable, he
lacks the *unum necessarium*, the reality of passion.

Before concentrating on the Shakespearian sonnet it will be
well to deal with Spenser's collection of 1595; for the *Amoretti*,
while they appeared in the full flood of Elizabethan sonneteering,
stand apart from the other poetry of their time, as all Spenser's
poetry does.

Whether Spenser invented his rhyme-scheme (ABABBCBC

CDCDEE) we cannot say; it was used more than once, with characteristic firmness of touch, by Daniel (dealt with later in this chapter). But perhaps only Spenser could, or would, have chosen it as the form for a whole sonnet-sequence. The difficulty of finding so many rhymes, and interlacing them so closely, was less to him than to others, for the same reasons which determine all his poetic practice; his unusual facility in rhyme, his total abundance of words and flowing rhythms. The primal gift is magical, a mystery we cannot explore; but Spenser's exploitation of it, in rhyme as elsewhere, is only made possible by his having 'writ no language'. Archaisms, nonce-words, distortions of common speech, are nowhere more useful to Spenser than in helping him to fulfil his usually complicated rhyme-schemes. If his unscrupulousness here gives some of the peculiar charm of his verse, it is nevertheless also a bar to some other effects, operating against Spenser's success in certain kinds of forms. The sonnet is one of these. It gives little scope for the charm of diffuse, vague, atmospheric poetry; on the other hand, it continually presses for concision and subtle modulation. Spenser's expletives and vague epithets, and his addiction to such rhymes as 'memory', 'chastity', 'eternity', 'posterity', 'moniment', 'wonderment' (see Sonnet LXIX), are among the assets that cease to be assets in writing sonnets. Where Spenser succeeds, it is when he is able to create his own kind of remote and shadowy, yet tender, vision within the narrow space of fourteen lines. Could anything be more characteristic, more exquisite, yet more outstanding in its context, than Sonnet LXX?

> Fresh spring the herald of loves mighty king,
>   In whose cote armour richly are displayd
>   all sorts of flowers the which on earth do spring
>   in goodly colours gloriously arrayd.
> Goe to my love, where she is carelesse layd,
>   yet in her winters bowre not well awake:
>   tell her the joyous time wil not be staid
>   unless she doe him by the forelock take.
> Bid her therefore her self soone ready make,
>   to wayt on love amongst his lovely crew:

> where every one that misseth then her make,
> shall be by him amearst with penance dew.
> Make hast therefore sweet love, whilest it is prime,
> for none can call againe the passed time.

The poem is piercingly beautiful, with the diffused lightness and sweetness, and yet the apparent vagueness and wastefulness, that we find elsewhere in English perhaps ohly in Shelley. The details might seem to invite condemnation: such imprecise epithets as 'fresh', 'mighty', 'goodly', 'joyous', 'lovely', 'sweet'; a lack of clear visualization in 'the cote armour' and the 'winters bowre'; the whole linguistic texture of loose phrases and expletives ('all sorts', 'the which', 'do', 'gloriously', 'amearst with penance dew', 'whilest it is prime'). Yet what could be more successful in its emotive effect, the evocation of the atmosphere of spring, the thoughts of love, the sense of an old world renewed, yet with the past and the dead still present in youth and life – sadness and sweetness mingled? Spenser's genius was not wholly at ease in the sonnet-form. Yet in the instances in which his poetry prevails over the pattern, he leaves impressions we find nowhere else in Elizabethan verse.

No two forms of poetic genius could be less alike than Spenser's and Shakespeare's. Yet a reading of *Amoretti* leaves us convinced that Spenser's sonnets are mysteriously closer to Shakespeare's than to those of any other Elizabethan. It is not only that these are the only two sequences of the period by great poets, and by poets who would be recognized as great without them. This does indeed give a common quality, which may be traced in the overflowing ease and abundance with which both poets write: their sonnets are composed *de longue haleine*, they take a deep breath, and speak out their fourteen lines with a confident impetus that we do not find, for example, in Sidney. Apart from this there is no doubt that Shakespeare read *Amoretti* at a time when he had discovered his own use for the sonnet, and that much of Spenser's feeling and atmosphere, and some of his phrasing, entered into Shakespeare's creations. It would take more space than I have to substantiate this; but in at least one sonnet ('Like as the waves make towards the pebbled shore')

Shakespeare has picked up an opening formula from Spenser;[1] and many lines or quatrains or concluding couplets in Spenser have the touch that Shakespeare makes his own. In both sequences we are present at the birth of a new form, and a new mood: if Spenser's type of sonnet is less logical, less stripped for action, than Shakespeare's, it is nevertheless a personal vehicle for a kindred vision of love, in which Platonic idealism takes on a new power. Both poets earnestly aspire to a liberation of spirit through human love which was as yet unparalleled in England.

The first intimations of Shakespeare's use of the sonnet must, however, have come to him earlier; they are to be found in the 1591 volume of *Astrophel and Stella* in the additional sonnets pirated from Daniel, and in Daniel's own consequent editions of *Delia* in 1592 and 1594.

To discuss *Delia* as a whole, and to try to reconstruct closely the evolution of Daniel's style, is not necessary, if we wish to isolate what he gave Shakespeare: the most 'Shakespearian' sonnets are conveniently linked, and form the climax of the sequence. Sonnet XXX and the six that follow, of which five form a chain, are unmistakably Shakespeare's inspiration for many of the earlier sonnets in his own book. Daniel was a diligent poetic craftsman and experimenter, within his limits; and *Delia* shows a variety of forms, though the Shakespearian predominates, and succeeds best. There are a few sonnets in the strict Italian form, which would appear to be early, and several in Spenser's form, which would appear to be late.

Yet Daniel was undoubtedly at his best, and attained the highest poetry he was ever to reach, in the form which Surrey had founded and Sidney half-disdained. He was the first to show its peculiar possibilities both in melody and in movement of thought. Thus we may note his exploration of its capacity for double rhymes (XVII, XXVI, and XXVII, and intermittently elsewhere); for the dramatic statement of a passionate impulse or of a calm or fervent resolution (VII, XX, XXXVI, XLIII, and Nos. XXXV and XLVI); for the embroidery of a conceit within a quatrain; and for the concentrated richness of phrase which Sidney had initiated. All these were to be taken further by Shakespeare.

As for that central group of seven (Nos. XXX–XXXVI), it certainly gave the note for Shakespeare's laments on time and transience, as well as his promise of poetic immortality, themes which belong far more to the sixteenth century, and perhaps more particularly to France, than to the older Petrarchan tradition. Daniel's sonnets of beauty and time, decay and fame should be read as a group; it is difficult to select one in which their quality is summed. Set any one of them beside any one of Shakespeare's, and Daniel's lower concentration and more conventional pitch appear at once. But who can miss the Shakespearian note in any of them? No. XXXIII may serve as an example:

> When men shall finde thy flowre, thy glory passe,
> And thou with carefull brow sitting alone:
> Received hast this message from thy glasse,
> That tells thee trueth, and saies that all is gone.
> Fresh shalt thou see in mee the woundes thou madest,
> Though spent thy flame, in mee the heat remayning:
> I that have lov'd thee thus before thou fadest,
> My faith shall waxe, when thou art in thy wayning.
> The world shall finde this miracle in mee,
> That fire can burne, when all the matter's spent:
> Then what my faith hath beene thy selfe shalt see,
> And that thou wast unkinde thou maiest repent.
> Thou maist repent, that thou has scorn'd my teares,
> When Winter snowes uppon thy golden heares.

Together with Sidney's two 'Shakespearian' sonnets, the farewell to lust and the farewell to love which he did not himself include in *Astrophel and Stella*, Daniel's sonnets of the early 1590s are a preparation for Shakespeare. The hidden forces making for the emergence of the Shakespearian form were constant both in the first and in the latter half of the century; Sidney gave the Italian form a new start, but the evolution away from it was rapid. In the 1580s and early 1590s we find the literary context out of which Shakespeare's sonnets grow.

Yet if this is true, and can be shown to be true, it is nevertheless not surprising that it has never been judged important (except by Sidney Lee): Shakespeare's Sonnets are incommensurate with those of any other poet of his century; the fact that technically they are the consummation of a line of poetic experiments looks pale beside their living eloquence and passion.

Shakespeare's poetic sovereignty might be said to be enough to account for the pre-eminence of the Sonnets: they are the overflow of the life and mind of this genius, as Petrarch's were the overflow of *his* life and mind. In an English modification of Petrarch's form, Shakespeare created a series of poems comparable only to those of Petrarch. All that goes between fades into insignificance. These two writers transfused their inner life into the sonnet. Shakespeare's moral and imaginative experience being what it was, it inevitably challenges a comparison with that which had been crystallized by Petrarch 250 years earlier. It is only by means of such a comparison that we can see how much the sonnet-form needed a new imaginative impulse, and how Shakespeare was able to give it.

Petrarch's conception of love was in essence that of Dante: Beatrice or Laura brought to the imperfections of their unsatisfied lovers a tender severity which would lead them to God. But Petrarch's realization of this is less majestic, less intellectual, less complete, than Dante's; and the medieval vision is missing in the sixteenth-century Italians who revived Petrarch. What remains has many virtues; but the intellect is dormant, and the love-experience in all these later poets has become relatively commonplace.

We may see this clearly by looking at *Astrophel and Stella*. Sidney's emotions and reflections are basically ordinary, if not commonplace. Our feeling that this is so is indeed one of the charms of the sequence: here is reality, a young man's reality, amid all the conventions, the literary intentions, the ingenuous or self-conscious fancies. The Petrarchan tradition had long since lost all but a tinge of medieval intensity; it remained a serviceable instrument for the projection and adornment of that most constant of human experiences: the working-out of love between man and woman. The various experiments with the sonnet in sixteenth-century Italy, – Della Casa's solemnity of diction, Tasso's richness of colour and ornament, Marino's glossy sensationalism – can be regarded as attempts to compensate for the 'ordinariness' which lies at the core of all these later love-sonnets.

But in Shakespeare there is an exploration of new possibilities; love has been liberated from its nominal limits. 'Two loves I have of comfort and despair' gives the key to the whole sequence. By taking for his 'good angel', his guiding star of virtuous love, not a Laura, not a Beatrice, but a young man, his friend, Shakespeare re-introduces an idealism equal to that of Dante or Petrarch: it may even appear more exalted than theirs, and is certainly more perilous. Whereas with Dante and Petrarch poetry is but the medium in which accepted spiritual realities are embodied, with Shakespeare poetry, the poetic imagination, becomes the means of knowing and possessing spiritual realities: it is not only the way, but the truth and the life. Shakespeare's love is a matter of living in and through imagination, or 'proving upon the pulses' the power or the weakness of beauty, truth, devotion, in day-to-day, year-by-year, experience. It is this which gives their searching edge to the sonnets of both happiness and unhappiness: to such poems as 'When in disgrace with Fortune and men's eyes' and 'When to the sessions of sweet silent thought', as well as to 'Some glory in their birth, some in their skill' and 'Farewell, thou art too dear for my possessing'. Dante or Petrarch could not have written:

> What is your substance, whereof are you made,
> That millions of strange shadows on you tend?

Those 'millions of strange shadows' were born of Shakespeare's own imagination, forced to explore a passion which could not be consummated in any other way. A new moral sensibility, a new kind of devotion (and a singularly gratuitous one), are wrought out in the Sonnets. There were no conventions, no precedents in the tradition of love-poetry, for the central reality of Shakespeare's passion. Such conventions as he takes up – for example, sonnets on absence, on going a journey, on not being

able to sleep, or sonnets promising immortality through poetry
(as studied by J. B. Leishman)[2] — are almost negligible in their
context. For one thing, they are used with the force and freedom
of Shakespeare's personal rhetoric, and consequently transformed. For another, they are usually conventions of mere circumstance or occasion or expression, dramatic settings for an emotion
which they project, but do not interpret. One of the less
'poetical', less richly ornamented, Sonnets will perhaps illustrate
the quality of Shakespeare's emotion more clearly than 'Being
your slave, what should I do but tend', or 'Let me not to the
marriage of true minds'.

> When thou shalt be dispos'd to set me light,
> And place my merit in the eye of scorn,
> Upon thy side against myself I'll fight,
> And prove thee virtuous, though thou art forsworn.
> With mine own weakness, being best acquainted,
> Upon thy part I can set down a story
> Of faults conceal'd, wherein I am attainted;
> That thou in losing me shalt win much glory:
> And I by this will be a gainer too;
> For bending all my loving thoughts on thee,
> The injuries that to myself I do,
> Doing thee vantage, double-vantage me.
>   Such is my love, to thee I so belong,
>   That for thy right myself will bear all wrong.
>
>   (LXXXVIII)

So Shakespeare's imagination reaches out to a fantasy, an
extravagance of generosity; it is the love-relationship itself that
commits him and incites him to such hyperbole, both of style and
sentiment. There is here nothing resembling the idealism of
Petrarch or the *dolce stil novo*, so often decried as strained and
artificial; Petrarch's conception of service, of devotion, of
spiritual endeavour in love, is practical, commonsensical and
balanced – part of an accepted religious and social
ideal – compared with Shakespeare's gratuitous offer of self-
sacrifice.

The old moral order which had inspired Dante and Petrarch had receded into the past; the travails of the new moral order are registered in poetry for the first time by Shakespeare, not only, as all the world knows, in the plays, but also in the various phases of the Sonnets. What is new in them enabled Shakespeare to raise to new heights the declining tradition of the Petrarchan sonnet. But if it had not been for that long and well-tried tradition, and for the favour it suddenly enjoyed in the 1590s, Shakespeare might never have written his Sonnets at all. The tradition gave him something approaching a *genre* within which to begin writing, though we tend to falsify our criticism if we regard sonnet-sequences as a *genre*. At their most intense Shakespeare's Sonnets have a startling novelty; they convey some realities of the experience of being in love with almost frightening force. Shakespeare re-created the love-sonnet in English, but he did so by means of a sensibility so exceptional that his love-poetry could produce no tradition, and had to wait until the Romantic period for a full understanding of its power.

SOURCE: *Elizabethan Poetry, Stratford-upon-Avon Studies*, II (1960) 11–29.

NOTES

1. See nos XXXIV, LXVII and LXXXIX in *Amoretti*, and also Shakespeare's nos CXVIII and CXLIII.
2. See *Elizabethan and Jacobean Studies, presented to F. P. Wilson* (1959).

Joan Grundy

SHAKESPEARE'S SONNETS AND THE ELIZABETHAN SONNETEERS (1962).

In a sonnet addressed to Spenser, Keats remarks,

> The flower must drink the nature of the soil,
> Before it can put forth its blossoming.

This describes very well Shakespeare's relationship to his fellow-sonneteers. However different the blossom he produced, their work, their example, provided the soil from which it sprang. The relationship is a complex one, and I wish to examine only one aspect of it here, namely Shakespeare's attitude to the accepted 'poetic' of the sonnet-sequence, in the hope that this may throw light upon the way in which the tradition has been adapted to suit an individual talent.

Convention is so much the ruling power in the Renaissance sonnet-sequence that even the principles and assumptions upon which the sonneteer claims to be writing are themselves a part of the convention. Thus the 'poetic' which I am about to outline is in its context what we might call the governing conceit, consistent and true only within its own largely artificial limits. The sonneteer for the most part wears a double mask – as poet, no less than as lover. One would not wish to take his critical statements out of their context and add them to Gregory Smith's collection of Elizabethan critical essays. Within their context, however, in the special world, the charmed if not always charming circle which we enter whenever we open a collection of Elizabethan sonnets, they are valid. And occasionally, when the poet is using the convention without being confined within it, they acquire a validity beyond it, and conceit becomes statement.

Fundamental to the sonnet-writer's poetic is the idea of the poem as a speaking picture. It is used with varying degrees of awareness and emphasis, sometimes being set at the very start of the sequence, as in Sidney's

Loving in truth, and fain in verse my love to show,
That She, dear She, might take some pleasure of my pain,
Pleasure might cause her read, reading might make her know,
Knowledge might pity win, and pity grace obtain,
I sought fit words to paint the blackest face of woe;

at other times being introduced later with apparent casualness so that it perhaps appears as no more than one image among many: for example, in Spenser's *Amoretti* it appears in sonnet xvii, in Griffin's *Fidessa* in sonnet xix. But whatever emphasis the poet gives to the idea in the form of the conceit or its actual placing or development, it appears to be always present in his mind as the shaping and directing idea of the poem as a whole. The picture may be of the beloved's beauty or of the lover's sufferings, but usually combines both: thus Barnes, using the common variant of the picture in the mirror, writes

Mistress! Behold in this true speaking Glass,
Thy Beauties graces! . . .
But, in this Mirror, equally compare
Thy matchless beauty, with mine endless grief.
(*Parthenophil and Parthenophe*, 1 1–2, 9–10)

and Daniel puts the position clearly:

Then take this picture which I heere present thee,
Limned with a Pensill not all vnworthy;
Heere see the giftes that God and nature lent thee,
Heere read thy selfe, and what I suffred for thee.
(*Delia*, xxxiiii 5–8)

'Heere see . . .', 'Heere read . . .': each implies, and is eloquent of the other: the vivid picture of her beauty testifies to the extent of his pain; the picture of his pain bespeaks the greatness of her beauty; or, as Henry Constable puts it,

> payne in verse
> Loue doth in payne, beautie in loue appeare.
> *(Sonnets,* III iii 6)

Pain, love, and beauty, each expressive of the other, are thus the subject of the sonneteer's portrait-art. As we have already noticed, a common variation of this basic idea is that of the poem, not as a painted picture, but as a mirror. The two images are so close as to be often fused: thus Griffin asserts,

> My Pain paints out my love in doleful Verse.
> (The lively Glass wherein she may behold it!),
> *(Fidessa,* XIX 1–2)

and even Sidney answers his own question,

> How can words ease, which are
> The glasses of thy daily-vexing care?

with the thought, 'Oft cruel fights well pictured-forth do please' *(Astrophel and Stella,* XXXIV 2–4). Whichever image is used, the emphasis is on expressiveness, on the fullness and truthfulness of the representation. Sometimes it is suggested that the poet's face or heart provides a more effective reflection of the lady's beauty than the mirror she holds in her hand: this is well known from Spenser's 'Leaue lady in your glasse of christall clene' *(Amoretti,* XLV 1), or Daniel's 'O why dooth *Delia* credite so her glasse' (XXIX 1). Face, heart, and poem receive and give back the lady's beauty, sometimes directly, sometimes indirectly, and, with a neat duality worthy of Dorian Gray, self-portraiture and the portraying of the beloved are seen as at once separate and the same. The sonneteer's self-consciousness is as an artist: he creates, and is constantly asserting that he creates. If the poem is a mirror, it is one which he likes to look both at and *into*, and before which he never tires of parading. However humble as a lover, he is

usually proud and even boastful as an artist: Delia's picture is
'limned with a Pensill not all vnworthy', and it is 'with a feeling
skill' that Sidney 'paints his hell'. The only exception to this self-
confidence is likely to be when the lover claims that the subject is
beyond the power of art to express, as in Spenser's assertion that
her 'glorious pourtraict' 'cannot expressed be by any art' –

> A greater craftesmans hand thereto doth neede,
> that can expresse the life of things indeed –
>
> (XVII 13–14)

or as in Chapman's,

> Her virtues then above my verse must raise her,
> For words want art, and Art wants words to praise her.
>
> (A Coronet for his Mistress Philosophy, VIII 13–14)

As Hallett Smith has pointed out in his Elizabethan Poetry in
relation to Sidney, the sonnet-writer is usually aware of addressing two audiences, his beloved, and the general public, and at
times plays off one against the other. Most sonneteers indeed
present us with a triangular relationship, with 'the world' playing
an indispensable role of spectator, usually admiring, but capable
on occasion of criticism and envy too, as for instance in Amoretti,
LXXXV,

> The world that cannot deeme of worthy things,
> When I doe praise her, say I doe but flatter.

Daniel especially keeps 'the world' in view: 'had she not been
faire and thus vnkinde', 'the world had neuer knowne' of his
sorrows; as it is, the world may mark and judge:

> Let this suffice, the world yet may see;
> The fault is hers, though mine the hurt must bee.
>
> (XV 13–14)

And his poems abound in such statements. For Daniel, as for

Spenser and others, this world audience comprises future, and even occasionally past, as well as present generations. It is here that the idea, particularly characteristic of *Delia*, of the poem as a 'monument' comes in: monument, mirror, and picture are closely linked, since it is the picture in the mirror that will preserve the beauty of the beloved for future generations to see. Implicit in all such claims upon the world's attention is the idea that the beloved is the nonpareil for beauty and, usually, for cruelty also: this in its turn makes the lover the unique exemplar of suffering, so that altogether it is not surprising that the spectacle should provide material for 'the worlds wonder' (a common phrase in sonnet-literature).

This poetic of the sonnet-form is not, of course, an English creation. The ideas are for the most part commonplaces of sonneteering wherever it is practised, even by Petrarch himself. But the Elizabethan sonneteers exemplify it so fully that it is reasonable to suppose that Shakespeare's acquaintance with it came principally through them. His kinship with them in this respect, his willingness to be one of them by accepting their basic assumptions, needs little demonstration. His poem is a love-poem, and its central purpose is, according to his oft-repeated statements, to blazon the beloved's beauty, for future generations even more than for present ones. Thus it too aims to be a speaking picture, of that lasting kind which serves as a monument:

> So long as men can breathe, or eyes can see,
> So long lives this and this gives life to thee
>
> (XVIII 13 – 14)

> Your monument shall be my gentle verse,
> Which eyes not yet created shall o'er-read.
>
> (LXXXI 9 – 10)

That the beloved is regarded as the nonpareil, 'the very archetypal pattern and substance' of beauty and truth, to quote J. W. Lever,[1] cannot be adequately illustrated by a few lines: the idea is the base and fabric, the very life-blood, of these poems. All these ideas, except that past generations, not future ones, are in

question, are brought together in sonnet CVI, with its concluding
emphasis on wonder:

> For we, which now behold these present days,
> Have eyes to wonder, but lack tongues to praise.

The reader needs little reminder of such celebrated passages.

This, however, is only a beginning. Shakespeare, in his usual
comprehensive way, shares a common platform with other
sonneteers. But he does not stay there. He develops and expands
some elements and rejects others, so that we are led to conclude,
in this as in so many respects, 'This is, and is not, a Petrarchan
sonnet-sequence'. Thus he makes little use of the idea of the poem
as a mirror. His awareness of it is clear from sonnet CIII, which
may be compared with the sonnets of Spenser and Daniel quoted
earlier:

> Look in your glass, and there appears a face
> That over-goes my blunt invention quite.   (6–7)

He recognizes too its close association with the 'eternalizing'
theme; at least, his use of the image in a different context suggests
this:

> Thou art thy mother's glass, and she in thee
> Calls back the lovely April of her prime.
>
> (III 9–10)

His otherwise complete neglect of it is probably to be connected
with his attitude to the closely-related idea of the poem as a
painted picture. Even this idea, although it seems implicit in his
claims concerning his poetry's immortalizing powers, is never
explicitly accepted, except in sonnet XVI, where it is subordinated
to the idea that the young man should perpetuate himself
through generation: 'And you must live, drawn by your own
sweet skill'; and in sonnet CI, which questions the validity of such
activity. The reason why Shakespeare does not commit himself
explicitly to the idea seems to be that he cherishes a higher

ambition: he has what we might call a Pygmalion complex and
hopes that somehow the image he creates may be real. Thus there
is constant emphasis upon the *life* that will be preserved in his
verses, for which the lines already quoted from sonnet XVIII may
serve as one example among many. The idea of poetry conferring
a 'life beyond life' through fame is, of course, familiar enough,
although actually (in Elizabethan sonnet-literature as a whole)
the theme is not so popular as may be supposed from the
frequency with which we meet it in Shakespeare and Daniel. Nor
is it normally used with the urgency, the desired near-literalness
of the word 'life', that it has in Shakespeare. Thus while Daniel
chiefly implies that his verse will be a *record* of the past, and will
confer the kind of immortality that comes through fame,
Shakespeare seems to be reaching out after something more truly
vital; his desire, however impossible of achievement, is by
recreating his loved one within the medium of language to stay
the flux of time. Daniel is talking of the permanent recording of
the past, Shakespeare mainly of its arresting. Daniel, for instance,
emphasises the perpetuating of Delia's *name* (in the sense of
fame) – in sonnets XXXV, XXXIX, XLVI, XLVII, XLVIII – whereas
Shakespeare talks about preserving the young man's life, truth,
self, being, but never, in this context, merely his name.[2] The
conventional notion of the portrait is thus always dissolving in his
verse into something less rigid and definable, yet at the same time
it provides a point of departure, or area of reference, for these
transcendencies. The poem is to be a picture, but not a *mere*
picture.

The increased emphasis on the *life* to be conferred by his
portrait replaces, in Shakespeare's verse, the normal sonneteer's
emphasis upon his own '*feeling* skill': the identification of beauty,
love, and pain is not made. Shakespeare does write about his own
sufferings, but un-self-consciously and without self-pity. His love
is, literally, not self-regarding; he has therefore no interest in
displaying or surveying it in his verse, and no grounds for
equating self-portraiture with the portraying of the beloved. This
introduces a fundamental change: the sonnet-sequence in
Shakespeare's hands loses its affinity with the love-complaint.
Here are no 'tears of fancie', no 'blackest face of woe'. The

contrast with Daniel's *Delia* is particularly striking, in view of their many affinities. Daniel leaves us in no doubt concerning the character of his poem: these are 'fatal anthems, lamentable songs', 'wailing verse', the product of an 'afflicted Muse'. Indeed, his description of his verse as 'A wailing deskant on the sweetest ground', played by the Muse upon his heart-strings (XLVII), aptly summarizes the triangular relationship under discussion. Shakespeare, on the other hand, speaks of himself in sonnet XXX as possessing 'an eye, unused to flow', and, as far as this sequence is concerned, this is true.

Something of the same self-effacement is seen in his attitude to that fashionable judge and arbitrator in the sonneteer's drama, 'the world'. J. W. Lever has observed that 'the world' supplies the role almost of a fourth personage in Shakespeare's sequence; we ourselves have already noted its appearance in the work of his fellow-poets. At times he does write of it as the interested spectator of his personal drama, but on two occasions at least he produces a significant variation on the common theme of the world, unenchanted and, in the poet's eyes, coldly envious and censorious, condemning his excessive praise of his beloved as flattery. In each case, Shakespeare turns the idea against himself. Thus in sonnet LXXI he warns his beloved,

> But let your love even with my life decay,
> Lest the wise world should look into your moan
> And mock you with me after I am gone.   (12–14)

And in sonnet CXLVIII, on the dark lady, he asks,

> If that be fair whereon my false eyes dote,
> What means the world to say it is not so?   (5–6)

where, ironically, the world is right. But, generally speaking, he shows a notable lack of interest in what the world thinks of himself, or of his sonnets. There is nothing akin to Daniel's

> Beholde the message of my iust complayning,
> That shewes the world how much my griefe imported,
> (*Delia*, L 3–4)

or even to Lodge's

> Show to the world, though poor and scant my skill is,
> How sweet thoughts be, that are but thoughts of Phillis.
> (*Phillis*, I 13–14)

It is, rather, he himself who looks on, and views the world in its relationship to his beloved. The latter is 'the world's fresh ornament' (1 9). Sometimes he is in direct relationship with the world, and of equal stature with it:

> Ah! if thou issueless shalt hap to die,
> The world will wail thee, like a makeless wife;
> The world will be thy widow, and still weep
> That thou no form of thee hast left behind,   (IX 3–6)

sometimes the world shrinks to nothingness in comparison with him:

> For nothing this wide universe I call,
> Save thou, my rose, in it thou art my all.   (CIX 13–14)

Such statements bring 'the world' into the sonnet-drama, not as spectator, but as participator. It would perhaps be going too far to suggest that Shakespeare was aware of all this; but he has, it would appear, in such instances subtly transformed a familiar and fairly rigid feature of the sonnet convention, and given it new depth and vibrancy.

Finally, there is that fairly large group of sonnets to be considered, in which Shakespeare reflects on his own practice and compares it with that of others. Similar discussions occur in only one other Elizabethan sequence – *Astrophel and Stella*. Shakespeare and Sidney alone among Elizabethan sonneteers[3] question the aims and methods, in other words the values, of the Petrarchan convention. Among continental writers, as Sidney probably knew, anti-Petrarchanism was one of the recognized and legitimate stances; its adoption did not entail any expulsion from the tribe, or any desire for expulsion. The question we are

faced with in both Sidney's case and Shakespeare's is: How far do
they really *mean* what they say? Are we still within the enclosed
circle of convention, where no lies are told because nothing is
affirmed, or have we broken away from it? Is Shakespeare, as
Richard B. Young has suggested Sidney is doing in 'You that do
search for every purling spring' (xv), raising the critical problem
of sincerity for merely rhetorical purposes?[4] We seem in examining such sonnets to be on a circular journey, wondering where
finally to halt; whether Art or Nature should have the last word.
And it may be that there is a kind of naïve sophistication in
immediately supposing it to be Art. The problem in
Shakespeare's case and Sidney's is not, however, identical, since
if we take, as we must, the poet's general practice into
consideration, we are more likely to concede Shakespeare's
claims to have avoided the faults he censures than we are
Sidney's. True, he does more than warble his native woodnotes
wild, but he has not that *exhibitionism* of style which is a normal
characteristic of the Petrarchan poet, good or bad. At the same
time, his critical comments do often recall Sidney's, both in
content and expression, and it seems likely that there was some
conscious imitation or reminiscence here. Sonnet XXI and the
celebrated sonnet CXXX ('My Mistress eyes . . .') have much in
common with sonnets III and VI of *Astrophel and Stella*. There is the
same scornful enumeration of the hyperboles of the fashionable
sonneteer, and the same assertion of the writer's own simplicity
and the sufficiency of his subject. But Shakespeare's argument is
more straightforward than Sidney's. He is merely asserting that
the beauty of his beloved will stand comparison with the best,
though not with sun and stars and so on; Sidney under a show of
modesty is claiming superior powers of expression for himself:

> For me, in sooth, no Muse but one I know,
> Phrases and problems from my reach do grow,
> And strange things cost too dear for my poor sprites.
> How then? even thus – in Stella's face I read
> What Love and Beauty be, then all my deed
> But copying is, what in her Nature writes.   (III 9–14)

These lines, however, may also be compared with a passage in Shakespeare's eighty-fourth sonnet:

> Lean penury within that pen doth dwell
> That to his subject lends not some small glory;
> But he that writes of you, if he can tell
> That you are you, so dignifies his story,
> Let him but copy what in you is writ,
> Not making worse what nature made so clear,
> And such a counterpart shall fame his wit,
> Making his style admired every where.
>
> (LXXXIV 5–12)

This is Shakespeare at his most Sidneyan: the central image, that of copying Nature's writing, is the same, and the conclusion, that this will make the writer famous for his style, is actually more typical of Sidney than it is of Shakespeare. (See, for example, *Astrophel and Stella*, sonnets XV and XC.) Even here, however, there is an essential difference in attitude. The implication in Sidney's sonnet that the poet has become a new and more successful kind of plagiarist -- Nature's ape, not Pindar's -- is missing in Shakespeare's. Instead, the point Shakespeare is making is that it is impossible for him to enhance his subject; he will do enough if he can but reproduce it. In other words, the centre of interest in Sidney's sonnet, for Sidney, is his own achievement; in Shakespeare's, it is his subject, and the key words are 'if he can tell / That you are you'. And this difference in emphasis, in orientation of interest, is typical. Sidney's strictures upon other sonneteers are really secondary to his main theme in his 'critical sonnets' (I, III, XV, XXVIII, for example), which is not a condemnation of eloquence, but an expression of his joy at having found a shorter way to it, having found its very source in fact, in Stella. Shakespeare too acknowledges that his beloved gives his pen 'both skill and argument' (sonnet C; Sidney, in sonnet XV, has the phrase 'love and skill'), but he is generally more attentive to the latter than the former. Sidney's Muse, unlike Shakespeare's, is never 'tongue-tied' (except in the situation described in the opening sonnet, when he 'took wrong ways'). It is exuberant and confident, airily overlooking (for the most part – sonnet L is an exception) the 'intolerable wrestle with words and meanings' that is involved even in copying Nature, as indeed Sidney himself overlooks it in the *Apology*. Shakespeare, on the other hand, is so conscious of the inadequacy of words that at one point he reaches the conclusion that it 'shall be most my glory, being dumb' (LXXXIII 10). Of course, Shakespeare does write; Sidney does wrestle with words. But the attitudes they take up are characteristic and significant. Sidney begs 'no subject to use eloquence' (XXVIII); he does not need to, since he has one, so to speak, at his finger-tips ('And Love doth hold my hand and makes me write', XC). Shakespeare, on the other hand, begs no eloquence for his subject, since it requires none.

This leads us back to the consideration of Shakespeare's quarrel with his fellow-sonneteers, in particular his 'rival poets'. Shakespeare's criticisms are more drastic than Sidney's, which, as we saw, are at one level scarcely criticisms at all, their main purpose being to praise Stella and at the same time to commend his own verse. For Shakespeare his own 'true plain words' and 'what strained touches rhetoric can lend' his rivals' verse are at genuine and open war. How close his expression comes to Sidney's is shown by the comparable lines in Sidney's fifteenth sonnet,

> those far-fet helps be such
> As do bewray a want of inward touch. (XV 9–10)

Yet essentially his position is close to that of Wordsworth in the preface to the *Lyrical Ballads* – much closer than Sidney's is. He refuses to 'interweave any foreign splendour of his own' with the beauty of his beloved, knowing that this is more likely to impair than to enhance it:

> I never saw that you did painting need
> And therefore to your fair no painting set.
>   (LXXXIII 1–2)

This is the error into which his rivals have fallen:

And their gross painting might be better used
Where cheeks need blood; in thee it is abused.

(LXXXII 13—14)

In the sonnets in which he treats this theme (LXXII — LXXXV, CI, CIII, and to some extent, XXI, XXXII, and LXXIX), Shakespeare shows an obsessive anxiety, quite lacking in Sidney, lest the colours of rhetoric should falsify the picture of his beloved. He is not merely being superior about his fellow-sonneteers: he is expressing his own artistic dilemma. This seems concentrated for him in the idea of 'praise'. This is the problem he faces: how to present the beloved directly, without praising, or how to praise without seeming to flatter. Sidney certainly had raised the question, but only incidentally:

What may words say, or what may words not say,
Where Truth itself must speak like Flattery?

(XXXV 1—2)

He had concluded:

Not thou by praise, but praise in thee is rais'd.
It is a praise to praise, when thou art prais'd.

(*ibid.* 13—14)

Shakespeare does not find the answer so easily. In sonnet XXI he seems to equate praise with hyperbole and therefore with flattery, concluding 'I will not praise that purpose not to sell.' Yet in sonnet LX he places his hopes on it:

And yet to times in hope my verse shall stand,
Praising thy worth, despite his cruel hand.

(13—14)

In sonnet LXXXII his concern is that this worth is 'a limit past my praise'; in CIII he asserts rather the futility of such praising:

> The argument all bare is of more worth
> Than when it hath my added praise beside!

In LXXXIV he shows himself suspicious of praise of the wrong kind; the poem begins

> Who is it that says most? which can say more
> Than this rich praise, that you alone are you?

and ends

> You to your beauteous blessings add a curse,
> Being fond on praise, which makes your praises worse.

There is praise and praise: that fact explains much, not only in Shakespeare's criticism of his fellow-sonneteers, but also in his whole relationship to them, and the personal adjustments he makes to the convention.

It is no new discovery that the love that Shakespeare expresses in his sonnets is of a peculiarly selfless kind: the point has often been made. What I hope has emerged from the foregoing comparison is that this fact governs his attitude to the conventional sonneteering 'poetic' in every aspect of it, and equally determines the use to which he puts it. There are, of course, sonnets in which he is merely playing the fashionable game – sonnets XLIII–XLVI, for instance, which employ the fashionable themes of sleeplessness, absence, and the war between eye and heart – in which he does exhibit the ordinary sonneteer's self-concentration, as he does also, to ironic effect, in many of those concerning the dark lady. But in the core of the sequence – the sonnets concerning the young man – he both re-examined the sonneteer's 'poetic', and gave it, through his practice, a philosophical and critical depth that it had not possessed before. In this, as in so much else, he turned the dreams and fancies of his predecessors into truths, for truth, not fancy, was his subject.

SOURCE: *Shakespeare Survey*, No. 15 (1962) ed. Allardyce Nicoll, pp. 41–9.

NOTES

1. *The Elizabethan Love-Sonnet* (1956) p. 184.
2. In sonnet CVIII, he has the line 'Even as when first I hallow'd thy fair name', but this is clearly a deliberate echo of the Lord's Prayer, taking up the phrase 'like prayers divine' in line 5.
3. Drayton occasionally shows something of the same critical spirit, but not often, and he may be directly imitating Sidney.
4. Richard B. Young, *English Petrarke: a Study of Sidney's Astrophel and Stella* (Yale, 1958) p. 6.

M. M. Mahood

LOVE'S CONFINED DOOM (1962)

I

The present trend of criticism is bringing Shakespeare's poems and his plays together. A dramatic element is recognized in short poems of many kinds – Shakespeare's sonnets, Keats's odes, the lyrics of Yeats. Like plays they attempt to give through some fiction (the truest poetry is the most feigning) form, and so meaning, to experiences whose real-life occasions are now lost to us and are, in any case, none of our business. A sonnet cannot help in the interpretation of a play, nor can the play throw any light on the sonnet's meaning, if the two works are thought of as belonging to different grades of imitation; if the sonnet, for example, is a snippet of biography or a poetic exercise. But if the two kinds of poetry are regarded, despite their differences in magnitude, as products of the same imaginative process, then our reading of the one can illumine our understanding of the other. In particular, these cross-references can lead us to a fuller understanding of the main theme of the sonnets: the complex and profoundly disturbed relationship of the poet with the friend to whom most of the sequence is addressed.[1]

Sonnet XXXIII provides an example of the elucidation that such cross-references can afford:

> Full many a glorious morning have I seen
> Flatter the mountain-tops with sovereign eye,
> Kissing with golden face the meadows green,
> Gilding pale streams with heavenly alchemy;
> Anon permit the basest clouds to ride
> With ugly rack on his celestial face,
> And from the forlorn world his visage hide,

Stealing unseen to west with this disgrace:
Even so my sun one early morn did shine
With all-triumphant splendour on my brow;
But out, alack! he was but one hour mine;
The region cloud hath mask'd him from me now.
Yet him for this my love no whit disdaineth;
Suns of the world may stain, when heaven's sun staineth.

It is not at all easy, in reading this, to grasp what the friend has done — if the clouds represent some blot on his reputation with the world at large, or the relationship of poet and friend has been clouded by the friend's unkindness. Is the clouding involuntary or deliberate? The grammatical structure of the second quatrain leaves us in doubt whether the sun hides his visage, stealing away in shame, or whether, untouched himself, he simply permits the clouds to hide it. 'Celestial' implies that the friend, like the sun, belongs to the immutable order of heavenly bodies who are not themselves affected in any way by the rack of clouds passing below them in the sublunary world's insubstantial pageant. Yet if the friend merely allows his glory to be eclipsed and is himself in no way blemished it is hard to see what Shakespeare intended by 'disgrace', since the word whenever used by him (with the possible exception of 'And then grace us in the disgrace of death' in *Love's Labour's Lost*, where it can mean 'disfigurement') has a derogatory meaning. 'Stain' also is a teasingly imprecise word. It can mean to darken, or even to eclipse or to be eclipsed (as in *Antony and Cleopatra*, III iv 27), though a much commoner meaning is to blemish or to become blemished.

If we turn to the plays for parallels in thought, diction or imagery which may throw light on Shakespeare's intention in sonnet XXXIII, we are immediately struck by two passages which bear a close resemblance to the second quatrain of the sonnet. When Richard II appears on the walls of Flint Castle, Hotspur exclaims

See, see, King Richard doth himself appear,
As doth the blushing discontented sun
From out the fiery portal of the east,

> When he perceives the envious clouds are bent
> To dim his glory and to stain the track
> Of his bright passage to the occident.

To which the Duke of York adds

> Yet looks he like a king: behold, his eye,
> As bright as is the eagle's, lightens forth
> Controlling majesty: alack, alack, for woe,
> That any harm should stain so fair a show!
>
>   (III iii 62–71)

The verbal resemblances between this and sonnet XXXIII are close, but no closer than others to be found in a passage of *Henry IV, Part I*. Hal, parting from his Eastcheap companions, lets the audience into the secret of his relationship with them:

> Yet herein-will I imitate the sun,
> Who doth permit the base contagious clouds
> To smother up his beauty from the world,
> That, when he please again to be himself,
> Being wanted, he may be more wonder'd at,
> By breaking through the foul and ugly mists
> Of vapours that did seem to strangle him.
>
>   (I ii 220–6)

In the first passage the sun image is used of a weak man who, for all his show of controlling majesty, is controlled by his subjects; in the second, of a strong man who conceals his true nature for reasons of policy. This contrast heightens rather than solves the contradictions of sonnet XXXIII. But fortunately the plays also offer a number of parallels with the sonnet's magnificent opening quatrain which may take us a little further in understanding the poem.

The first of these is in *Henry VIII*, when Wolsey, disgraced by the King ('That sun, I pray, may never set!'), laments that

> No sun shall ever usher forth mine honours,

> Or gild again the noble troops that waited
> Upon my smiles.   (III ii 410–12)

The context is one of betrayal; however hard Wolsey seeks, like
the poet in sonnet after sonnet (for example, xxxv, which is
closely connected with xxxiii and in which 'Thy adverse party is
thy advocate') to justify the King, every audience is perturbed by
Henry's treachery. The use of 'gild' is significant. Shakespeare
nearly always employs the word in a derogatory sense to suggest
the brilliance that masks corruption: 'England shall double gild
his treble guilt'; 'men are but gilded loam'; 'the gilded puddle';
'gilded tombs do worms infold'. Goneril is 'this gilded serpent'.
Even a seemingly neutral use of the word turns out to be
ambiguous. When Antony sends a jewel to Cleopatra after his
parting with her, the queen greets the messenger with the words

> coming from him, that great medicine hath
> With his tinct gilded thee.
>
> (I v 36–7)

Gold is cordial. Antony is life-giving, 'sovereign' like the sun. Yet
at this moment he is bound for Rome and marriage with Octavia.
A mainspring of the play's action is Cleopatra's uncertainty as to
whether Antony is dust a little gilt or gilt o'er-dusted. This is
exactly the uncertainty in which the poet of the sonnets stands in
relation to his friend.

'Alchemy', like 'gild', was not a word which necessarily
implied deception to the sixteenth-century reader. But it too is
used by Shakespeare in contexts of betrayal. As J. W. Lever has
shown² there is a meaningful resemblance between the opening
of sonnet xxxiii and the lines in *King John* in which the King,
having treacherously abandoned the cause of Constance and her
son Arthur by agreeing to the French match, declares of the
marriage day

> To solemnize this day the glorious sun
> Stays in his course and plays the alchemist,

Turning with splendour of his precious eye
The meagre cloddy earth to glittering gold.

(III i 77–80)

Even more interesting is the way the word is used in *Julius Caesar*:

O, he sits high in all the people's hearts:
And that which would appear offence in us,
His countenance, like richest alchemy,
Will change to virtue and to worthiness.

(I iii 157–60)

Although Cassius gives warm assent to this 'right well conceited' description of Brutus, the play itself leaves us in lasting doubt over the effect of such alchemy. Does it in fact turn the assassination into a golden deed, or does it only gild over the conspirators' guilt? Public virtue, Shakespeare hints here and elsewhere in the plays, never cancels out private wrong, and the noblest Roman of them all is branded with the lasting reproach of *Et tu, Brute*.

To Coleridge the opening of sonnet XXXIII represented one mark of the poetic imagination at its best: its ability to transfer a human and intellectual life to images of nature.[3] Just as Venus's sense of loss at Adonis's departure is precisely matched by the experience of watching a shooting star vanish in the night sky, so Shakespeare finds in the treacherous overclouding of a bright summer's day the exact image for his disappointment in his friend's deliberate coldness. This disappointment is not the almost impersonal regret felt by Hotspur and York at Richard's weaknesses; it is the personal pain that Henry V could give his old companion, Falstaff. So much is suggested by the beginning of sonnet XXXIV — 'Why didst thou promise such a beauteous day', where the hurt is scarcely healed by the tears the friend sheds. 'And they are rich and ransom all ill deeds' may well be spoken with deep irony to the man who thinks his patronage can pay for his unkindness. For in italicizing the word 'Flatter' in his quotation, Coleridge unerringly indicated the tone of sonnet XXXIII and the succeeding sonnet. Flattery forebodes treachery. What Shakespeare dreads in his friend is not the folly of youth – that he is almost eager to condone – but the cold strength of maturity.

II

If Thorpe's arrangement of the sonnets has any significance, sonnet xxxiii represents the first cloud across the friendship, and the poet never subsequently speaks with the simple trust that we find, say, in sonnet xxix. When Shakespeare later made use of the image of the rising lark which supplies the unforgettable sestet of that sonnet, he gives it a bitter setting; it becomes the incidental music to Cloten's attempt to corrupt Posthumus's wife. And when, within the sonnet sequence itself, Shakespeare returns in sonnet xci to the theme of love's riches as compensation for the world's neglect – 'And having thee, of all men's pride I boast' – the final, misgiving couplet quite alters the sonnet's effect:

> Wretched in this alone, that thou mayst take
> All this away and me most wretched make.

Another sonnet concerned with the friendship's value is the forty-eighth, which contrasts the care the poet has taken to stow away his material wealth on leaving for a journey with the way his most precious possession of all, the friend himself, is left 'the prey to every vulgar thief':

> Thee have I not lock'd up in any chest,
> Save where thou art not, though I feel thou art,
> Within the gentle closure of my breast,
> From whence at pleasure thou mayst come and part.

The lingering monosyllabic line 'Save where thou art not . . .' is heavy with mistrust. Such a mistrust is experienced by the Helena of *A Midsummer Night's Dream*, whose affection has been so freely and foolishly given and who still cannot quite believe, when all the mistakes of a midsummer night are over, that Demetrius is hers:

And I have found Demetrius like a jewel,
Mine own, and not mine own.

(IV i 195–6)

The motif of a treasure in a casket which occurs several times in
the sonnets is of course an integral part of *The Merchant of Venice*.
Here the critics draw our attention to one particularly close
parallel. Bassanio, making his choice of the leaden casket,
moralizes over the way the world is still deceived with ornament:

So are those crisped snaky golden locks
Which make such wanton gambols with the wind,
Upon supposed fairness, often known
To be the dowry of a second head,
The skull that bred them in the sepulchre.

(III ii 92–6)

Sonnets LXVII and LXVIII also protest at the deceptions of the time,
which are held to accord ill with the friend's 'truth'. His beauty is
his own as beauty was in the days

Before the golden tresses of the dead,
The right of sepulchres, were shorn away,
To live a second life on second head;
Ere beauty's dead fleece made another gay.·

The poet's intention seems to be that both Bassanio and the friend
should stand for truth in a naughty world. Sonnet LXVII in fact
strengthens this connection by saying that nowadays Nature is
bankrupt – 'Beggar'd of blood to blush through lively veins';
and Bassanio's wealth, he tells Portia, all flows in his veins. But
though he is frank enough to tell her this when he first comes
wooing he does not then tell her what he later confesses, that he is
'worse than nothing' and that he is in fact indebted to Antonio for
coming like a day in April 'To show how costly summer was at
hand'. It is unfashionable at present to regard Bassanio as a
fortune-hunter, yet in this same scene Gratiano puts the facts of
the matter honestly enough when he says 'We are the Jasons, we

have won the fleece'. If generations of critics have been perplexed
by the discrepancies between Shakespeare's apparent intentions
in portraying Bassanio and the character who emerges from the
play, the reason may be that Shakespeare's presentation of the
character is related to a real-life discrepancy between what he
wishes his friend to be and what he fears he is. So in the sonnets,
with their many verbal parallels to *The Merchant of Venice*:
Shakespeare strains in sonnet LXVII and sonnet LXVIII to dissociate
his friend from the corruption of the times and in sonnet LXIX
blames those times for adding to his friend's fair flower 'the rank
smell of weeds'; yet the collection as a whole shows him to be
haunted by the fear that his friend is all the time a lily that festers.

Such a re-reading of *The Merchant of Venice* in the light of the
sonnets helps us towards an answer to the question with which the
play opens: why is the Merchant himself so sad? Already in the
first scene Antonio hints at the true source of his sadness:

> My ventures are not in one bottom trusted,
> Nor to one place; nor is my whole estate
> Upon the fortune of this present year:
> Therefore my merchandise makes me not sad.
>
> (I i 42–5)

Discriminatory stress here falls on *bottom, place, merchandise*;
Antonio has not entrusted all his wealth to one ship, but he has
entrusted all his affection to one man and is obsessed by thoughts
of the hazards he runs in this venture. In the story, as Shakespeare
shapes it out of the casket tale and the tale of the cruel bond,
Bassanio is faithful to Antonio, whose fears are therefore
groundless. But they are none the less real to the audience.
Antonio begins as he ends, the odd man out, awakening in the
audience a sympathy which is extraneous to the play's general
effect and so quite different from any emotions which Shylock
may arouse. In Antonio's readiness to stake all for his friend, his
parting from him, his letter, his willing resignation, we find the
dramatic expression of that 'fear of trust' at which Shakespeare
hints also in Bassanio's speech on ornament, and which runs

through so many sonnets to find, perhaps, its most eloquent expression in sonnet XC:

> Ah, do not, when my heart hath 'scaped this sorrow,
> Come in the rearward of a conquer'd woe;
> Give not a windy night a rainy morrow,
> To linger out a purposed overthrow.
> If thou wilt leave me, do not leave me last,
> When other petty griefs have done their spite,
> But in the onset come; so shall I taste
> At first the very worst of fortune's might.

The same fear of trust may be the case of a similar disproportion in another of Shakespeare's middle comedies, *Twelfth Night*. The Antonio of that play feels for Sebastian a devotion which belongs to an altogether different order of experience from the Duke's infatuation with Olivia or Olivia's mourning for her dead brother. Viola's silent passion comes within reach of it, and for this reason she is deeply moved by Antonio's reproaches to her for not yielding his purse (a situation handled with cheerful heartlessness in *The Comedy of Errors*). Bewildered as she is by this meaningless demand, she can recognize his anguish of disillusion, an anguish oddly misplaced in Illyria:

> Let me speak a little. This youth that you see here
> I snatch'd one half out of the jaws of death,
> Relieved him with such sanctity of love,
> And to his image, which methought did promise
> Most venerable worth, did I devotion . . .
> But O how vile an idol proves this god!
> Thou hast, Sebastian, done good feature shame.
> In nature there's no blemish but the mind;
> None can be call'd deform'd but the unkind:
> Virtue is beauty, but the beauteous evil
> Are empty trunks o'erflourish'd by the devil.
>
> (III iv 393–404)

Two persistent themes of the doubting sonnets – the youth's

beauty, promising 'most venerable worth' and the poet's wor-
shipping devotion – are to be found here, and Antonio's speech
of further reproach in the last act adds another: the contrast
between the speaker's spendthrift affection and the friend's
careful calculations of the risks involved:

> His life I gave him and did thereto add
> My love, *without retention or restraint,*
> All his in dedication; for his sake
> Did I expose myself, pure for his love,
> Into the danger of this adverse town;
> Drew to defend him when he was beset:
> Where being apprehended, his false cunning,
> *Not meaning to partake with me in danger,*
> Taught him to face me out of his acquaintance,
> And grew a twenty years removed thing.
>
> (v i 83–92)

This relationship of Antonio to Sebastian stands up like a great
inselberg of eroded experience in the green landscape of comedy.
And in a history play of the same period, *Henry V*, surprising
prominence is given to the theme of trust betrayed, in Henry's
eloquent reproaches to the traitor Scroop. The loosely episodic
construction of the play is not injured by the stress Shakespeare
lays on an incident which is briefly treated by the chroniclers. But
this emphasis once again suggests that Shakespeare was haunted
by the fear that his self-possessed friend would one day repudiate
him:

> O, how hast thou with jealousy infected
> The sweetness of affiance! Show men dutiful? . . .
> Free from gross passion or of mirth or anger,
> Constant in spirit, not swerving with the blood,
> Garnish'd and deck'd in modest complement,
> Not working with the eye without the ear,
> And but in purged judgement trusting neither?
> Such and so finely bolted didst thou seem:
> And thus thy fall hath left a kind of blot,

To mark the full-fraught man and best indued
With some suspicion. I will weep for thee;
For this revolt of thine, methinks, is like
Another fall of man.   (II ii 126–42)

Among the sonnets, sonnets XC – XCIV, a sequence of mounting
mistrust which most of the rearrangers leave undisturbed, and
which culminates in the much-discussed 'They that have power',
come very close in theme and tone to Henry's speech. Sonnet
XCIII speaks, with all the bitterness of *Twelfth Night*'s Antonio, of
the youth's deceptive beauty, and like Henry V the poet here
associates outer fairness and inner corruption with original sin; so
calamitous and yet so inescapable does the friend's betrayal
appear to him:

But heaven in thy creation did decree
That in thy face sweet love should ever dwell;
Whate'er thy thoughts or thy heart's workings be,
Thy looks should nothing thence but sweetness tell.
How like Eve's apple doth thy beauty grow,
If thy sweet virtue answer not thy show!

iii

The sonnets we have hitherto discussed are among the least
conventional in the sequence. In many of the more conventional
ones, however, it is noticeable that Shakespeare is making use of
the convention to relieve or to escape from his intolerable doubts
of his friend's loyalty. Thus one of the oldest themes which the
sonnet absorbed from medieval love poetry, the poet's abject self-
abasement before the god-like nature of the friend or mistress,
eases the poet's dread of betrayal by supplying a justification for
it. Such a rationalization of fear is found, alongside the
melancholy which the fear induces, in Shakespeare's depiction of
Antonio in *The Merchant of Venice*. His words at the trial –

I am a tainted wether of the flock,
Meetest for death: the weakest kind of fruit

Drops earliest to the ground; and so let me:

(IV i 114–16)

are as movingly unconvincing as is sonnet LXXXVIII:

> With mine own weakness being best acquainted,
> Upon thy part I can set down a story
> Of faults conceal'd, wherein I am attainted,
> That thou in losing me shalt win much glory.

Glory of this kind is won by Hal at the end of the second part of *Henry IV* when he repudiates Falstaff; and there are several sonnets in which the relationship between the young, handsome and conspicuous friend seems closely to parallel that of the Prince of Wales and his reprobate old companion. Of these sonnet XLIX comes nearest to the culminating scene of *Henry IV, Part II*:

> Against that time, if ever that time come,
> When I shall see thee frown on my defects,
> When as thy love hath cast his utmost sum,
> Call'd to that audit by advised respects;
> Against that time when thou shalt strangely pass
> And scarcely greet me with that sun, thine eye,
> When love, converted from the thing it was,
> Shall reasons find of settled gravity,
> Against that time do I ensconce me here
> Within the knowledge of mine own desert,
> And this my hand against myself uprear,
> To guard the lawful reasons on thy part:
> > To leave poor me thou hast the strength of laws,
> > Since why to love I can allege no cause.

At the end of the play, love is converted from the thing it was when Hal, succeeding to the throne, declares 'I have turned away my former self' and takes as his new counsellor the strength of laws in the person of the Lord Chief Justice. If we take, from the back of the gallery or the back of history, a long view of the Hal - Falstaff relationship, the rejection is justified. But the

sonnet gives us a sombre close-up of the matter from the
viewpoint of the rejected companion, in which cold prudence
shows itself in the 'advis'd respects' (a phrase already used of
majesty in *King John*) and in the profit-and-loss calculations with
which the friend casts his utmost sum. The reasons of settled
gravity serve, to borrow a telling phrase from sonnet LXXXIX, 'to
set a form upon desired change'. Gravity belongs to the court and
in particular to the Lord Chief Justice who tells Falstaff 'There is
not a white hair on your face but should have his effect of gravity'.
'What doth gravity out of his bed at midnight?' Falstaff asks when
a nobleman of the court comes to summon Hal to a reckoning
with his father; and gravity is dismissed by levity while the scene
of reckoning is played out as an Eastcheap farce. But in the
charade, Falstaff is soon turned out of the role of Hal's father; and
the royal resolution – 'I do, I will' with which Hal encounters
Falstaff's plea not to banish honest Jack is put into effect when the
new-crowned Henry V passes 'strangely'. The Lord Chief Justice
follows, to waken Falstaff rudely from his long dream in which
he, and not the Lord Chief Justice, will replace Hal's father –

> Thus have I had thee, as a dream doth flatter,
> In sleep a king, but waking no such matter.
>
> (Sonnet LXXXVII)

In the play as well as the poems, Shakespeare seeks to exorcize the
haunting fear of betrayal by showing such betrayal to be justified
in the light of prudence, a cardinal virtue, and of policy, the
wisdom of governors. But the reproach of disloyalty remains,
breaking out in the sonnets through ambiguous words and
phrases, and perplexing for centuries the audiences of *Henry IV*.

Readers who are distressed by the self-abasing tone of such
sonnets may turn with relief to those that make use of a contrary
convention and promise the friend immortal life in the poet's
verse. Yet many of these 'eternizing' sonnets are not so much the
expression of confidence as of fear, the same persistent fear of the
friend's treachery. In anticipation of that betrayal, the poet tries
to perpetuate his friend in his verse as he now is and while he is
still the poet's friend. He seeks 'To make him seem long hence as

he shows now' (sonnet CI). But what he seems and shows may be quite other than what he actually is, and some of these sonnets are as profoundly ironic as the Duke's words to Angelo in the last act of *Measure for Measure*, when the deputy still appears 'unmoved, cold, and to temptation slow':

> O, your desert speaks loud; and I should wrong it,
> To lock it in the wards of covert bosom,
> When it deserves, with characters of brass,
> A forted residence 'gainst the tooth of time
> And razure of oblivion.
>
> (v i 9–13)

Because the characters of brass may ultimately speak of the friend as someone very different from the man the poet knows, the poet insists on his power to perpetuate him in his verse, not as a paragon of all the virtues – in fact we are told very little about the young man, as all Shakespeare's biographers have cause to complain – but simply as the poet's friend –

> But you shall shine more bright in these contents
> Than unswept stone besmear'd with sluttish time.
>
> (Sonnet LV)

Sluttish time not only neglects the gilded monuments but actually besmears them; the poet is fighting to preserve his friend against 'all-oblivious *enmity*' and beyond that, it may be conjectured from the same sonnet's ambiguous final couplet, from the ultimate truth of his nature which the poet dreads to see discovered:

> So, till the judgement that yourself arise,
> You live in this, and dwell in lovers' eyes.

So too in the greatest 'eternizing' sonnet, the Ovidian sonnet LX, Time appears as the enemy not only of the youth's beauty but of his virtue too. Time feeds on the rarities of Nature's truth, and the eclipses which fight here against the glory of maturity can be, as they are in sonnet XXXIII, the darkened reputation which comes even in a man's lifetime from 'envious and calumniating time'.

The ravages of Time are the subject of sonnet LXIV — 'When I have seen by Time's fell hand . . .'. But here there is no promise of an immortality in verse to offset the melancholy close:

> Ruin hath taught me thus to ruminate,
> That Time will come and take my love away.
>> This thought is as a death, which cannot choose
>> But weep to have that which it fears to lose.

Commentators on this sonnet are much struck by the resemblance between its second quatrain and the speech of King Henry in *Henry IV*, *Part II* beginning 'O God! that one might read the book of fate'. Both passages picture the sea's encroachment upon the land and the land's upon the sea. It is worth following Henry's speech in the play a little further, to see what application he makes of the image:

> O, if this were seen,
> The happiest youth, viewing his progress through,
> What perils past, what crosses to ensue,
> Would shut the book, and sit him down and die.
> 'Tis not ten years gone
> Since Richard and Northumberland, great friends,
> Did feast together, and in two years after
> Were they at wars. It is but eight years since
> This Percy was the man nearest my soul,
> Who like a brother toil'd in my affairs
> And laid his life and love under my foot.
>> (III i 53–63)

Time will also come and take Shakespeare's love away — by death perhaps, although in the natural course of things the poet would die the earlier; the *Henry IV* passage shows rather that Time may take him away as it took Northumberland from Richard and has taken Hotspur from Henry. Here again then destructive time is equated, as Derek Traversi has said, with the 'necessary flaw at the heart of passion'.[4]

So the millioned accidents of time creep in, the poet says in sonnet cxv, between men's vows and 'Divert strong minds to the course of altering things'. In this last sonnet, however, the vicissitudes of time are made to serve a new turn of thought by explaining how it has been possible for the poet's love to increase. This sonnet therefore belongs with those that make use of a third conventional idea of love poetry and of the sonnet in particular, the constancy of the poet's love. Whatever the friend may do, the poet's affection will last for ever and a day. There is thus a natural transition from this sonnet to the boast of sonnet cxvi that love is not love 'Which alters when it alteration finds'. Sonnets cvii and cxxiv also belong to this group, and when, after all that has been written about these two difficult poems, one rereads them in their place in the sequence it is hard to see how the 'love' they celebrate could ever have been taken to mean the friend himself and not Shakespeare's affection for the friend. The 'confin'd doom' of cvii can surely only mean the limits which cynical onlookers have set to Shakespeare's friendship, limits suggested perhaps by a knowledge of the friend's true nature. But in defiance of these prophecies, the poet claims his love is not 'the child of state' —

> It fears not policy, that heretic,
> Which works on leases of short-number'd hours.

The friend's love may well be diverted from its true allegiance by policy; he has already revealed himself as a calculating young man, and the time may come when he will cast his utmost sum and, knowing his estimate, will reject the poet. But in contrast the poet's love stands 'hugely politic'; it embraces the whole state of existence and to him it is inconceivable that he could ever 'leave for nothing all this sum of good' —

> For nothing this wide universe I call,
> Save thou, my rose; in it thou art my all.

Sonnet cix, from which these lines are quoted, presents the poet 'like one that travels' bringing 'water for my stain'. Verbally it

closely parallels the passage in *Henry IV, Part II* from which T. W.
Baldwin begins his study of the relationship between the poems
and the plays:[5]

> FALSTAFF   But to stand stained with travel, and sweating with
> desire to see him; thinking of nothing else, putting all affairs else in
> oblivion, as if there were nothing else to be done but to see him.
> PISTOL   'Tis 'semper idem', for 'obsque hoc nihil est:' 'tis all in
> every part.
>
> (v v 25–31)

In this of course Falstaff's devotion is anything but disinterested,
and I have already suggested that it is one of Shakespeare's ways
of evading the fear of trust to present Falstaff as a character who
deserves the dismissal he gets. But Falstaff does not alter where he
alteration finds. He believes that he will be sent for soon at night
and when that last hope is gone, Falstaff himself has nothing left
to live for: 'The king hath killed his heart.'

IV

In suggesting that the deep fear of love's confined doom and the
various ways of coming to terms with that fear – by accepting
the justice of the doom, by stressing poetry's power to escape
devouring time and by protesting the poet's own unchanging
loyalty – are the motive forces of most of the sonnets between
XXXIII and CXXIV, and an important element in several of
Shakespeare's middle plays, I have run the risk, especially where
the plays are concerned, of appearing to be a biographical
speculator. But while I am convinced the fear of trust is a factor to
be reckoned with in our reading of the poems and plays, I would
not suggest following this clue out of the text and into
Shakespeare's life. We know too little about the labyrinthine
processes by which experience is transformed into the work of art.
The warning of a Victorian editor of the sonnets, Robert Bell, is
apposite: 'the particle of actual life out of which verse is wrought
may be, and almost always is, wholly incommensurate to the
emotion depicted, and remote from the forms into which it is
ultimately shaped'.[6] Some trifle light as air may have rendered

Shakespeare the man jealous of a friend's affection and so created the tormented 'I' of the sonnets as well as the two Antonios and certain aspects of Falstaff. If the recognition of the 'fear of trust' as a strong element in the sonnets and middle plays throws no clear light on Shakespeare's biography, it might be expected to help in the critical evaluation of these works. But here we meet a long standing difference of opinion between those critics – they are mostly practising poets like Yeats, Auden and Empson – who hold that poetry should be the clear expression of mixed feelings and those others, and they include some of the best commentators on the sonnets, who feel that ambiguities of tone and verbal meanings constitute a defect because they indicate the poet has insufficiently realized his experience in a poetic form. For these critics the lack of moral explicitness in, say, *The Merchant of Venice* and *Henry IV* will always be a blemish on these plays, and they are likely to prefer *Integer vitae* to 'They that have power', or the perfect control of 'When in disgrace with fortune . . .' to the sounding imprecision of 'Not mine own fears . . .'. If I here stop short of an evaluative conclusion to these few observations on the Sonnets and middle plays, it is not because I feel such evaluations can be dismissed as a matter of taste, but because they need a definition of critical principles that lies outside the scope of the present essay. And even when we are furnished with such principles we are likely to find that in critical evaluation, as in biographical inquiry and other activities of scholarship, we may come to the pericardium, but not the heart of truth.

SOURCE: *Shakespeare Survey*, No. 15 (1962) ed. Allardyce Nicoll, pp. 50–61.

NOTES

1. See especially J. W. Lever, *The Elizabethan Love Sonnet* (1956). The many studies of parallels between plays and sonnets are summarized in Hyder Rollins's Variorum edition (1944), ii, pp. 63–9. To the works

there cited should now be added T. W. Baldwin, *The Literary Genetics of Shakespeare's Poems and Sonnets* (1950).

2. Lever, *The Elizabethan Love Sonnet*, pp. 221–2.
3. *Biographia Literaria*, ed. J. Shawcross, II, pp. 17–18.
4. *Approach to Shakespeare* (1946) p. 46.
5. Baldwin, *The Literary Genetics of Shakespeare's Poems and Sonnets*, p. 157. Actually use is not made, in Baldwin's study, of the striking resemblance between these passages, which is discussed by J. W. Lever, op. cit., p. 238, nor of the resemblance between sonnet XLIX and *Henry IV*.
6. Quoted by Hyder Rollins, op. cit., II, 139.

Jan Kott

SHAKESPEARE'S BITTER ARCADIA (1964)

The Sonnets can be interpreted as a drama. They have action
and heroes. The action consists of lyrical sequences which slowly
mount to a tragedy. There are three characters: a man, a youth
and a woman. This trio exhaust every form of love and go
through all its stages. They exhaust all the variants and forms of
faithlessness, every kind of relationship, including love, friendship, jealousy. They go through the heaven and hell of love.
The diction of the Sonnets, however is not Petrarchan, and
another epithet would be more apt here: the characters go
through Eden and through Sodom.

The fourth character of the drama is time. Time which
destroys and devours everything. Greedy time which has been
compared to gaping jaws. It devours the fruits of human labour
and man himself.

O time, swift despoiler of created things! How many kings, how many
peoples hast thou brought low! How many changes of state and
circumstance have followed since the wondrous form of this fish died
here in this hollow, winding recess? Now destroyed by time, patiently
thou liest within this narrow space, and with thy bones despoiled and
bare art become an armour and support to the mountain which lies
above thee.[1] . . .

. . . Time is the foremost actor in any tragedy.

> When time is old and hath forgot itself,
> When waterdrops have worn the stones of Troy,
> And blind oblivion swallow'd cities up,
> And mighty states characterless are grated
> To dusty nothing.   (*Troilus and Cressida*, III ii)

That was Cressida. No Shakespearian play is so close to the
Sonnets, with its bitter images of the inevitable end of love.[2]

> Injurious time now, with a robber's haste,
> Crams his rich thievery up, he knows not how.   (IV iv)

That was Troilus. In the Sonnets, as in *Troilus and Cressida*, time,
the 'great-siz'd monster of ingratitudes' (III iii), 'injurious Time',
is against the lovers. It destroys cities and kingdoms as well as love
and beauty, breaks the oaths of princes and lovers' vows.

> . . . Time, whose million'd accidents
> Creep in 'twixt vows, and change decrees of kings.
>   (Sonnet CXV)

Let us invoke Leonardo once more. He speaks of the same
voracious time:

O time, thou that consumest all things! O envious age, thou destroyest
all things and devourest all things with the hard teeth of the years, little
by little, in slow death! Helen, when she looked in her mirror and saw
the withered wrinkles which old age had made in her face, wept, and
wondered to herself why ever she had twice been carried away. O Time,
thou that consumest all things! O envious age, whereby all things are
consumed![3]

Three Leonardian images contain three kinds of time. Geological
time: the time of the earth, of oceans and mountain erosion;
archaeological time, for all history becomes archaeology in the
end: of the pyramids, destroyed cities, kingdoms of which only
the names have remained; and, finally, human time in which
grave stands next to cradle and all faces are mortal.

> Against my love shall be, as I am now,
> With Time's injurious hand crush'd and o'erworn;
> When hours have drain'd his blood and fill'd his brow
> With lines and wrinkles . . .
>   (LXIII)

The three Leonardian kinds of time can always be found in Shakespeare. When the earth is covered with blood, human time becomes again the inhuman time of nature. It is then that blind Gloster takes leave of the deranged Lear:

> O ruin'd piece of nature! This great world
> Shall so wear out to nought.   (*King Lear*, IV vi)

The three kinds of time, inter-linked one with another, are continually invoked in the Sonnets. That is why the Sonnets are a great prologue.

>   . . . where, alack,
> Shall Time's best jewel from Time's chest lie hid?
> Or what strong hand can hold his swift foot back?
> Or who his spoil of beauty can forbid?   (LXV)

. . . The Sonnets are a prologue in yet another sense. They are the prologue to Shakespeare's erotic poetry, or at least to the erotic aspects of the comedies of his early period. The real theme of the Sonnets is the choice, or rather the impossibility of choice between the youth and the woman, the fragile boundary between friendship and love, the fascination with all beauty, the universality of desire which cannot be contained in or limited to one sex. The same theme, treated in a variety of moods, from *buffo* to a most serious approach, from ambiguous and spoilt idyll to mockery and derision, will return in *The Two Gentlemen of Verona*, in *Love's Labour's Lost*, in *As You Like It* and in *Twelfth Night*, in the undercurrent of *The Merchant of Venice*, in the loving friendship and brutal rejection of Falstaff by Henry V.

Ambiguity in the Sonnets is at the same time a poetic and an erotic principle. Compared with Shakespeare's Sonnets, the sonnets of Petrarch seem transparent and pure as crystal, but cold, artificial, contrived. Beauty and goodness are permanent values in them, never to be questioned; the conflict is between the body and the mind. In Shakespeare's Sonnets this rigid division into physical and spiritual is blurred. Good intermingles with evil, beauty with ugliness, desire with revulsion, passion with

shame. There are other divisions, too, at once more baroque and
more modern. Passion looks at itself; indecision is the food of
pleasure; insight does not kill passion but inflames it even more.
Eroticism here is exact and precise, sharpened by observation,
aggravated by self-analysis.

> . . . although to-day thou fill
> Thy hungry eyes even till they wink with fulness,
> To-morrow see again, and do not kill
> The spirit of love with a perpetual dulness.
> Let this sad interim like the ocean be
> Which parts the shore, where two contracted new
> Come daily to the banks . . .
>
> (LVI)

The erotic partner here is real and fictitious at the same time; the
eye wages a struggle with the heart, day with night, touch with
sight. The partner is bodily present and yet created by imagination and desire. Eroticism is the pupil of Renaissance
painting, and itself becomes in turn the school of a new
sensibility.

> Since I left you, mine eye is in my mind;
> And that which governs me to go about
> Doth part his function, and is partly blind,
> Seems seeing, but effectually is out;
> For it no form delivers to the heart
> Of bird, of flower, or shape, which it doth latch;
> Of his quick objects hath the mind no part,
> Nor his own vision holds what it doth catch;
> For if it see the rud'st or gentlest sight,
> The most sweet favour or deformed'st creature,
> The mountain or the sea, the day or night,
> The crow or dove, it shapes them to your feature.
>
> (CXIII)

. . . The Sonnets are a dramatic prologue for a third reason.
The Dark Lady will be transformed in turn into Julia of *The Two
Gentlemen of Verona* and into Rosaline of *Love's Labour's Lost*; later
she will serve as a model of the harsh and sensuous Hermia in *A*

Midsummer Night's Dream. We shall find her in Cressida: pure and faithless, affectionate and mocking. Perhaps it is to her that Rosalind in *As You Like It* is indebted for her audacity, and Viola in *Twelfth Night* for her determination in amorous exaltation. Julia, Rosalind and Viola have disguised themselves as boys. Viola has become Cesario, Rosalind has turned into Ganymede. The Dark Lady of the Sonnets has unexpectedly become the fair 'master–mistress'. Her charm is irresistible. She seduces men and women alike: the former as a girl, the latter as a boy. She is an almost perfect androgyny. This is how Viola of *Twelfth Night* describes herself:

> I am all the daughters of my father's house,
> And all the brothers too . . .
>
> (II, iv)

SOURCE: extracts from *Shakespeare our Contemporary* (1964); revised ed., paper back, 1967) pp. 191–3, 196–7, 205–6.

NOTES

1. Leonardo da Vinci's *Notebooks*, trans. E. McCurdy (New York, 1935) p. 136.
2. A detailed list of all the images of time in the Sonnets and in *Troilus and Cressida* was made by Caroline Spurgeon in *Shakespeare's Imagery* (Cambridge, 1935).
3. Leonardo's *Notebooks*, p. 52.

Inga-Stina Ewbank

SHAKESPEARE'S POETRY(1971)

. . . Unlike his fellow-sonneteer Sidney, Shakespeare left no Apology for Poetry; unlike such of his fellow-dramatists as Nashe, Greene, Jonson, Chapman or Webster, he left no comments outside his plays on what he thought good drama and good poetry should be like. From the plays we can learn something of what he thought they should *not* be like. Mocking of 'taffeta phrases, silken terms precise, / Three-piled hyperboles, spruce affectation, / Figures pedantical' plays a large part in *Love's Labour's Lost*, and most of the other love comedies contain references to literary affectations and mannerisms. Not many agree that *Titus Andronicus* is a parody on 'the height of Seneca his style' as practised by the tragic dramatists of the late 1580s and the early 90s, but the verse of the Mousetrap in *Hamlet* certainly is; and the 'very tragical mirth' of the Pyramus and Thisbe interlude in *A Midsummer Night's Dream* takes off the cruder forms of contemporary dramatic and non-dramatic literature – even, some would say, Shakespeare's own *Romeo and Juliet*. But in none of these cases is the literary satire the main point: it is part of and subordinated to a dramatic exploration of the false as against the genuine, fiction as against reality. Deliberately 'bad' Shakespearean poetry is sometimes functional *rather than* parodic. The nurse's mock-Senecan fulminations against the 'woeful, woeful, woeful day' in *Romeo and Juliet*, IV v serve to set Juliet's mock-death here off from her real one in the last scene. Othello's departure from his real self, at the point where he definitely succumbs to Iago's persuasions, is measured by his assumption of the voice of the conventional Revenger:

Arise, black vengeance, from the hollow hell.

> Yield up, O love, thy crown and hearted throne
> To tyrannous hate! Swell, bosom . . .
>
> (*Othello*, III iii 451–3)

If the 'poetic' of the plays is often negatively stated and always embodied in the dramatic whole, the sonnets more clearly show Shakespeare reflecting on his own poetic practice and comparing it with that of others. For example, Shakespeare refuses to 'glance aside / To new-found methods, and to compounds strange' (LXXVI), and he has ambivalent feelings about 'the proud full sail' of the Rival Poet's 'great verse' (LXXXVI). As Joan Grundy has pointed out, Shakespeare and Sidney alone among Elizabethan sonneteers question the aims and methods of the Petrarchan convention which they inherited. But Shakespeare's, unlike Sidney's, questioning is not so much a literary quarrel as part of a larger concern with rendering the real image of the person he is writing of and to and for – the Youth (I – CXXVI) and the Dark Lady (CXXVII – CLII). His poet's prayer is: 'O, let me, true in love, but truly write' (XXI); and to write truly means to show 'that you alone are you' (LXXXIV). Even in the best-known piece of mockery of Petrarchan love-poetry, 'My mistress' eyes are nothing like the sun' (CXXX), the mockery itself is the staircase by which we climb to the real point of the poem, the celebration of the 'rareness' of the Lady:

> And yet, by heaven, I think my love as rare
> As any she belied with false compare.

Explicitly, then, in the sonnets, Shakespeare is striving for a subordination of the style to the subject matter. Ideally, the style *is* the subject:

> O, know, sweet love, I always write of you,
> And you and love are still my argument; (LXXVI)

> In others' works thou dost but mend the style,
> And arts with thy sweet graces graced be;
> But thou art all my art. (LXXVIII)

That this is not merely an echo of Sidney's 'Look in thy heart and write', but is meant as well as said, is shown by the texture and structure of the individual sonnets. Whatever the 'true' facts behind the 1609 volume of *Sonnets* – and this is not the place to enter into the controversy about the identities of Mr W. H., the Fair Youth, the Rival Poet and the Dark Lady – it remains a poetically true record of two different love relationships, with the fluctuations of mind and mood involved in each. In the first 126 sonnets the Youth is re-created, not in static perfection but dramatically pitted against the enemies that threaten: the flatterers without, his own unfaithfulness within and – all around – the very condition of man as he is subjected to inexorable Time. The greater the threat, the keener the imaginative realization of the enemy's attack and the poet's counter-attack:

> Like as the waves make towards the pebbled shore,
> So do our minutes hasten to their end;
> Each changing place with that which goes before,
> In sequent toil all forwards do contend.
> Nativity, once in the main of light,
> Crawls to maturity, wherewith being crown'd,
> Crooked eclipses 'gainst his glory fight,
> And Time that gave doth now his gift confound.
> Time doth transfix the flourish set on youth,
> And delves the parallels in beauty's brow,
> Feeds on the rarities of nature's truth,
> And nothing stands but for his scythe to mow.
>   And yet to times in hope of my verse shall stand,
>   Praising thy worth, despite his cruel hand.
>
> (LX)

J. W. Lever, in a particularly fine analysis of this sonnet, has shown how it 'achieves its own poetic miracle by taking an entire chain of images from the speech of Ovid's Pythagoras [in the *Metamorphoses*] and fusing them at white heat with the themes of the sonnet sequence'. In sonnets like this we have the implicit application of Shakespeare's explicit poetic. But we have it in lesser sonnets, too. Even in the lines which I quoted from Sonnet LXXVIII, the style embodies the meaning. The pretty pattern of sound and sense in 'arts with thy sweet graces graced be' resolves itself into the monosyllabic plainness of 'but thou art all my art', where yet the crucial pun on 'art' shows that the plainness is carefully controlled artifice. It is artifice of a lower imaginative order than that behind the careful structuring of evocative images in Sonnet LX; but in neither poem does the style simply illustrate or decorate a thought. The greatest sonnets, whether to the Youth or to the Lady, *enact* the impact of the beloved on the poet, through their diction, their imagery, their rhythm and their structural pattern – whether it be the rise from despondency to jubilation through 'thy sweet love rememb'red' in Sonnet XXIX, or the downward movement to the realization that 'Time will come and take my love away' of sonnet LXIV, or the tug-of-war impulses of 'Th' expense of spirit in a waste of shame' in Sonnet CXXIX.

Already we have seen that when Shakespeare sets about applying his sonnet poetic – the fusion of subject and style, matter and manner – this involves qualities which are dramatic as well as poetic. It involves the arrangement of words and images into a pattern which is formal, not merely in the external sense that it consists of three quatrains and a clinching couplet, but in the sense that it imitates an action. And it involves the rendering of the general through the particular, so that the beloved's image, 'most rich in youth', is part of the consciousness that 'every thing that grows / Holds in perfection but a little moment' (xv). Both these are essential, and common, to all great dramatists. But there is also another, perhaps peculiarly Shakespearean, quality involved. Read as a whole, the *Sonnets* show an apparently paradoxical combination of a tremendous interest in words and belief in their power with a kind of humbleness about the possibilities of language.

The very desire to show 'that you alone are you' makes the poet conscious of the inadequacy of poetry:

> Who will believe my verse in time to come, . . .
> If I could write the beauty of your eyes

And in fresh numbers number all your graces,
The age to come would say 'This poet lies;
Such heavenly touches ne'er touch'd earthly faces.'
So should my papers, yellowed with their age,
Be scorn'd, like old men of less truth than tongue.

(xvii)

The truth–tongue opposition in that last line reminds us of a
key *motif* in *Richard II*. Richard D. Altick, in an important study
of 'symphonic imagery' in this play, shows how

that words are mere conventional sounds molded by the tongue, and
reality is something else again, is constantly on the minds of all the
characters.

Most critics agree that *Richard II* is a milestone in Shakespeare's
poetic–dramatic development, and that the play – like its
poet-hero – is uniquely self-conscious about the power *and*
limitations of language. But the sonnets' questioning of language
reverberates right through to the end of Shakespeare's career. In
Sonnet xxiii, the intensity of the poet's emotion outruns words
altogether:

O, let my looks be then the eloquence
And dumb presagers of my speaking breast;
Who plead for love, and look for recompense,
More than that tongue that more hath more express'd.
O learn to read what silent love hath writ!
To hear with eyes belongs to love's fine wit.

Shakespeare is here talking about what in *The Winter's Tale* he
puts into a stage-image, when he makes the reunion of Leontes
and Hermione wordless. In that scene he shows his awareness, as
a dramatist, of realities which language cannot get at, not even
the subtle tool of his own poetry.

Part of Shakespeare's poetic belief is that what *is* cannot always
be said. . . .

. . . It would be very wrong to give the impression that
Shakespeare, like some modern dramatists, was preoccupied

with the non-meaning of language and the impossibility of communication. The plays themselves, through to Prospero's eloquent farewell to his art, are evidence enough to the contrary. Through the sonnets there surges a powerful belief in his own verse, gathered into explicit assertion in the group that deals with the immortalizing of the Friend by his poetry – supremely in Sonnet LV:

> Not marble nor the gilded monuments
> Of princes shall outlive this pow'rful rhyme;
> But you shall shine more bright in these contents
> Than unswept stone, besmear'd with sluttish time.

In this sonnet he makes new a commonplace conceit which Renaissance poets took over from Ovid (thus proving his point by the very writing of the poem). In other sonnets, such as 'Let me not to the marriage of true minds/Admit impediments' (CXVI), it is by the perfect handling of some of the simplest words in the language that he makes his assertion of belief both in his subject and in his poetry. The reason why it is important to stress Shakespeare's sense (to us perhaps unwarranted) of the limitations of his poetry is that it is part of the poetic, in the deepest sense, of the sonnets and of the plays. The poetry not the poet matters, and the poetry matters as the true image of its subject. The reason why the sonnets are the greatest love poems in the language is also the reason why Shakespeare is the greatest poetic dramatist. We could call it selflessness – and critics have often drawn attention to the lack of self-assertion in Shakespeare's sonnets, compared to those of his contemporaries. We could borrow Keats's phrase and call it 'negative capability'. In either case we are talking of the man whose 'nature is subdu'd / To what it works in, like the dyer's hand' (Sonnet CXI). . . .

SOURCE: extracts from 'Shakespeare's Poetry', in *A New Companion to Shakespeare Studies*, ed. Muir and Schoenbaum (1971) pp. 101–4, 105–6.

C. F. Williamson

THEMES AND PATTERNS IN SHAKESPEARE'S SONNETS (1976)

The traditional approach to the structure of Shakespeare's sonnets as a total sequence, and more particularly to the relationship between sonnets I–CXXVI and CXXVII–CLIV, has been to look for a pattern of historical events in which the Poet,[1] the Young Man and the Dark Lady were involved. Shakespeare, however, explicitly states that the essence of the love he is celebrating is its independence of the world of happenings and so of change:

> . . . it was builded far from accident,
> It suffers not in smiling pomp, nor falls
> Under the blow of thralled discontent . . .
> But all alone stands hugely politic,
> That it nor grows with heat, nor drowns with showers.
>
> (CXXIV)[2]

This is not to deny the existence of a physical reality, a physical context, but to affirm that the value of the relationship lay elsewhere. Is it possible then to discover some other structural principle in the poems, an organization thematic rather than biographical?

In a reading – or, better still, repeated readings – of the sonnets, the dominant impression, although one certainly has a sense of events and situations somewhere in the background, is surely of an expanding awareness of the nature of love. Here the printed order of individual sonnets is not of crucial importance. It is possible, even probable, that Shakespeare's understanding of the nature of love did not move steadily forward; what was seen clearly on one occasion may have been clouded on another, certainty may have given way to doubt, and doubt again to certainty. But for the reader understanding is cumulative in richness and in depth, growing to a total awareness rather than conveying a linear sense of a series of events. Familiarity with the poems also brings to light a number of parallels between the two main groups of sonnets. Some of these parallels are on the level of convention or indeed of mere commonplace. In sonnets XLVI and XLVII the Poet debates the respective claims on the Young Man of his eyes and heart: in sonnets CXXXI and CXXXII he distinguishes between the tyrannical attitude of his mistress's heart and the compassionate appearance of her dark eyes, which seem to mourn his wretchedness. He praises the Young Man in sonnets LXVII and LXVIII because in an age of 'false painting' he alone makes 'no summer of another's green', while in sonnet CXXVII the Dark Lady is shown to be fair although swarthy because at least her appearance owes nothing to others in an age given to 'Fairing the foul with art's false borrowed face': and in all three poems the Poet looks for his ideal to a previous age when beauty had no need to have recourse to art. Sonnets VIII and CXXVIII both take music as their starting point, but Shakespeare extends this conventional idea to make the persons addressed epitomise music. The opening of sonnet VIII, 'Music to hear . . .', is usually understood as an ellipsis for 'Thou whom to hear is music' or 'Thou who art music to hear'; in CXXVIII the Dark Lady is addressed directly as 'thou, my music'. The effect of the trope in the two poems is, however, almost diametrically opposite. In VIII the musical opening leads on to ideas of concord, unity and order, realised in the family relationships of husband, wife, and child; whereas in CXXVIII the music provokes, though admittedly on a fairly playful level, erotic feelings which were widely assumed in Shakespeare's day to be subversive of order and concord.

In sonnet XXI the Poet rejects conventional comparisons to express the beauty of the Young Man –

> . . . then believe me, my love is as fair,
> As any mother's child, though not so bright
> As those gold candles fixed in heaven's air:

and in sonnet CXXX he admits that his mistress falls short of the stock objects of poetical comparison, and yet ends by affirming her beauty in his own eyes:

> I grant I never saw a goddess go,
> My mistress when she walks treads on the ground.
> And yet by heaven I think my love as rare,
> As any she belied with false compare.

Other parallels arise inevitably from the triangular relationship between the Poet, the Friend and the Dark Lady. Sonnet XL, 'Take all my loves, my love, yea take them all', in which he surrenders his mistress to the Young Man, chimes with CXXXIV, 'So now I have confessed that he is thine . . .'; and in XLII and CXXXIX the Poet employs similar expressions in trying to accept the situation. In sonnets XXXV, CXLIX and CLII he confesses to having surrendered his own integrity in defending the truth and constancy of his Friend and his Mistress:

> All men make faults, and even I in this,
> Authorizing thy trespass with compare,
> My self corrupting salving thy amiss . . .
> Thy adverse party is thy advocate
>
> (XXXV)

> . . . I against my self with thee partake
>
> (CXLIX)

> . . . I have sworn deep oaths of thy deep kindness;
> Oaths of thy love, thy truth, thy constancy . . .
> For I have sworn thee fair: more perjured I,
> To swear against the truth so foul a lie.
>
> (CLII)

Other likenesses emphasize the difference between the relationship with the Young Man and that with the Mistress. The quality of self-abasement that has been singled out as the distinctive feature of Shakespeare's love for the Friend by such critics as C. S. Lewis and J. W. Lever[3] is powerfully expressed in sonnet LVII:

> Being your slave what should I do but tend,
> Upon the hours, and times of your desire?

The apparently innocent word 'desire' becomes less so when it emerges that the Poet suspects that he is being kept waiting while the Young Man is making love to the Dark Lady, and this meaning gives an ironic point to a parallel in sonnet CLI, where the Poet admits his physical enslavement to the Mistress:

> . . . flesh stays no farther reason,
> But rising at thy name doth point out thee,
> As his triumphant prize, proud of this pride,
> He is contented thy poor drudge to be,
> To stand in thy affairs, fall at thy side.

The last two lines read like a travesty of 'Being thy slave', and indeed their *doubles entendres* strongly underline the contrast between the selflessness of one relationship and the degradation of the other. Similarly, sonnet CXVI, which could be seen as attempting a formal 'Definition of Love', can be set alongside CXXIX, 'Th' expense of spirit in a waste of shame', which performs the same service for lust. Furthermore, the desire for death expressed in sonnet LXVI, 'Tired with all these for restful death I cry', has a parallel in sonnet CXLVI, 'Poor soul the centre of my sinful earth', with the important difference that whereas the situation in sonnet LXVI is mitigated by the Poet's love for the Young Man, in sonnet CXLVI the despair of earthly things is total.

In fact, nearly half of the poems in the Dark Lady group (I am ignoring CLIII and CLIV which do not seem an integral part of the sequence) have clear parallels in those addressed to the Friend, and more could probably be found. Although some of these correspondences spring inevitably from the historical facts of the relationship between the Poet, the Friend and the Mistress, they seem more concerned with and certainly throw more light on the quality of the experience or, rather, the two contrasting experiences involved.

Unquestionably Shakespeare was acutely conscious of and at times deeply disturbed by the dual nature of human love, at once physical and spiritual. This unease is apparent in *Venus and Adonis*, where the physical voracity of the goddess is described in terms which may well reflect and are certainly calculated to provoke distaste if not revulsion (cf. lines 55–8, 547–58). On the other hand, there is in the comedies a clear recognition of the need to accommodate the two elements – it is in marriage implied, for example, by the bawdy plays on *rings* in the fifth act of *The Merchant of Venice*. But an alternative to reconciliation was segregation, and a number of writers of the time argued that love between members of the same sex could achieve a disinterested purity impossible in heterosexual relationships. Sir William Cornwallis made the point well in his essay 'Of Love'[4]: '. . . that which comes nearest to loue is this, man with man agreeing in sexe: I cannot thinke it is so betweene man and woman, for it giues opportunity to lust, which the purenesse of Loue will not endure'. A more explicitly evaluative distinction is made in Lyly's *Endymion*: 'The loue of men to women is a thing common and of course: the friendshippe of man to man infinite and immortall' (III iv).[5] A similar evaluation is found in Spenser:

> For naturall affection soone doth cesse,
> And quenched is with Cupids greater flame:
> But faithfull friendship doth them both suppresse
>
> (*Faerie Queene*, IV, 9, 2)

Spenser elaborates this distinction in the tenth canto of Book IV where in the Temple of Venus examples of male friendship – Hercules and Hylas, David and Jonathan, and others – are singled out for special honour:

> All these and all that euer had bene tyde
> In bands of friendship, there did liue for euer,
> Whose liues although decay'd, yet loues decayed neuer.
>
> (IV, 10, 27)

Such attitudes justify seeing the basic division of the sonnets into one group addressed to the Young Man and another addressed to the Dark Lady (a division which most critics consider acceptable if not authorial) as representing a hiving off of physical sexuality into the relationship with the Dark Lady which relieves that with the Young Man of any taint of physical impurity. After all, if narrative considerations were uppermost, the end would have been better served by integrating the Mistress sonnets into the Young Man group, but there seems no evidence that the sonnets were ever so intercalated. The division, therefore, suggests that – taking the sonnets as a whole – what matters is a thematic rather than a narrative structure.

Seen in this light, the placing of the notorious sonnet XX becomes strategic. In sonnets I – XVII the Poet has addressed the Young Man less from the personal point of view than as a spokesman for all human beings who regard beauty as something too precious to be lost:

> From fairest creatures we desire increase,
> That thereby beauty's rose might never die
>
> (I)

Sonnets XV to XVII effect a transition. In XV poetry is put forward as an alternative to 'breed' as a means of achieving immortality; but in sonnets XVI and XVII it is admitted to be an inadequate alternative. Sonnet XVIII, however, sounds a new note of confidence:

> So long as men can breathe or eyes can see,
> So long lives this, and this gives life to thee.

And in XIX the Poet boldly puts himself forward as the Young Man's lover and champion; we hear no more of marriage:

> Yet do thy worst old Time: despite thy wrong,
> My love shall in my verse ever live young.

The Poet's personal interest in the Young Man thus established, it is important, if the separation between the sonnets concerned with a non-physical relationship with the Young Man and those concerned with a physical passion for the Dark Lady is at all authoritative and not merely accidental, that Shakespeare should make clear at the outset the true nature of this affection. This sonnet xx does with an explicitness that has lured critics into a variety of interpretative extravagances, largely because of their preoccupation with the poems as a record of actual events. But such explicitness is perfectly appropriate if it is meant to serve a thematic rather than a narrative organization.

A preoccupation in sonnets I–CXXVI, as in much of Shakespeare's work, is the relation between appearance and reality. At first sight the Young Man's beauty appears to be matched by his truth:

> But from thine eyes my knowledge I derive,
> And constant stars in them I read such art
> As truth and beauty shall together thrive
> If from thy self, to store thou wouldst convert:
>   Or else of thee this I prognosticate,
>   Thy end is truth's and beauty's doom and date.
>
> (XIV)

> O how much more doth beauty beauteous seem,
> By that sweet ornament which truth doth give . . .
>   And so of you, beauteous and lovely youth,
>   When that shall vade, by verse distills your truth,
>
> (LIV)

In the Young Man appearance and reality correspond as they always did in the pre-lapsarian state, and the Poet is prompted to see him as representing to a degenerate age the qualities of a Golden Age before the Fall. This, I think, is implied in sonnet XIV in the idea that the Young Man is the sole example of the perfect union of truth and beauty. Elsewhere Shakespeare is more explicit. In sonnet LXVII the Young Man is the exemplar of true beauty in a time of 'false painting', whom Nature

> stores, to show what wealth she had,
> In days long since, before these last so bad.

In sonnet LXVIII the religious note is sounded in the resonance of the word 'holy':

> In him those holy antique hours are seen,
> Without all ornament, it self and true,
> Making no summer of another's green,
> Robbing no old to dress his beauty new,
> And him as for a map doth Nature store,
> To show false Art what beauty was of yore.

Not only did appearance and reality correspond in the unfallen state but objects were valued instinctively at their true worth; love therefore always had a rational basis. So for the Poet love is the appropriate reaction to the Young Man's beauty. As the relationship progresses, however, and the Poet's understanding of the Young Man deepens, the correspondence of truth and beauty crumbles; the Young Man proves lascivious and treacherous. The Poet tries desperately to maintain a rationality in the relationship, arguing on the one hand that in loving the poet's mistress the Young Man is in effect loving the poet himself (sonnets XL, XLII); and, on the other hand, that the Young Man is too beautiful not to attract love, and too kind to refuse it (sonnet XLI):

> Take all my loves, my love, yea take them all,
> What hast thou then more than thou hadst before?
> No love, my love, that thou mayst true love call,
> All mine was thine, before thou hadst this more:
> Then if for my love, thou my love receivest,
> I cannot blame thee, for my love thou usest
>
> (XL)

> Loving offenders thus I will excuse ye,
> Thou dost love her, because thou know'st I love her,
> And for my sake even so doth she abuse me,

Suff'ring my friend for my sake to approve her . . .
But here's the joy, my friend and I are one,
Sweet flattery, then she loves but me alone.

(XLII)

Gentle thou art, and therefore to be won,
Beauteous thou art, therefore to be assailed.

(XLI)

'Sweet flattery' indeed! It is clear that the Poet does not convince himself. The Young Man has become a prey to the internal corruption of fallen humanity.

The external threat that resulted from the Fall was, of course, Time, and throughout the sonnets this occupies much of Shakespeare's attention. Towards the end of the Young Man group (and the nature of the argument demands that, whatever the printed order, these poems must come late) he moves towards a solution in terms of the maturation of experience:

Alas why fearing of time's tyranny,
Might I not then say 'Now I love you best,'
When I was certain o'er incertainty,
Crowning the present, doubting of the rest?
  Love is a babe, then might I not say so
  To give full growth to that which still doth grow.

(CXV)

O benefit of ill, now I find true
That better is, by evil still made better.
And ruined love when it is built anew
Grows fairer than at first, more strong, far greater.

(CXIX)

Many critics have noticed, particularly in what I take to be the later poems, the way in which the term 'love' is used sometimes of the Young Man, sometimes of the Poet's feelings, sometimes ambiguously, the two meanings appearing now to merge, now to separate. In so far as what the Poet is celebrating ceases to be the Young Man (who is 'mortal, guilty', and therefore subject to change) and becomes his own love, which nevertheless seems in, for example, sonnet CXXIV, almost to detach itself from the Poet and stand as an independent entity, Time has lost its ascendancy. The implication of the shift becomes clear in sonnet CXVI. Perfect mutuality – 'The marriage of true minds' – gives way to a situation where one party to the relationship proves fickle, just as the Poet's belief in the truth of the Friend has been replaced by the recognition of his treachery. The Poet had discovered that his Love / Friend was not true; the realisation that his Love / emotion remained true nevertheless leads to the recognition that true love is superior to time and change, and hence to the positive affirmation 'O no, it is an ever-fixed mark'. Time's effect on the Friend's truth (his 'alteration') and its threat to his beauty ('rosy lips and cheeks') have become irrelevant.

This is something for which the Poet claims no credit, nor indeed has he himself any personal immunity to Time's power. The sonnets show him fully aware that he is subject to ageing (sonnets XXII, XXXII, LXII, LXIII, LXXI, LXXIII, LXXIV), that he has his faults and is liable to change (sonnets XXXVI, LXXXVIII, CIX, CX, CXVII). Indeed sonnet CXV makes it clear that in the early stages of the relationship the Poet's fear had been lest *his own* love for his Friend should decline:

> Alas why fearing of time's tyranny,
> Might I not then say 'Now I love you best' . . .

In the event the Poet's constancy is something discovered, not worked for; given, not achieved. It is the recognition that neither change in the Friend nor his own mistreadings can destroy his love that justifies the superb confidence of sonnet CXXIII. Time has been defeated because human imperfection and mortality have become matters of indifference. The effects of the Fall have been vanquished by true love.

But a problem remains: why should a love for the impure and the untrue become transcendent in a way that a love for the embodiment of beauty and truth did not?

The Renaissance appears to have found little difficulty in accepting the idea of a multi-natured God, a concept eloquently expressed by Donne in his *Devotions upon Emergent Occasions*, speaking particularly of the interpretation of the Scriptures but in a way that cannot but extend to the nature of God himself:

My *God*, my *God*, Thou art a *direct God*, may I not say a *literall God*, a *God* that wouldest bee understood *literally*, and according to the *plaine* sense of all that thou saiest? But thou art also (*Lord*, I intend it to thy *glory*, and let no *prophane misinterpreter* abuse it to thy *diminution*), thou art a *figurative*, a *metaphoricall God too*: a *God* in whose words there is such a height of *figures*, such *voyages*, such *peregrinations* to fetch remote and precious *metaphors*, such *extensions*, such *spreadings*, such *Curtaines* of *Allegories*, such *third Heavens*, of *Hyperboles*, *so harmonious eloqutions*, so *retired* and so *reserved expressions*, so *commanding perswasions*, so *perswading commandements*, such *sinewes* even in thy *milke* and such *things* in thy *words*, as all *prophane Authors*, seeme of the seed of the *Serpent*, that *creepes*, thou art the *Dove*, that flies.[6]

Donne's 'direct God' was the God who expressed his rational, orderly nature in the perfect economy of the created universe but who, when that was disrupted by the Fall, could in his other nature redeem the situation by an act of defying human rationality in the Incarnation, the paradox of God made Man, Immortal mortal, the Omnipotent Ruler incarnate as the helpless child in the manger ('The *Word*, and not able to speak a word? How evill agreeth this,' said Andrewes),[7] the supreme illogicality of God manifesting his love more richly for men who had shown themselves unworthy of it than for unfallen man, and in doing so revealing most fully the essential divinity of His nature. As Hooker presents it, the rule of Justice, under which Man would have received immortality as the due reward for obedience, was superseded by the dominion of Grace, which offers redemption for disobedience.[8]

If, as the Scriptures taught and the Renaissance believed, Man is created in the image of God, he should be capable of reaching, however rarely, something approaching this quality of love. Probably the supreme literary example is Cordelia who, when Lear invokes the rule of justice, saying she has good cause to hate him, replies in words that are at once manifestly false and yet triumphantly true 'No cause, no cause' (IV vii). And this I believe is the quality of love that the Poet, to his own awe and wonderment, discovers in the course of time that he felt for the Young Man. Ironically, Cordelia's words echo the end of Sonnet XLIX where the Poet excuses the Young Man in advance for ceasing to love him on the grounds of his own unworthiness:

> To leave poor me, thou hast the strength of laws,
> Since why to love, I can allege no cause.

In the event, of course, it is the behaviour of the Young Man, not of the poet, that threatens to destroy the relationship.

In Sonnet XLII, it is apparent that the Poet's deepest concern at learning of the Young Man's liaison with the Dark Lady springs from the likelihood that he will lose his Friend rather than his Mistress. The intensity of this fear is accounted for by the nature of his love. In many of the plays we are presented with a love that sees in its object a kind of guarantee of the goodness and meaning of life. The degree of commitment involved in such a love brings with it correspondingly great risks, terribly manifested in Othello's 'And when I love thee not / Chaos is come again'. Sonnets XXIX, XXX and LXVI show clearly that the Poet's love for the Young Man was of this nature. Without it, life appeared not worth living, and therefore the prospect of the collapse of the relationship was intolerably painful. But of course the relationship did not collapse. The Poet went on loving (whether the Young Man did too is not clear and indeed seems not important) and found, like Cordelia, that in love assessments of guilt and desert are beside the point. Such a love was all the more precious because, like that of the Phoenix and the Turtle in Shakespeare's poem of that name, it partook, in its very irrationality, of God's love for fallen man.

But what meanwhile of the Dark Lady? Although there is more confusion in sonnets CXXVII–CLIV than in the earlier group, there seems to be a thematic logic in proceeding from the sonnets which deal mainly with external appearance to those which probe further into the inner nature. Sonnets CXXVII and CXXX are

primarily concerned with what the Lady looks like. In sonnet
cxxvii Shakespeare specifically refers to the two themes which
have been discussed in relation to the Young Man, appearance
and reality and the 'old age', a phrase often suggestive of a
Golden Age of Innocence. The Poet argues that although by the
standards of 'the old age' the lady's swarthy appearance cannot
be counted beautiful (and of course blackness has age-old
associations with evil) the fact that, unlike most women, her
appearance owes nothing to art gives her a beauty of integrity,
while her blackness can be justified as mourning for the death of
true beauty:

> In the old age black was not counted fair,
> Or if it were it bore not beauty's name:
> But now is black beauty's successive heir,
> And beauty slandered with a bastard shame . . .
> Therefore my mistress' eyes are raven black,
> Her eyes so suited, and they mourners seem,
> At such who not born fair no beauty lack . . .

Thus, the Poet argues, in a fallen world the Dark Lady has
succeeded in reversing the traditional association of black with
falseness and fairness with truth; in spite of appearances, black is
beautiful because it is true. In sonnet cxxx, however, the Poet
insists that although his lady is not physically beautiful (her
breasts are 'dun', her breath 'reeks'), he implies, with surely
deliberate understatement, that his love for her is at least as
strong as that of the average lover.

In sonnets cxxxi and cxxxii the Poet deplores the lady's
cruelty, and draws a distinction between her tyrannical heart
(her inner nature) and her compassionate eyes (external appearance) whose blackness seems to mourn the Poet's unhappiness. Her appearance is fair although she is black, but her
conduct is black although she is fair:

> In nothing art thou black save in thy deeds.   (cxxxi)

If, however, the attitude of her heart could be brought into harmony with the aspect of her eyes, the Poet would be prepared to celebrate this conformity of inner reality to external appearance as the only true beauty:

> O let it then as well beseem thy heart
> To mourn for me since mourning doth thee grace,
> And suit thy pity like in every part.
> Then will I swear beauty herself is black,
> And all they foul that thy complexion lack.   (cxxxii)

As the character of the Dark Lady becomes more fully open to him, however, the conceit that her black eyes mourn his unhappiness becomes unserviceable. Not only has the Poet known all along that his Mistress was in fact not beautiful, but he has also had strong suspicions that her morals were equally shady. Whereas he had been anxious to sustain as long as possible a belief in the correspondence in the Young Man between beauty and Truth, in the case of the Dark Lady his aim has been to preserve the illusion that she possessed good qualities in spite of her appearance. Only thus could he avoid the conclusion that the attraction he felt for her was essentially irrational – hence the continued arguments that she is really beautiful because her appearance is 'true' in that it owes nothing to cosmetics, or because her blackness mourns for the demise of true beauty or for his own unhappiness. In sonnet cxlviii he excuses his self-delusion on the grounds that tears of sorrow have clouded his vision, but the hollowness of the argument is exposed in the final couplet, where he shows himself fully aware of the faults he has been pretending he could not see:

> O cunning love, with tears thou keep'st me blind,
> Lest eyes well-seeing thy foul faults should find.

Characteristically, however, he does not rest in excuses, and in sonnet cxlvii frankly confesses the irrationality of his attitude, recognising the hopelessness of trying to reconcile the Dark Lady's appearance with the possession of good qualities; and in

sonnet CLII he bitterly reproaches himself for his own betrayal of
the truth:

> My thoughts and my discourse as mad men's are,
> At random from the truth vainly expressed.
>   For I have sworn thee fair, and thought thee bright,
>   Who art as black as hell, as dark as night.   (CXLVII)
>
> For I have sworn deep oaths of thy deep kindness:
> Oaths of thy love, thy truth, thy constancy,
> And to enlighten thee gave eyes to blindness,
> Or made them swear against the thing they see.
>   For I have sworn thee fair: more perjured I,
>   To swear against the truth so foul a lie.   (CLII)

What forces him to face up to the unpleasant truth? Sonnet
CXXXVII suggests that he has been aware from the beginning of
the Dark Lady's promiscuity, but has been prepared to ignore it:

> Why should my heart think that a several plot,
> Which my heart knows the wide world's common place?

Almost certainly the turning point came with the knowledge not
just that the Dark Lady was playing him false, but that she was
playing him false with the Young Man. This was a situation he
could not turn his back on, and which forced him to a reappraisal
of his relations with the Dark Lady just as we have seen it forced
him to a reappraisal of his attitude to the Young Man. Parallel
strategies are employed to come to terms with the
situation – 'Loving offenders thus I will excuse ye' (XLII), 'Let
me excuse thee, ah my love well knows . . .' (CXXXIX). An
alternative solution to such specious arguments was to evade the
problem by a conspiracy of a silence, a kind of play-acting which
refused to recognise the two great enemies of the earlier group,
Time and falsehood:

> Thus vainly thinking that she thinks me young,
> Although she knows my days are past the best,

Simply I credit her false-speaking tongue,
On both sides thus is simple truth suppressed:

(CXXXVIII)

Or again an attempt could be made to accept the situation
through a wryly humorous recognition of the infidelity and
degradation the relationship involved:

> . . . flesh stays no farther reason,
> But rising at thy name doth point out thee,
> As his triumphant prize, proud of this pride,
> He is contented thy poor drudge to be,
> To stand in thy affairs, fall by thy side.   (CLI)

But all this will not do. The intensity of self disgust is too powerful
to be denied. The recognition cannot finally be avoided that
appearance and reality have in the event coincided (but not at all
as desiderated in sonnet CXXXII): the lady is black not only in her
looks but in her irredeemably fallen nature.

The movement in the first group of sonnets, from a celebration
of the union of truth and beauty (to which love is the rational
reaction) to a recognition of a widening gap between them
(which affords an opportunity for love to transcend human
rationality) has thus been reversed. An appearance which the
Poet had tried to persuade himself belied personality has proved
in the event to express it all too accurately. But the 'love' that has
resulted, although it too is irrational (the rational reaction to
what is ugly and treacherous is loathing), is not transcendent.
That he loved the Friend in spite of his imperfection pointed
toward the Redemption; that he loved the Dark Lady in spite of
himself and of her imperfections confirmed the Fall. The pain in
the love for the Friend was lest it should be lost; the anguish in the
desire for the Mistress was because it could not be escaped.
Shakespeare has grasped with devastating honesty the implications of abandoning that reason which in a fallen world is the
most reliable substitute for unfallen man's intuitive sense of what
is fitting. Two paths lie open: one leads to an experience
repeating in little God's supreme redemptive love; the other,

sonnet CXLIV suggests, leads to damnation. In this poem the references to the good and bad angels and to hell are not merely a combination of hyperbole and veiled obscenity. Indeed the sonnet begins not as a poem about two *people*, but about two *loves*, where the emphasis seems to be on the emotions, not the objects of affection. The two loves are 'like two spirits', which in turn become embodied in two actual persons:

> Two loves I have of comfort and despair,
> Which like two spirits do suggest me still,
> The better angel is a man right fair:
> The worser spirit a woman coloured ill.
> To win me soon to hell my female evil,
> Tempeth my better angel from my side,
> And would corrupt my saint to be a devil,
> Wooing his purity with her false pride.   (CXLIV)

The 'man right fair' and the 'woman coloured ill' become almost morality or allegorical figures, representing on the one hand the love of sonnet CXVI, the point of stability and source of reassurance in a world of flux, and, on the other, the degradation which finds its starkest expression in sonnet CXXIX, 'Th' expense of spirit in a waste of shame', which, significantly, ends a reference to 'the heaven that leads men to this hell'.

The vision that therefore emerges from the two groups of sonnets is of Man slung in the void between damnation and the Glory of God, capable of experiencing a love which partakes of the divine nature, but also of a degrading lust such as that in the grips of which Milton's Satan begot Death on Sin; capable in a way of cooperating in the continuing act of the redemption, capable too of re-enacting the Fall in which the lower faculties overthrew the higher; and, perhaps the crowning irony, capable of experiencing both at the same time and within the same triangular relationship. To such a dilemma there can be no human solution, and, after the power and intensity of such a vision, the impulse towards withdrawal expressed in sonnet CXLVI, 'Poor soul the centre of my sinful earth', seems inevitable.

SOURCE: *Essays in Criticism*, XXVI 3 (July 1976) 191–207.

NOTES

1. Since Shakespeare's Sonnets may be no more autobiographical than, say, Donne's *Songs and Sonnets*, it seems advisable to refer to 'the Poet' in discussing what the poems express. For the manner of expression Shakespeare must of course be responsible.

2. All references to the Sonnets are to the New Cambridge edition, ed. J. Dover Wilson (Cambridge, 1966).

3. *English Literature in the Sixteenth Century Excluding Drama* (Oxford, 1954) pp. 303–5; *The Elizabethan Love Sonnet* (London, 1956) pp. 185–6.

4. *Essayes* (first ed. 1600; quotation from 1632 ed.) D1 v.

5. *Complete Works*, ed. R. W. Bond (Oxford, 1902) vol. iii, p. 50.

6. *Devotions upon Emergent Occasions*, ed. John Sparrow (Cambridge, 1926) p. 113 (Devotion 19, Expostulation).

7. *XCVI Sermons* (1629) p. 48 (Christmas Day, 1611).

8. *Laws of Ecclesiastical Polity*, Everyman ed. (London, 1965) vol. i, pp. 206–8.

SELECT BIBLIOGRAPHY

EDITIONS

T. G. Tucker (Cambridge, 1924).
Hyder E. Rollins, *A New Variorum*, 2 vols (Philadelphia, 1944).
Martin Seymour-Smith (London, 1963).
John Dover Wilson (Cambridge, 1966).

CRITICISM

W. H. Auden, Introduction to W. Burto (ed.), *The Sonnets* (Signet edition, London and New York, 1964).
John Berryman, 'Shakespeare at Thirty', *Hudson Review*, VI (1953), included in *The Freedom of the Poet* (London and New York, 1976).
Samuel Butler, Introduction to *Shakespeare's Sonnets Reconsidered and in part Rearranged* (London, 1899 and 1927) (includes the 1609 text).
Sir Edmund Chambers, *William Shakespeare: a Study of Facts and Problems*, 2 vols (Oxford, 1930); *Shakespearian Gleanings* (Oxford, 1944).
Patrick Crutwell, 'A Reading of the Sonnets', *Hudson Review*, V (1952/3); *The Shakespearian Moment* (London, 1953).
William Empson, *Seven Types of Ambiguity* (Harmondsworth, 1961); *Some Versions of Pastoral* (Harmondsworth, 1966): this volume contains an important essay on Sonnet XCIV – 'They That Have Power' – omitted here for reasons of space. The essay is also included in the Signet edition of *The Sonnets*.
Leslie Hotson, *Shakespeare's Sonnets Dated* (London, 1949) (and a reply by F. W. Bateson, 'Elementary My Dear Hotson! A Caveat for Literary Detectives', *Essays in Criticism*, I, 1951).
Edward Hubler, *The Sense of Shakespeare's Sonnets* (Princeton, 1952).
G. Wilson Knight, *The Mutual Flame: An Interpretation of Shakespeare's Sonnets* (London, 1961).
J. B. Leishman, *Themes and Variations in Shakespeare's Sonnets* (London, 1961).
J. W. Lever, *The Elizabethan Love Sonnet* (London, 1956).
M. M. Mahood, *Shakespeare's Wordplay* (London, 1957).

Philip Martin, *Shakespeare's Sonnets: Self, Love and Art* (Cambridge, 1972).

Allardyce Nicoll (ed.), *Shakespeare Survey*, No. 15, *The Poems and Music* (Cambridge, 1962).

John Crowe Ransom, 'Shakespeare at Sonnets', *Southern Review*, III (1937), included in *The World's Body* (London and New York, 1938).

The Riddle of Shakespeare's Sonnets: a text of the Sonnets with essays by Edward Hubler, Northrop Frye, Leslie A. Fielder, Stephen Spender, R. P. Blackmur, and the full text of Oscar Wilde's *The Portrait of Mr W. H.* (London, 1962).

ADDENDUM 1983

Gerald Hammond, *The Reader and Shakespeare's Young Man Sonnets* (Basingstoke and London, 1980).

Robert Giroux, *The Book Known as Q* (London, 1982).

S. C. Campbell, *Only Begotten Sonnets* (London, 1978).

NOTES ON CONTRIBUTORS

WILLIAM EMPSON: Professor of English Literature at Peking National University, 1947–52, at Sheffield University, 1953–71, and since then Emeritus Professor. His many published works include *Seven Types of Ambiguity* (1930), *Some Versions of Pastoral* (1935), *Milton's God* (1961) and *Collected Poems* (1961).

INGA-STINA EWBANK: Professor of English at Bedford College, University of London. She is a translator of Ibsen's plays into English and in 1976 delivered her inaugural lectures at Bedford College on *Shakespeare, Ibsen and the Unspeakable*. Among her other works is a study of the Brontë sisters, *Their Proper Sphere* (1966).

ROBERT GRAVES: Professor of English Literature at Cairo University in 1926, and Professor of Poetry at Oxford in 1961. He now lives in Mallorca. His numerous works include *Goodbye to All That* (1929), *I, Claudius* (1934), *The Common Asphodel: Collected Essays on Poetry, 1922–1949* and *Collected Poems, 1965–8*.

JOAN GRUNDY: Reader in English Literature at Royal Holloway College, University of London. Her most important published work is *The Spenserian Poets: a Study in Elizabethan and Jacobean Poetry* (1969).

G. K. HUNTER: currently Professor of English at Yale University and Honorary Professor at the University of Warwick. His several books of editorial scholarship include a volume on Shakespeare's *Henry IV Parts I and II* in the Casebook series and an important work on Lyly, *John Lyly: the Humanist as Courtier* (1962).

G. WILSON KNIGHT: since 1962, Emeritus Professor of English at the University of Leeds. His many publications include *The Wheel of Fire* (1930), *The Shakespearean Tempest* (1932), *The Starlit Dome* (1941), *The Crown of Life* (1948) and *The Mutual Flame* (1955).

L. C. KNIGHTS: formerly Professor of English at Sheffield and Bristol Universities, he was from 1965 to 1973 King Edward VII Professor at the University of Cambridge and is now Emeritus Professor. His many important works include *Drama and Society in the Age of Jonson* (1937), *Some Shakespearean Themes* (1959) and *An Approach to Hamlet* (1960).

JAN KOTT: born in Warsaw, he settled in the U.S.A. in 1966 and has been visiting Professor at Yale, 1966 / 7 and 1968 / 9; at San Francisco State College, 1967, and at Berkeley, 1967 / 8. Since 1969 he has been Professor of Comparative Drama at the State University of New York at Stony Brook. His two most important works of dramatic criticism are *Shakespeare our Contemporary* (trans. from Polish, 1964) and *The Eating of the Gods: an Interpretation of Greek Tragedy* (trans. from Polish, 1974).

M. M. MAHOOD: Professor of English and American Literature at the University of Kent at Canterbury since 1967. Her critical writings include *Poetry and Humanism: an Analysis of 17th-Century English Poetry* (1950) and *Shakespeare's Wordplay* (1957).

WINIFRED M. T. NOWOTTNY: Reader in English at University College, London. Her most important work is *The Language Poets Use* (1962).

F. T. PRINCE: he was appointed Professor of English at the University of Southampton in 1957 and his many works of editorial scholarship include the 1960 Arden edition of *Shakespeare: The Poems*. He has also published several volumes of poetry and one of his most important works of criticism is *The Italian Element in Milton's Verse* (1954).

JOHN CROWE RANSOM: Professor of Poetry at Kenyon College, Gambier, Ohio, 1937–58, and then Emeritus Professor until his death in 1974. A most influential critic of twentieth-century poetry, he edited the *Kenyon Review* from 1939. His many books include two major volumes of criticism, *The World's Body* (1938) and *The New Criticism* (1941). His *Selected Poems* appeared in 1955.

LAURA RIDING: living in America, Mrs Schuyler B. Jackson now writes as Laura (Riding) Jackson. She has made many pungent written statements about the nature of language and poetry and her own poetry is published in her *Collected Poems* (1938) and *Selected Poems: in Five Sets* (1970). She wrote, with Robert Graves, a novel, *No Decency Left* (1932) and critical works, *A Survey of Modernist Poetry* (1927) and *Contemporaries and Snobs* (1928).

C. F. WILLIAMSON: Lecturer in English at the University of Oxford, and Fellow of Jesus College, his main interests lie in Renaissance literature, and he is also preparing a book on Dickens.

YVOR WINTERS: critic, teacher and poet, he became in 1926 a graduate student at Stanford, California, and later Professor of English there until his death in 1968. *In Defense of Reason* (1947) is his principal volume of criticism. Among his many other works the most important are his *Collected Poems* (1952 and 1960), *The Function of Criticism* (1957) and *Forms of Discovery* (1967).

INDEX

Note. Figures in bold type denote essays or extracts.